Globalization
and Its Managerial
Implications

Globalization and Its Managerial Implications

Edited by
C. P. RAO

QUORUM BOOKS
Westport, Connecticut • London

Library of Congress Cataloging-in-Publication Data

Globalization and its managerial implications / edited by C.P. Rao.
    p.   cm.
    Includes bibliographical references and index.
    ISBN 1–56720–263–2 (alk. paper)
    1. International marketing.   2. International business enterprises—Management.
    3. Competition, International.   I. Rao, C.P.
    HF1416.G575   2001
    658'.04921—dc21   99–046052

British Library Cataloguing in Publication Data is available.

Library of Congress Catalog Card Number: 99–046052
ISBN: 1–56720–263–2

First published in 2001

Quorum Books, 88 Post Road West, Westport, CT 06881
An imprint of Greenwood Publishing Group, Inc.
www.quorumbooks.com

Printed in the United States of America

The paper used in this book complies with the
Permanent Paper Standard issued by the National
Information Standards Organization (Z39.48–1984).

10 9 8 7 6 5 4 3 2 1

Copyright Acknowledgments

To

Mohini, Kris, and Sri

for making it all purposeful

Contents

Introduction

C. P. Rao

Globalization has become a major environmental force shaping management theory and practice in recent years. With the fall of communism and the spread of democracy, globalization forces have intensified in shaping policies and behaviors of both nation-states and corporate entities all over the world. Globalization has also concurrently ushered in privatization and liberalization trends making it imperative for corporate management to deal with the new reality of operating in a global context. The globalization process is further aided by new technological developments in communications and information processing, in addition to the faster spread of these technologies worldwide. Increased information dissemination and unrestricted global mobility of financial and other factors of production and distribution are resulting in homogenization of values and norms, which in turn are creating global markets and concomitant managerial challenges. Every facet of management practice—including production, financing, marketing, sourcing, and human resource management—is affected by globalization trends.

The pervasive globalization trends in turn require visionary thinking, creativity, information focus, considerable investments, and organizational change so that corporate management can effectively respond to the emerging global challenges and opportunities. In today's global markets, while consumption patterns, consumer expectations, and overall consumer behavior patterns are becoming increasingly harmonized, certain infrastructural and cultural peculiarities of individual national markets continue to pose difficult managerial problems. Today's corporate management has to deal simultaneously with converging commonality and persistent diversity in various global markets. Such contrary trends created by globalization processes seem to require globalized strategies but localized marketing and management practices.

Depending upon the extent of globalization taking place in specific industries, management is finding that customer needs and behaviors the world over are increasingly homogenized. Following this development, both traditional and new competitors think and behave globally, forcing global orientation on the part of many other enterprises. Without such global orientation, enterprises may be missing out on the opportunities for substantial economies of scale or scope in their key value-creating activities. Hence, management is forced to perceive the world as a global village and formulate business strategies on an integrated worldwide basis. Further, they need to aggressively and effectively implement their global strategies with large investments, technological innovations, and strategic alliances. In general, global competitors are well-managed companies.

This volume addresses the managerial implications of the ongoing and intensifying globalization processes for business operations. Chapters dealing with six broad types of managerial issues germane to globalization processes are presented. Part I deals with the emerging business environmental issues for management, both from a global standpoint as well as from some of the unique environmental aspects of groups of countries that are entering the global economy, such as the former communist countries of Russia and Eastern Europe. Part II deals with micromanagement issues in the context of globalization. Some of the topics addressed are the internationalization process of firms, international industrial buying, and global sourcing.

One of the key characteristics of globalization in recent years has been the phenomenal increase in international trade. Globalization is making it imperative for companies both to export their products and services and also to source products and services globally. This has necessitated more active interaction between importers and exporters, even to the point of engaging in long-term relationships and strategic alliances. Hence, Part III of this volume deals with the various aspects of importer-exporter interaction issues. Success in today's global markets very much depends upon how successfully business operators manage their relationships with their counterparts in different parts of the world.

Communications in general, and international market communications in particular, have become key success factors in globalized markets. In Part IV, chapters relating to international market communication issues, with special focus on cross-cultural communications issues, are presented. Globalization implications for management vary by each sector of business. Some sectors, such as the services sector, the small and medium-sized business sector, and the information technology sector, experience uniquely different problems emanating from globalization processes. These sectoral management issues are explored in Part V.

Just as there are sectoral differences with regard to managerial implications of globalization, wide variations with regard to managerial implications of globalization can be found in different regions of the world. These regional market variations are explored in Part VI of the book.

PART I: ENVIRONMENTAL ISSUES

In recent years, globalization forces are significantly contributing to make the business environment very challenging. As new and vast overseas markets develop as a result of globalization, traditional environmental analysis tools have proved to be inadequate or need to be applied to the newly emerging overseas markets in order to comprehend the complexity of such business environments. Chapter 1, by Cordell and Breland, deals with the problems caused by varying national competition policies and practices and examines their impact on international trade and investment. They argue that it is no longer feasible for the international trading community, governments and business alike, to ignore the important effects that national competition policies have on international trade practices and market access. Chapter 2, by Ghauri, advocates the need to use cooperative strategies to compete effectively in a fast-changing global economy. Chapter 3, by Clake and Owens, discusses the strategic marketing management implications of the long-established international business concept of country of origin from the perspective of U.S. marketing statutes. Four legal tests for determining country of origin are detailed and practical examples provided to illustrate the strategic implications. In Chapter 4, Stanton and Rao propose a macrosegmentation scheme for the emerging Eastern European and former Soviet country markets. Given the massive size and diversity of these markets and the general paucity of information about them, the scheme of macrosegmentation suggested by the authors proves to be a useful first step in analyzing this important group of emerging markets.

PART II: MICROMANAGEMENT ISSUES

Globalization has intensified the need for business firms to internationalize their operations as quickly as possible. At the micro level, business firms experience unique management problems emanating from the globalization process. In Chapter 5, Sharma proposes a resource-based model of the internationalization process of firms. The author draws on three distinct research streams—resource-based strategy, the theory of the growth of firms, and behavioral organization theory—and presents a comprehensive integrated model of the internationalization of firms under conditions of globalization. Chapter 6, by Rao and Witt, deals with the interface between global sourcing and global marketing. While there is considerable literature on global marketing, there is a paucity of research dealing with global sourcing in spite of its increasing importance under current conditions of globalization. The authors argue that the knowledge related to global marketing will be greatly useful for global sourcing. Global sourcing is becoming a highly sophisticated activity with focus on a wide range of inbound activities involving the effective management of sourcing relationships. Chapter 7, by Servais', discusses both the monadic and the dyadic approaches to international sourcing. The author discusses the intricacies of international sourcing strategies by proposing and outlining a portfolio model with a network approach.

PART III: IMPORTER-EXPORTER INTERACTION ISSUES

As a result of globalization, international trade is increasing by leaps and bounds. This increased international trade has created greater opportunities for and challenges of interacting with various parts of the world. While there is considerable literature dealing with management of exports and export behavior of firms, there is very limited research dealing with importer-exporter interaction issues in today's global markets. Hence, Part III is devoted to such research. Chapter 8, by Karunaratna, Johnson, and Rao, deals with the impact of culture on the exporter–import agent contractual relationship. The authors developed a conceptual framework by integrating cultural dimensions with agency theory. Chapter 9, by Stanton, Rao, and Jou, reports empirical research results dealing with relationships between Taiwanese importers and exporters from the United States, Japan, and Western Europe. The perspective taken by the authors in this chapter is to look at the importer-exporter interaction process from the perspective of importers.

PART IV: MARKET COMMUNICATIONS ISSUES

Under conditions of globalization, market communications issues gained greater importance. Because of firms' efforts to reach global markets and to source globally, the communication complexities of reaching and persuading customers, employees, and suppliers of different country cultures have become major management concerns. These issues are addressed in Part IV. Chapter 10, by Rallapalli and Rao, provides a model for improving understanding of the role that culture plays in a sales interaction. The chapter focuses on improving sales training methods for sales people in order to deal effectively with customers from diverse cultural backgrounds. Chapter 11, by Hansen, describes the development of the measurement of advertising effectiveness in terms of three generations of changing audience characteristics on a global scale. Its focus is on international copy testing. Chapter 12, by Durvasula and Lysonski, deals with the global dimensions of beliefs toward advertising in general among the consumers across five diverse countries. Based on their empirical research investigation, the authors discuss the implications of their research for cross-national advertising practitioners and provide direction for future research on advertising beliefs on a global scale.

PART V: SECTORAL MANAGEMENT ISSUES

Part V presents chapters dealing with managerial implications of globalization for distinct business sectors. Three business sectors are addressed: small and medium-sized enterprises (SMEs), international alliances in the information technology (IT) sector, and the general insurance industry. Chapter 13, by Asundi, addresses the managerial implications of globalization for SMEs. It suggests different strategic approaches for SMEs to face the challenges posed by globalization. The IT industry has become the most dynamic industry worldwide in recent years. The dynamism of this industry is evident in its growth on a global scale. In Chapter 14, Rao addresses technology-based international alliances as the means for the IT industry's global expansion. The chapter explores the dominant managerial strategic motives for such alliances, and further suggests that technology alliances portend the beginning of a larger trend in the form of vertical integration of the important segments of the IT industry. Chapter 15, by Yorke and Andresen, discusses a normative framework for global expansion of insurance companies. With the World Trade Organization agreement, the globalization of service industries, including general insurance, is expected to be next frontier of international trade expansion.

PART VI: MANAGERIAL ISSUES IN REGIONAL MARKETS

As global markets expand in response to ever-intensifying globalization forces, vast new overseas markets are emerging. These emerging markets are in the process of transforming themselves into free market economies and exhibit different business environments for global business. In Part VI, some of these emerging markets and their business environments are explored. Chapter 16, by Wang, Rao, and Vorhies, investigates Chinese consumption-oriented personal values using a new measure, consumers' Perceived Attribute Importance (PAI), along four product categories: clothing, household appliances, household supplies, and food. Results of research using PAI suggested that Chinese consumption values displayed differences along the four product categories studied. Chapter 17, by Oumlil and Oumlil, critically evaluates the evolving European Union as a regionally integrated market. The authors examine the international marketing realities and their marketing management implications in the European Union context.

Part I

Environmental Issues

Chapter 1

Conflicting Competition Policies in a Globalized Business Environment: Prospects for International Cooperation and Convergence

Victor V. Cordell and Erin A. C. Breland

INTRODUCTION

This chapter presents an argument for the necessity of trading nations to begin negotiating agreements on cooperative competition policies at the multilateral level; it is divided into five sections. The first gives a brief summary of developments in the world trade environment as background for arguing the need for coordination of competition policy. It includes sections on the liberalization of trade in the post–World War II era and the recent trends toward trade restrictions. The second section discusses competition policies and briefly summarizes some of the differences in their characteristics and developments to illustrate the difficulties likely to arise in negotiating agreements on common competition policies.

The third section gives a political and economic rationale for why competition should be addressed. The importance of multinationals is discussed, and a case study on merger control requirements is given to illustrate the practical problems MNCs face with the current state of varying national competition policies. Arguments for the author's view on which nations should attempt to cooperate, on which issues, and under what forum are presented in the fourth section. The final section reaffirms the necessity of beginning negotiations on competition and summarizes the conclusions of the study.

THE STATE OF INTERNATIONAL TRADE

The Liberalization and Concurrent Restriction of World Trade

Through the creation of the General Agreement on Tariffs and Trade (GATT) in 1947 and its eight subsequent rounds of negotiation, the world's trading nations have reduced tariff levels to the point that, for most industries, they are no longer a significant barrier to trade. Not only through the GATT but also through the formation of regional trading blocs, cooperating nations have increased harmonization and, in some parts of the world, have virtually eliminated customs procedures and other formal border controls. These measures have made it easier for companies to conduct international trade and investment and to globalize their production, distribution, and general business operations.

As a result, world trade has increased substantially. In fact, in virtually every year of the postwar period, the growth of world merchandise trade has exceeded the growth of world merchandise output. Overall, the volume of world merchandise trade is estimated to have increased at an average annual rate of slightly more than 6 percent during the period 1950–1994, compared with close to 4 percent for world output. This means that for every 10 percent increase in world output, there has been on average a 16 percent increase in world trade.[1]

However, during the last 20 years, in an effort to keep markets closed without going against GATT principles, governments have created new policies with which to limit market access for foreign businesses. The introduction of orderly marketing arrangements (OMA), voluntary export restraints (VER), and voluntary import expansion (VIE) measures are three examples of such policies.[2] These so-called hard-core non-tariff barriers (NTB) have been erected by a wide range of countries, but the majority are imposed by the United States and members of the European Union while the exporting country most often targeted is Japan, with South Korea as the second.[3] In addition, a topic of much discussion now in many industrialized economies is the use of strategic trade policy to counter and correct market distortions introduced by trading partners.[4] Such policies do hold some legitimacy among economists,[5] based on economic principles and models; however, implementing a strategic trade policy is so doubtful that even the theory's biggest proponents stress caution in actually adopting it as a national policy.[6] Most are in agreement that granting the government the right and authority to pick and choose winners among not only industries but firms as well would be corrupted and distorted by rent-seeking firms, by power-seeking politicians, and by favor-seeking lobby groups.

Rationale for Restriction: The Situation in the United States

Despite warnings from economists, many politicians, particularly in the United States, seem to favor a restrictive industrial policy because it directly addresses the anxiety of their constituencies that Americans are losing their jobs due to "unfair" competition from foreign firms and that, as a result, their standard of living is being reduced.[7] Strategic trade does seem to rectify this grievance; however, what few politicians take into consideration is the benefits that American consumers receive from openness to foreign trade in the form of higher product quality and variety and lower prices than in most of the rest of the world. What politicians also do not consider is that, in addition to the disastrous effects of a trade war, there also exists a very real likelihood that, when faced with such blatant protectionism, other governments will either adopt their own strategic trade policies or will use other retaliatory measures against U.S. firms.

Both of these outcomes would harm consumers greatly and would cause a real decrease in their standard of living—initially through an increase in taxes to help subsidize the domestic industry, and later through an increase in the prices of products available for consumption due to the decrease in foreign competition. In addition, with the increase in the ratio of trade to GDP in recent years and the increasing dependence of the United States on foreign trade, the losses caused by retaliation would be devastating to many U.S. firms operating or selling abroad and would have ill effects on the domestic economy as a whole.

This theory and other similar industrial economics arguments reflect a growing belief that U.S. businesses need protection and support in order to remain competitive—that, without government intervention, U.S. firms will lose market share to foreign competitors, American jobs will be lost, employment will either decrease or shift to low-wage sectors, the standard of living will plummet, and America will become a second-class state. Many others, however, are of the belief that the private sector is generally better off when the government remains at arm's length. While the U.S. government has been necessary for, and highly successful at, negotiating reductions in tariffs and other market access issues, to translate this into success in planning the U.S. economy and the private sector's production schedule is as ludicrous as granting a CEO the right and ability to determine the country's social agenda.

On a global level, the emergence of strategic trade theory and the increasing use of NTBs illustrates a contradiction in the purported goals of the WTO member nations and their actual trade practices and policies. As Deardorff and McCulloch noted, "It seems perverse behavior on the part of the world's governments to work so hard to reduce inefficient restrictions in domestic markets only to recreate inefficiencies in the world markets through the imposition of highly inefficient trade barriers, such as VERs."[8]

COMPARATIVE COMPETITION POLICIES

Competition laws go by various names. In the United States they are called antitrust laws, while in the rest of the world they are called anti-monopoly, anti-competitive, or simply, restrictive business practices (RBPs). In the interest of continuity and clarity, throughout the rest of this chapter these will all be referred to simply as competition policies. Rather than to attempt to define the concept, it is sufficient merely to state their areas of coverage, namely, anti-competitive business practices, merger control, and state subsides. The focus of this chapter is on the regulation and investigation of proposed or completed corporate mergers or, simply, merger control. But all three aspects are covered in virtually all competition legislation in countries where such legislation exists. There are currently about 40 countries with some type of enforced competition law, including all members of the Organization for Economic Cooperation and Development (OECD) as well as Korea, Thailand, India, and others.[9]

An Illustration of Differing Motives and Views

The issue of coordinating competition policies is difficult to navigate since each country has in place its own policies, which stem from such varying factors as stage of economic development, accepted business practices, societal structure, and even national culture. How, for example, could an industrialized nation such as Germany converge its competition law with a trading partner like Brazil? How, for that matter, could Germany coordinate with the United States? Even given similar stages of development and market structure, the vast differences in national objectives and governmental roles in the private sector that still exist make cooperation a formidable task for both governments.

While it would be impossible to attempt to discuss the differences between all of the world's competition laws in this chapter, it is interesting and useful to mention a few aspects of different national policies in order to illustrate the difficulties and the possibilities that negotiators will face in the future.

The United States, Canada, the European Union, and Japan

In the United States, the first constitutional enactment of competition policy was the Sherman Act of 1890.[10] However, a basic distrust and dislike of state-controlled monopolies was exhibited as early as the Boston Tea Party of 1773.[11] Antitrust policy later emerged as an important part of the New Deal policy in the late 1930s and its enforcement increased with the enactment of the "New Sherman Act" at that same time. After interruption, during the war, it resumed its upward surge from 1945.[12] However, not until 1969 did the U.S. antitrust agencies start to use a pre-merger notification system, which was given statutory authority in 1976.[13]

History has shown that, in contrast to many other nations, Americans are generally resistant to government involvement in the private sector and are particularly averse to the idea of large trading companies that may monopolize the market. U.S. antitrust policy, like those of many others, is based on efficiency grounds, with the aim of maintaining competitive markets. The U.S. law also reflects this fundamental distrust of monopolies and state-run enterprises. The laws contain general language, which is interpreted and enforced on a case-by-case basis federally by the Department of Justice (DOJ) and the Federal Trade Commission (FTC) and locally by state attorneys general.

In contrast to the United States, Canada's Bureau of Competition Policy is responsible for implementing and enforcing a clearly spelled-out set of rules and definitions of anti-competitive behavior. Canada has also recently overhauled its competition law after nearly two decades of study, consultation, and thorough assessment of the policies of numerous other countries, which culminated in the passage of the Competition Act of 1986.[14]

The European Union (EU) is a unique example in which a Union-wide commitment to convergence in virtually all economic aspects has led to the need for a common competition law. In the EU, the Director General IV (DGIV) is responsible for the coordination of members' competition rules and for investigating and deciding cases that affect more than one member market (Van Bael 1987). In addition, each member nation still retains its own laws, but for intra-Union cases that pass a certain monetary threshold, mergers are reviewed by the European Commission (EC). However, in practice, there is a considerable amount of consultations with DGIV on a number of non-qualifying mergers as well. DGIV guidelines, similar to those of the United States, are based on competition and efficiency grounds, while some members' national policies, such as those of France and the United Kingdom, also allow for consideration of social concerns (see Appendix 1.2 at the end of this chapter).

The origins of the current EC policy are in the European Coal and Steel Community (ECSC), which was created in 1951 in order to create a bulwark against Soviet expansion. Because of fear that Germany's powerful steel and coal industries could again provide a basis for aggression, the ECSC was created to make Germany's steel-making potential available to all members.[15] The Union's current competition rules are embodied in Articles 85 and 86 of the 1957 Treaty of Rome.

Japanese law,[16] which borrows from the continental European systems, the American system, and the traditional Japanese system, has only recently included competition measures, and only after much external pressure has it begun to be based and enforced on grounds of competition. However, the *keiretsu* system of vertically and horizontally integrated companies that exists in Japan, which would clearly be illegal in many other countries, has been condoned, if not encouraged, by the Japanese government. This difference alone would pose immense difficulties in including Japan in any type of multinational agreement, since it would involve a complete restructuring of the country's production and distribution systems.

The Japan Fair Trade Commission (JFTC), which has often been accused of being ineffectual, has the legal authority to investigate and enforce Japan's Anti-Monopoly Law (AML). Despite recent criticisms, the JFTC has substantially increased not only the number of investigations but also the fines and penalties involved.

The AML was first introduced in 1947 in response to a recommendation by the Occupation Forces that the Japanese government enact a law that would serve as the basic law of competition. The original law was strict and, under considerable pressure from the Occupation Forces, was strongly enforced by the JFTC. After undergoing relaxation amendments in 1953 and 1960, which helped to promote incredible growth during the postwar years and was encouraged by the United States so that Japan could become a strong barrier against Soviet expansion, the AML began to be more strictly enforced through amendments in 1977 and 1991.

This very short assessment illustrates the wide variance in the nature and evolution of national competition laws and provides some sense of the difficulties that will inevitably be involved in coordinating them on an international level. Coordination will involve, in many areas, not only amendments to current laws but also restructuring of how business is conducted in countries such as Japan. It may also run counter to the goals of socialist systems that do not place as high a priority on competition and economic efficiency.

WHY COMPETITION? WHY NOW?

Quite simply, national competition rules should be addressed because the progress toward liberalization made under the auspices of the GATT does not apply directly to the private sector. Rather, the tariff reductions and other liberalizing measures deal with government-imposed restrictions, not with private sector–imposed restraints. As Graham has pointed out, "(i)t has long been acknowledged that whatever progress governments might be able to achieve in removing entry barriers posed by restrictions at the border on the exchange of goods and services, the benefits of this progress can be undone if certain private practices take the place of official restrictions."[17]

In addition, as can be seen now in the trade dispute between Eastman Kodak of the United States and Fujifilm of Japan, trade and competition issues are overlapping and are causing increased tension in bilateral relationships. The issue in this case is over the availability of shelf space for foreign products, namely film and photographic paper, which has to do with particular aspects of the Japanese distribution system, clearly a competition issue. If this issue goes to the Dispute Settlement Body of the WTO, which it likely will since Japan has maintained a position of not negotiating with the United States, the world community will then be faced with the dilemma of competition aspects that constitute trade barriers. The problem with this is that the WTO is not equipped to address such issues at this time.

Recognition by the International Trading Community

As previously mentioned, traditional trade-restricting border measures have largely been negotiated away during the years of the multilateral GATT rounds. It is generally accepted today in developed as well as developing nations that liberalized trade is the best alternative, given the economic and political realities of the world. Even the traditionally protectionist least-developed countries (LDCs) seem to have accepted this view, as is evidenced by their virtual abandonment of import substitution measures, their participation in the WTO, and their increased openness to foreign direct investment (FDI). In order to continue on this path toward liberalization and globalization, developed nations should now concentrate their efforts not on protection and trade-limiting measures such as those discussed earlier, but on measures that will increase the efficiency of trade and investment.

This has already been done in the WTO with the inclusion of the Trade Related Investment Measures (TRIMs), the Trade Related Aspects of Intellectual Property (TRIPs) and the General Agreement on Trade in Services (GATS) agreements in the final draft of the Uruguay round. This trend toward increasing the scope of trade liberalization was also suggested for competition measures in a November 1995 speech at the Conference on Antitrust in Rome, where WTO Director-General Renato Ruggiero described the "urgent need for analysis of links between competition policy and trade policy, notably to identify the problems that may require action and the options for such action."[18] The OECD has also recognized the importance of competition policies in international trade and has published an in-depth series of economic and policy studies on the subject.[19]

The importance of international trade and competition for the analysis of antitrust issues is stressed in the 1986 OECD *Recommendation for Cooperation in Areas of Potential Conflict between Competition and Trade Policies* and is incorporated in the U.S. Department of Justice's *Antitrust Enforcement Guidelines for International Operations* (1989) and Canada's *Merger Guidelines*. The Trade Minister for the European Commission, Sir Leon Brittan, has also taken an active role in pushing the issue onto the GATT/WTO agenda and even went so far as to create an International Antitrust Code Working Group in July 1993, which released a draft proposal designed specifically to be part of the GATT agreement.[20] Brittan also encouraged the inclusion of competition considerations in the December 1996 WTO ministerial talks in Singapore.

Liberalization, Globalization, and MNCs

The liberalization of trade and investment in the post–World War II era has led to the creation and rapid growth of multinational companies (MNCs). These companies do not fit into the classic model of industrial organization; rather, they epitomize globalization. By selectively setting up and operating divisions of research and development, production, assembly, and distribution, they are able to take advantage of the differences between nations' wage rates, technological capabilities, and educational levels, as well as traditional differences such as capital, climate, population, and other country-specific advantages.

An excellent example of the comparative advantage utilization of a true multinational is the creation of the Elevonic 411, a new product introduced by Otis Elevator, a division of United Technologies. In producing the Elevonic 41, Otis employed their worldwide resources, which resulted in an end product with door work done in France, small gear components sourced from Spain, electronic work performed in Germany, creation of a special motor in Japan, and systems integration from the United States. This case exemplifies the benefits to multi-

nationals in terms of resource utilization and is one of hundreds of cases oc-
curring increasingly in today's globalized marketplace.

However, national and international regulatory regimes have not kept pace
with the rapid growth of these companies. While conventional trade-restricting
border measures are obvious and negotiable, other national restrictive business
practices (RBP) are less visible and are therefore more difficult, but they require
international attention nonetheless.

Furthermore, while some type of regulation of the private sector is obviously
necessary, the beneficial contributions made by multinationals is now being recognized and appreciated. Industrialized countries have long been reliant on the
corporate taxes derived from multinationals to help fund national budgets, but
the developing nations have traditionally been wary of allowing FDI by multinationals for fear of the implied abuse of their market dominance. However,
with the introduction of notions of contestibility,[21] the old fears of dependence
upon multinationals have faded. These countries now realize that such companies can assist in building up the domestic economy and infrastructure, not only
by direct investment and technology transference but also by increasing a nation's foreign reserves and by more efficiently utilizing domestic resources.

With this more positive view of MNCs and an increased awareness on the
part of international policy makers that the number of MNCs are growing and
will continue to grow, given the challenges of global competition, measures to
assist them in operating efficiently have become desirable. Therefore, in order
to address the obstacles to trade and investment that multinational firms are now
facing in the global marketplace, it is only logical to address the issue of national
competition policies. The following section illustrates, by means of a case study,
the difficulty MNCs face when attempting to comply with the multi-jurisdictional requirements imposed on corporate mergers. The incredible amount of
overlap is shown, and the implied problems and costs to the firms involved are
obvious.

The Case: Gillette–Wilkinson Sword[22]

The current state of affairs for multinational corporations is, at best, difficult.
All companies involved in mergers must not only follow the national competition rules, they must also comply and provide information to the other governments involved and take into consideration any bilateral treaties or overriding
institutions that may be in force. There are different forms to fill out, different
deadlines for notification, different information requirements, different regulating bodies, different criteria and calculations for determining a final decision,
and different policies governing the confidentiality of company information. In
order to illustrate these differences, it is useful to examine a case study of a
merger that is becoming more representative of transactions in the 1990s.

On December 20, 1989, an agreement was reached between the world's number one firm in the wet-shaver market, Gillette, and a leading competitor, Wil-

kinson Sword. The following summary of the case illustrates the immense cost to, and the time consuming efforts of, the firms involved when trying to comply with overlapping national competition policies and procedures.

The Players

1. Stora Kopparbergs Bergslags AB Eemland Holdings NV, which owns the wet-shaver business called Wilkinson Sword (previously Eemland Management Services BV, then Swedish Match NV)
2. Gillette

Creditors

1. Copenhagen Handlesbank
2. Intermediate Capital Group
3. Morgan Guaranty
4. Lustrasilk UK Limited (a Gillette subsidiary)
5. Stora Kopparbergs Berglsags AB
6. Various senior creditors syndicated by Morgan Guaranty

The Transaction

1. The Gillette Company and other members of the Gillette group financed the purchase of Stora's consumer products division through a $630 million leveraged buy-out (LBO). The consumer products division included the Wilkinson Sword wet-shaving business, which had manufacturing facilities in the United Kingdom, Germany, Zimbabwe, and Brazil.
2. Having been previously advised by government officials that the competition rules of the United Kingdom, Germany, and the EC would likely prevent the buy-out since Gillette and Wilkinson Sword competed directly with each other in many countries, the Gillette Company bought the entire Wilkinson Sword wet-shaving business outside of the European Community from Eemland.

Investigations

1. Of the LBO where authorities in the EC and its member states were looking at the possible effect of Gillette's involvement in the Eemland:
   - European Commission (DGIV)
   - UK (Office of Fair Trading; Monopolies and Mergers Commission; Department of Trade and Industry, or OFT, MMC, and DOT)
   - Germany (Bundeskartellamt, or BKartA)
   - France (Ministère de l'Economie, des Finances, et du Budget; Conseil de la Concurrence)
   - Ireland (Department of Industry and Commerce; Fair Trade Commission)
   - Spain (Department for the Defence of Competition)
2. Of the non-EC acquisition where authorities were looking at the effects on competition:
   - United States (Department of Justice)
   - Canada (Bureau of Competition Policy)

- New Zealand (Commerce Commission)
- Australia (Trade Practices Commission)
- Brazil
- Switzerland (Cartel Commission)
- South Africa (Competition Board)
- Sweden (Competition Ombudsman)

Outcomes

1. Of the LBO and Gillette's acquired influence over Eemland within the EC: Due to the incredible opposition faced and the inevitable negative decisions, expected and later issued, from the European Commission, the United Kingdom, Germany, and France, Eemland sold Wilkinson Sword division to Warner-Lambert. If they had not done so, a divestiture order from all countries and the Commission would have forced a dissolution of the merger. Only Ireland and Spain did not oppose the transaction.

2. Of the non-EC acquisition of Wilkinson Sword:

   - *United States*: In response to a case filed with the USDOJ, which contended that the transaction violated US Antitrust law (Section 7 of the Clayton Act, 15 USC s. 18), Gillette, Eemland, and Wilkinson rescinded Gillette's acquisition of Wilkinson Sword business in the U.S. market.

   - *Canada*: Before an investigation could be completed, Gillette transferred the beneficial ownership in Wilkinson Sword's Canadian business to Eemland's Wilkinson Sword Gmbh subsidiary, which was acquired by Warner-Lambert on the same day.

   - *New Zealand*: The Commerce Commission gave clearance for the transaction on 16 November 1990.

   - *Australia*: In 1994 the case was proceeding to a final hearing.

   - *Switzerland*: The Commission conducted an investigation and found no harm.

   - *South Africa*: Since the Wilkinson Sword business in South Africa is owned by a subsidiary of South African Breweries, the Board requested further information of the transaction but took no further action.

   - *Sweden*: The Office of the Competition Ombudsman conducted a preliminary investigation of the transaction only. Minimal effects were found and so no prohibition order was made.

After looking at the incredible amount of overlap of procedures and investigations of international corporate mergers as demonstrated in this case, it becomes obvious that some form of cooperation, even if it is only procedural (e.g., common deadlines for notification, similar criteria for decisions, common informational forms, etc.), would certainly make the process more efficient, less time consuming, and less costly to all parties involved.

Economic Rationale for the Importance of Competition Policies

In market-based economies the ability of prices to adjust based on supply and demand is crucial for determining not only the most efficient domestic industries but also the most efficient producers. Under this type of system, firms that produce products that are in demand increase investment and build new production facilities, which in turn promote increases in production and supply. Firms that supply products whose demand has declined will stop producing and supply will decrease. In this way, needed products will be supplied effectively and the production of unneeded products will decline so that the optimum allocation of resources in a society is achieved.

However, in order to achieve this kind of market response there must be numerous firms producing competitive products, and there must be unrestricted competition among all firms. In other words, there cannot be a monopoly or a cartel arrangement if the market price is to respond to the supply and demand function and the system is to work effectively. For this reason, market-based economies have competition laws to ensure that firms compete, rather than collude, with each other.

Problems arise because, as previously mentioned, the nature of firms as well as industrial and trade economics has evolved to include considerations of dynamic and strategic relationships while competition policies have not. Previously, the economic theory of international trade primarily dealt with flows of goods between nations in perfectly competitive environments. New trade and industrial economic theories have begun to address imperfectly competitive and dynamic environments where firms act based on the actions of their competitors. However, most of the intellectual basis for antitrust policy still rests largely upon the theory of industrial organization in a closed economy in which all consumers and producers are domestic and where the presence of international competition is largely ignored.[23]

This unparalleled development in the globalization of business and national policy adjustment has led to a precarious situation. The new trade theory[24] contains many options, including the subsidization of target industries and governmental tolerance of firm dominance or other RBPs, which effectively allows firms to use their market power to achieve advantageous outcomes at the expense of other nations. In this sense, action (or inaction) in accordance with a nation's competition policy may very well be beneficial to that nation; however, the beggar-thy-neighbor effects that occur will not go undetected and will not be allowed to persist indefinitely, which will lead to the same negative effects previously discussed (e.g., retaliation).[25]

The gains from an international approach to competition policy are numerous and complimentary. Possible benefits are a reduction in national and private friction caused by anticompetitive practices, harmonization of policies resulting in reduced business costs, economic efficiency gains benefiting consumers and also encouraging the creation and development of new firms, and more technology transference as a result of the reduction in the number of cartels and monopolies. Keeping in mind the foreseeable and the possible gains from convergence, the questions then become: at what level should the problem of competition law disparity be addressed and what commonalities between nations' current policies are likely to be successfully negotiated? These questions are further explored in the following section and recommendations are made.

RECOMMENDATIONS: WHO? WHAT? WHERE? HOW?

In this section, it is argued that nations that meet the criteria under "who?" will be most successful at negotiating a competition agreement under the auspices of the OECD if they begin with the least controversial issue, merger control policies, and build on that agreement later to include other, more controversial issues.

Who?

It would seem that most trading nations would have a vested interest in increasing competition and, further, that firms would agree and encourage the adoption of a more transparent competition policy. This, however, does not hold true for two main reasons. First of all, as in the case of cooperation leading to further liberalization in many other areas, firms already established in markets or protected by competition measures in their own markets are certainly not receptive to the notion of increasing their competition and risking their dominant position. However, this is precisely why liberalization should occur.

Second, as far as participating nations are concerned, as mentioned earlier, the relatively small number of the countries that actually have (and enforce) competition laws precludes the inclusion of a large number of countries in any type of agreement. For example, to attempt to include the LDCs in any discussion on competition would be fruitless, as their need for such policies are basically nonexistent. Additionally, countries that traditionally protect their industries and shelter them from excess competition are also unlikely to cooperate fully, given that it is not in their interest to do so.

Therefore, it is expected that nations that (1) are already active participants in international trading regimes, (2) are advanced industrialized, (3) are among the leading exporters and importers of world trade, and (4) have consumer orientations will be the most likely to be successful at cooperation. This hypothesis is presented graphically in Appendix 1.1 at the end of this chapter.

The logic behind these assumptions is rather simple. If governments are already cooperating on issues such as tariff reduction and quota elimination in international regimes, then they are likely to be cooperative on other issues, such as competition. Following this, if countries are advanced industrialized, they presumably have a greater interest in, and possibly a dependence on, international trade. Therefore, they should also have an interest in increased access to, and freedom in, foreign markets. In addition, countries that already have competition rules in place are largely industrialized.

The interest in market access is magnified if a country maintains a high level of investment in a trading partner's country, since similar policies would reduce the confusion and difficulty of conducting business between the two countries. Finally, nations that have a strong consumer orientation are more likely to be interested in free trade since coordination on competition policies and practices would lead to greater transparency and ease of market entry. This, in turn, would increase competition, which encourages better quality, increased selection, and lower prices of goods available to consumers. Consumer-oriented countries have a greater interest in increasing competition and trade by coordinating their policies than do countries that are more industry or state oriented and whose governments have an interest in protecting domestic companies and markets.

A preliminary study discovered that there are currently at least sixteen countries that, to a certain degree, fit the criteria just described. They are all OECD members and are all industrialized. They have consumer orientations, as evidenced by the fact that "competition" concerns are the basis for decisions on mergers in most countries (see Appendix 1.2). As previously discussed, increased competition benefits consumers and, therefore, for this study, this is an adequate measure of consumer orientation. Also, all of the countries conduct a high degree of international trade, as shown in their trade to GDP ratios (see Appendix 1.3). Appendix 1.4 also shows that all sixteen have a high level of participation in international economic agreements. In fact, they are all signatories to no fewer than 93 such agreements.

What?

Nations will probably be the most successful at negotiating an agreement on aspects that are not only *common* to all but also *similar* in each nation's domestic law. After an extensive review of the literature on comparative competition laws, it was clear that merger control is the one aspect of existing policies that appears to have the least amount of disparity. As Horlick has also noted,

merger control probably is the easiest form of competition policy for regulators to implement. [Since] (m)echanically, all that is needed is a pre-notification requirement—hardly likely with many other types of anticompetitive behavior. In most instances, few deep-seated complaints about merger policy will arise.[26]

Indeed, the similarities between the characteristics and goals of merger control policies are great, particularly in the OECD nations.[27] Negotiation on merger control would focus on five main areas: notification requirements, time limits for review and decisions, criteria for decisions, confidentiality requirements, and consequences. As illustrated in Appendix B, the amount of commonality and overlap and, therefore, the possibility for convergence is substantial.

How?

How should nations attempt to negotiate? In a perfect world, it would be ideal if the world's largest trading nations were able to sit down and in a few months agree on a comprehensive, all-encompassing plan for convergence to a single international policy on competition. However, this is obviously not the case. After taking into consideration the economic and political realities of the world, we find that there are three practical alternatives for policy makers: *sector-specific agreements*, *GATT-like growth*, or *specific-aspect agreements*.

The first option is to concentrate on one sector at a time, as is currently being done under the auspices of the WTO in the negotiations on telecommunications. However, this type of segmented policy formation can lead to serious problems when there is overlap among sectors, as is likely to occur in the area of high-technology goods, which are currently of great concern. In addition, this type of approach could easily result in a massive patchwork of inconsistent and burdensome regulation.

The second option is to create a regime based on the GATT model, a General Agreement on Competition Policies (GACP) or, more specifically, a World Merger Body that would apply internationally agreed-upon substantive criteria to multinational mergers and would follow the one-stop principle of the EC Merger Regulation, thereby eliminating the problems of multiple investigation and of conflict.[28] In this scenario, signatories would commit to change their domestic rules to bring them in accordance with GACP principles. However, in addition to the free-rider problem that would likely exist in this situation, where member nations would receive the benefits of membership based on the Most Favored Nation (MFN) principle without necessarily converging their own policies, the GATT precedent of a long and arduous negotiation process does not offer much hope to policy makers and trade officials who need fast solutions to the problems that their domestic companies are facing abroad.

This problem is particularly substantial in the United State, where trade law requires the U.S. Trade Representative (USTR) to evaluate and, if found to be legitimate, investigate any petition filed by a U.S. entity and negotiate resolutions with the foreign governments involved. Therefore, with this type of legislated guarantee of action available to businesses, one can imagine that it would be extremely difficulty for the USTR to convince a U.S. company facing "unfair" competition practices abroad to wait for years until a GACP can be fully negotiated.

The third alternative, which is the recommendation of this chapter, is to begin by attempting to negotiate one aspect of competition law at a time, beginning with the area that is common to the most nations, either RBPs, merger control, or state subsidies. This approach is also flawed because it promises to be slow and would likely take many years to bring all aspects into an agreement. However, it would likely be the most effective for the following reasons: (1) only negotiating members would reap the benefits of cooperation (thus no free-riders), (2) initial agreements could be more comprehensive, as opposed to merely setting out general principles; (3) a strictly defined policy area of negotiation would be set out initially so that the specific industry involved would not be as important; and (4) it is a way to utilize the GATT method of "building up" an agreement and laying a foundation for future cooperation, while actually accomplishing short-term goals, which will be evident immediately. Of course, one must consider that the immediate outcomes may not be desirous, but it will at least illustrate weaknesses that can be addressed and improved upon in later, more important negotiations.

Where? OECD, WTO, or Bilateral Arrangements?

Various fora have been suggested for negotiating the issue of competition policy and its relationship to international trade, the most often suggested site being the OECD. Indeed, the issue has already been researched and written about extensively under the OECD. The Committee on Competition Law and Policy was formed, and in 1986 a recommendation[29] was made and adopted regarding policy principles and procedures of member countries with the aim of minimizing policy conflicts. This is only logical, as the members make up the majority of nations having enforced competition policies. However, some question the extent to which the OECD can be of use beyond this scope, given the voluntary nature of the institution. But, given the unlikely outcomes of attempts at the other possibilities, the OECD remains the best forum for such discussions.

In order to ensure the widest coverage, the WTO would be the ideal setting in which to introduce competition aspects of international trade. Indeed, this has been suggested not only in the United States[30] but also by Sir Leon Brittan of the EC.[31] Not only would the binding aspects of the WTO ensure compliance with mutually agreed upon provisions, but the coverage would be virtually worldwide. However, one should keep in mind that, realistically, GATT negotiations, while having been very effective, can largely be characterized as "mercantilist bargaining," whereby a nation grants concessions only if it must and only if the expected gains are greater than the concession made. Given that the nations with such policies make up less than one-sixth of the voting members of the WTO (counting the EC as one vote) and that the rest of the members have an equal vote and will not likely care to have the developed world's practices forced upon them while they are struggling to grow, it is improbable that the issue will go very far without considerable concessions being made. Here, once again, the MFN clause, which is fundamental to the WTO, gives rise to the problem of free-riders.

A significant problem with the way the GATT agreement stands today is that the GATT does not apply to private business practices unless they have been supported by the government. Additionally, GATT's reach is limited to action or inaction by governments that affect the conditions of competition in their markets. It does not apply to export cartels or actions by governments themselves that have detrimental effects on competition in export markets.[32]

The third alternative is to pursue bilateral agreements. This has already been done to some extent with the creation of a number of agreements regarding merger control. The United States, for example, has agreements with the EC, Germany, Australia, Canada, and Mexico. France and Germany, and Australia and New Zealand (ANZCERTA) also have agreements. However, these are basically agreements on notification procedures and cooperation on assuring enforcement of national laws, except in the case of ANZCERTA, which also contains information-sharing provisions. As such, they are not attempts at co-ordination of merger policies.

CONCLUSION

In the past 50 years a massive elimination of formal barriers to international trade and investment has occurred, which has facilitated an increase in the amount of international trade and investment as well as an increase in the number of multinational corporations. Through liberalization, the world has effectively become borderless in the sense that R&D, production, distribution, accounting, and sales transactions take place in any number of countries so that companies can, and do, operate irrespective of national borders.

In this new globally integrated economy, not only private producers but also governments engage in competition through the use of industrial policies such as those proposed by strategic trade theorists. In order to avoid this return to protectionism, business and government leaders should focus not on trade re-stricting measures but rather on addressing issues that can be solved through positive change and liberalization. One possibility is to harmonize competition measures. Such a contentious and broad topic is unlikely to be agreed upon in the foreseeable future, but there are manageable aspects of competition policies that can be addressed and converged relatively painlessly.

Given the increased prominence and importance of MNCs in international trade, governments should begin to look closely at the important effects that differing competition policies have in limiting business expansion and distorting trade and investment flows through the imposition of inefficient, overlapping multi-jurisdictional antitrust requirements of individual nations. This is particularly true in the area of merger controls, where, with little change required, there is the possibility of coordinating policies to include common notification requirements, forms, and deadlines.

In a best-case scenario, governments would begin to discuss and agree on competition *principles*, which are fundamental to reaching a more widely applicable common policy, for now to come under the auspices of the OECD and perhaps in future years, under the WTO. However, in order to address the problems that multinationals are now facing in a realistic and timely manner, it is the recommendation of this chapter that the OECD members begin to seriously negotiate with the aim of reaching a binding agreement on, at the very least, administrative issues of merger control. This should include provisions that will increase information sharing, reduce administrative and investigative overlap, and reduce the cost and burden to the firms and the government agencies involved. This will, in turn, increase global competition, increase economic efficiency, and promote the further liberalization of international trade and investment.

Appendix 1.1
Modeling Success in Negotiating a Comomon Competition Policy

Country characteristics

- Level of industrialization
- Degree of international trade
- Consumer orientation
- Level of participation in international economic agreements
- Political considerations

Willingness to negotiate

Success in reaching an agreement on a common competition policy

Economic Efficiency Gains

Reduced Business Costs

Increased Competition

Appendix 1.2
Summary of Merger Notification and Review Requirements

Country	System of Notification	Notification Thresholds	Time Limit for Initial Decision	Time Limit for Final Decision	Criteria for Decision	Confidentiality	Risk of Failure to Notify
Australia	Voluntary			Up to 45 days for decision by Trade Practices Commission. Parties have 21 days following TPC decision to appeal. Appeal must be heard by Tribunal within 60 days.	Substantial lessening of competition in a market.	Discretionary	Post-closing divestiture.
Austria	Compulsory	Post-merger notification where enterprises have combined share of at least 5 percent of domestic market.		Not applicable.			
Belgium	Compulsory	Combined annual turnover of more than 1 billion francs and more than 20 percent of relevant market.	One month.	75 days after the decision to begin the second phase.	Acquisition or strengthening of a dominant position and public interest criteria.	Assured	Fines from 20,000 to 1 million Belgian francs.
Canada	Compulsory	Combined assets/sales in, from or into Canada of C$ 400 million; target assets value or sales in/from Canada of C$ 35 million.		Seven days (short form), 21 days (long form: 10 days for a tender offer).	Competition	Assured	Fine, imprisonment, divestiture.
France	Voluntary	Combined market share of 25 percent or combined sales in France of FF 7 billion and each of two or more parties has sales in France of FF 2 billion.	Two months.	Six months.	Economic and social balance.	Assured	Post-closing divestiture.

Country		Criteria			Review basis	Clearance	Sanctions
Germany	Compulsory	Pre-merger: worldwide sales of DM 2 billion of any party; or DM 1 billion worldwide sales by each of two or more parties (also post-merger if worldwide combined sales of DM 1 million).	One month (for merger proposals only).	Four months (one year for post-merger notification).	Competition (in case of prohibition by the FCO, exemption by the Minister of Economics on general economic policy grounds possible).	Generally assured	Fine, invalidity of transaction.
Greece	Compulsory	Prenotification for horizontal mergers in sectors to be designated for enterprises with combined market share of 30 percent or aggregate turnover of at least ECU 65 million (post-merger notification for mergers having more than 10 percent market share or more than ECU 10 million aggregate turnover).	One month.	Two months (may be extended).	Competition-related.	Assured	Fine of up to 15 percent of aggregate turnover for failure to prenotify; up to 3 percent for failure to post-notify.
Ireland	Compulsory	Each of two or more parties has assets worth £Ir 10 million or sales of £Ir 20 million.	One month.	Three months.	Competition and common good.	Assured	Fine, invalidity of transaction.
Italy	Compulsory	Aggregate sales in Italy of L 500 billion or target company sales exceed L 50 billion.	30 days.	45 days after reference (can be extended).	Competition.	Assured	Fine, post-closing divestiture.
Japan	Compulsory	True mergers or acquisitions of the whole or a substantial part of an ongoing business in Japan.	30 days.	90 days.	Competition.	Assured	Fine, post-closing divestiture.

21

Appendix 1.2 (continued)

System of Country	Notification	Time Limit for Notification Thresholds	Initial Decision	Time Limit for Final Decision	Criteria for Decision	Confidentiality	Risk of Failure to Notify
New Zealand	Voluntary	Nil.	10 working days.	60 working days.	Market dominance and public benefit including economic efficiency.	Assured	Pecuniary penalties, post-closing divestiture, damages should the courts conclude that the merger creates or strengthens a dominant market position.
Portugal	Compulsory	Mergers where enterprises have combined turnover of at least Esc 30 billion or where they control at least 30 percent of the relevant market.	50 days.	50 days, to which can be added 30 + 15 days.	Competition-related.	Assured	Fine, initiation of proceeding, lack of legal effects until authorization is given.
Spain	Voluntary	Combined market share in Spain of 25 percent or combined sales in Spain of Ptas 20 billion.	One month.	Six months after.	Competition-related.	Assured	Post-closing divestiture.
Sweden	Compulsory	Aggregate turnover in excess of SKr 4 billion.	One month.	Further three months to bring case before Stockholm City Court.	Competition and detriment to public interest.	Assured	Fines.

22

					Public interest.	Generally but qualified by some exceptions.	Post-closing divestiture.
United Kingdom	Voluntary	Assets acquired worth £30 million or combined 25 percent market share in United Kingdom.	20 working days (may be extended up to 45 days).	Fixed for each case (maximum six months).	Public interest.	Generally but qualified by some exceptions.	Post-closing divestiture.
United States	Compulsory	One party has worldwide sales or total assets of $100 million and other has $10 million of sales or total assets, and acquiror will hold securities and assets worth in excess of $15 million or representing 15 percent of outstanding voting securities or assets as a result of the acquisition.	30 days.	20 days after compliance with second request.	Competition.	Assured	Periodic penalty payments, post-closing divestiture or other equitable remedies.
European Community (EC)	Compulsory	Combined sales worldwide of ECU 5 billion and sales of ECU 250 million in European Community for each of at least two parties unless each of them achieves more than two-thirds of its EC turnover within one and the same Member State.	One month.	Four months.	Competition-related.	Assured	Fine, periodic penalty payments, divestiture.

23

Appendix 1.3
Trade-to-GDP Ratio, 1993

Country	Ratio
Egypt	
Argentina	
Brazil	
India	
Japan	
United States	
Peru	
Turkey	
Mexico	
Australia	
Colombia	
Spain	
China	
Poland	
South Africa	
Italy	
Germany	
France	
United Kingdom	
Venezuela	
Indonesia	
Russia	
Chile	
Canada	
Korea	
Greece	
New Zealand	
Finland	
Sweden	
Iceland	
Denmark	
Switzerland	
Portugal	
Hungary	
Philippines	
Israel	
Austria	
Norway	
Thailand	
Taiwan	
Czech Republic	
Netherlands	
Ireland	
Jordan	
Belgium/Lux.	
Malaysia	
Hong Kong	
Singapore	

Horizontal axis: 0, 20, 40, 60, 80, 100, 120, 140

Source: International Institute for Management Development (IMD), *World Competitiveness Yearbook 1996* (Lausanne, Switzerland: IMD, 1996).

24

Appendix 1.4
Country Participation in International Economic Agreements

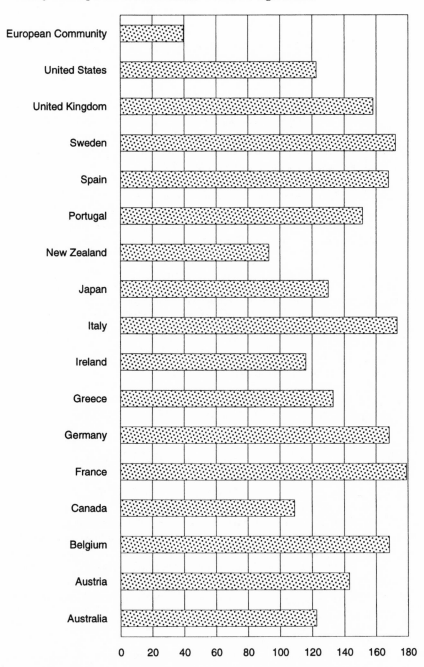

Source: Bernard Coles, ed., *Global Economic Co-operation: A Guide to Agreements and Organizations*, 2nd ed. (Cambridge, MA: United Nations University Press, 1994).

NOTES

1. WTO (1995), p. 15.

2. For an excellent study on the effects of these "hard-core" non-tariff measures, see OECD (1993).

3. OECD (1993), p. 9.

4. Strategic trade theory simply states that, due to existing imperfect competition, governments may justifiably intervene in certain "target" industries (those which produce positive externalities), and that, if they do, the nation will benefit not only socially, from the externalities created by the industry, but also economically since intervention can tilt the terms of oligopolist competition to shift excess returns from foreign to domestic firms by more than the cost of the protection (e.g., the subsidy).

5. Spencer (1986); Tyson (1992).

6. Brander (1986); Harris (1989); Krugman (1993).

7. This populist phenomena is most pointedly illustrated by the surprising large and loyal support of the nationalistic politician Pat Buchanan in the 1996 Republican primary.

8. Deardorff and McCulloch (1987) p. 218.

9. Matsushita (1993).

10. Horlick (1993), p. 65.

11. See Labaree (1964), p. 91, where he notes that "opposition to the tea shipment had quickly divided into two themes: (1) if the tea tax is submitted to, other taxes would soon follow, (2) if the East India company succeeded in establishing a monopoly over trade in one commodity, it would soon monopolize all the foreign commerce of America."

12. Matsushita (1993), p. 78.

13. American Bar Association (1991), pp. 167–168.

14. Horlick and Mayer (1995).

15. Swann (1970), p. 19.

16. Information on the Japanese Competition law is drawn entirely from Matsushita (1993), ch. 2.

17. Graham (1994), p. 109.

18. Internet site: http://www.unicc.org/wto/Pressrel/rome1.htm.

19. Many such publications are listed in the Reference list for this chapter.

20. *International Antitrust Code Will Be Studied by GATT Members*, 65 Antitrust & Trade Reg. Rep. (BNA) 259 (August 19, 1993).

21. Contestibility refers to the notion that, in a dynamic world, a firm that fails to constantly upgrade technologies and other firm-specific assets will likely be replaced by aggressive rivals so that the power of MNCs, which developing countries once feared, is illusory since firms are only powerful as long as they perform satisfactorily [Graham (1994), p. 107].

22. All information for this case study was taken from Richard Whish and Diane Wood, *Merger Cases in the Real World—A Study of Merger Control Procedures* (Paris: OECD, 1994), pp. 66–83.

23. Ordover and Goldberg (1993), p. 86.

24. For a complete discussion of the so-called new trade theory or strategic trade theory, *see* Krugman et al. (1986).

25. Graham (1994), p. 108.

26. Horlick and Meyer (1995), p. 68.

27. See Appendix 1.2 for a summary of the aspects of merger control policies in sixteen OECD nations as well as the EC.

28. See the comments of Rill and Metallo in *Globalization of Competition: The Case for Convergence*, in the October 1992 proceedings of the Fordham Corporate Law Institute, p. 15.

29. Recommendation of the Council for Cooperation between Member Countries in Areas of Potential Conflict between Competition and Trade Policies [C (86) 65 (Final)].

30. Draft ICC Statement on Present and Future Agenda of the WTO in Preparation for the First WTO Ministerial Conference, March 5, 1996. International Chamber of Commerce, Doc. no. 103/182; Thompson (1994); Fox (1994).

31. Brittan (1992), p. 54.

32. Hoekman and Mavroodis (1994), p. 22.

REFERENCES

American Bar Association (1991). *Report of the ABA Section of Antitrust Law Special Committee on International Antitrust.* Chicago: American Bar Association.

American Bar Association: Section of International Law and Practice (1995). "Report to the House Delegates, Using Antitrust Laws to Enhance Access of U.S. Firms to Foreign Markets." *The International Lawyer*, 29(4) (Winter): 945–957.

Brander, James A. (1986). "Rationales for Strategic Trade and Industrial Policy." In Paul R. Krugman (ed.), *Strategic Trade Policy and the New International Economics.* Cambridge, MA: MIT Press, ch. 2.

Brittan, Leon (1992). *European Competition Policy: Keeping the Playing-Field Level.* Brussels: Brassey's for the Centre for European Policy Studies.

Deardorff, Alan V. and Rachel McCulloch (1987). "Why Do Governments Prefer Non-Tariff Barriers?" *Carnegie-Rochester Series on Public Policy*, 26 (Spring): 191–222.

Fox, Eleanor (1994). "Competition Law and the Next Agenda for the WTO." In *New Dimensions of Market Access in a Globalising World Economy.* Paris: OECD, ch. 18.

Graham, Edward M. (1994). "Competition Policy and the New Trade Agenda." In *New Dimensions of Market Access in a Globalising World Economy.* Paris: OECD, ch. 12.

Harris, Richard G. (1989). "The New Protectionism Revisited." *Canadian Journal of Economics*, 22(4): 751–778.

Hoekman, Bernard M. and Petros C. Mavroodis (1994). "Competition, Competition Policy and the GATT." *The World Economy*, 17(2): 121–151.

Horlick, Gary N. (1993). "How the GATT Became Protectionist: An Analysis of the Uruguay Round Draft Final Antidumping Code." *Journal of World Trade*, 27(5): 5–18.

Horlick, Gary N. and Michael A. Meyer (1995). "The International Convergence of Competition Policy." *The International Lawyer*, 29(1) (Spring).

Krugman, Paul R. (1987). "Is Free Trade Passé?" *Journal of Economic Perspectives*, 1(2): 131–144.

——— (1993). "The Narrow and Broad Arguments for Free Trade." *American Economic Review, Papers and Proceedings*, 83(2): 362–366.

Krugman, Paul R. et al. (1986). *Strategic Policy and the New International Economics.* Cambridge, MA: MIT Press.

Labaree, Benjamin Woods (1964). *The Boston Tea Party.* New York: Oxford University Press.

Matsushita, Mitsuo (1993). *International Trade and Competition Law in Japan.* Oxford: Oxford University Press.

Nicolaides, Phedon (1994). *Trade and Competition Policies: Comparing Objectives and Methods.* Paris: OECD.

Ordover, Janusz A. and Linda S. Goldberg (1993). *Obstacles to Trade and Competition.* Paris: OECD.

Organization for Economic Cooperation and Development (OECD) (1993). *Obstacles to Trade and Competition.* Paris: OECD.

Spencer, Barbara (1986). "What Should Trade Policy Target?" In Paul R. Krugman (ed.), *Strategic Trade Policy and the New International Economics.* Cambridge, MA: MIT Press, ch. 4.

Swann, Dennis (1970). *The Economics of the Common Market.* Harmondsworth, UK: Penguin.

Thompson, Graeme A. (1994). "Trade and Competition Policy Linkages: Some Ideas on a Framework for the Future." In *New Dimensions of Market Access in a Globalising World Economy.* Paris: OECD, ch. 16.

Tyson, Laura D'Andrea (1992). *Who's Bashing Whom? Trade Conflict in High Technology Industries.* Washington, DC: Institute for International Economics, chs. 1 and 2.

United Nations Conference on Trade and Development (1994). *Handbook of International Trade and Development Statistics: 1993.* New York: United Nations.

World Trade Organization (WTO), Economic Research and Analysis Division and the Statistics and WTO. Information Systems Division (1995). *International Trade: Trends and Statistics.* Geneva: WTO.

Chapter 2

Using Cooperative Strategies to Compete in a Changing World

Pervez N. Ghauri

INTRODUCTION

At no time in modern economic history have countries been more economically interdependent, have greater opportunities of international trade existed, or has the potential for increased demand been greater than now. Yesterday's competitive market battles were fought in Western Europe, Japan, and the United States; today's competitive battles have extended to Asia, Eastern Europe, and Latin America as these emerging markets open to trade. More and more of the world's people, from the richest to the poorest, are now participating in the world's wealth through global trade. Bonded together by satellite communications and global companies, consumers in every corner of the world are demanding an ever-expanding variety of goods. The worldwide economic growth and rising standards of living in almost all parts of the world have led to an increasingly competitive marketplace. This heightened competition has forced companies from all over the world to find new ways to build and maintain their competitive strength. As a result, the level and intensity of competition has changed.[1]

The most profound change in the first postwar period is the emergence of successive waves of Asian newly industrializing countries (NICs) as key players in the world economy. These countries are bringing new competition to Western nations and fostering the notion of a "loss of competitiveness" in the developed countries. This has had a number of effects. First, foreign direct investment (FDI) in these countries changed in nature, and its conceptualization ceased to regard the host economy as purely a malleable object. Second, as outward-oriented policies replaced protectionism, emerging country multinationals became salient and the analysis of their strategies became important. Third, the policies of host governments toward inward investment have been shaped by the increasing interdependence of global economic activity. Asian emerging countries went beyond NIC states to become full global competitors, and the post-communist nations began to enter the world economy as new NICs. The danger facing many economies was that of being left on the fringes as globalization drew countries together, either through expanded world trade and FDI or through the creation of trading blocs (the European Union, NAFTA, ASEAN-AFTA). Some of these issues, such as privatization, the emergence of China, and the Asian crisis, have made scholars and policy makers rethink their strategies.

In terms of strategic decision making, firms undertake FDI to achieve three main objectives:

1. *Market seeking.* Firms invest in countries where they see a large and/or rapidly growing market; for example, recent investments in China and India.

2. *Efficiency seeking.* Firms invest in countries where they can achieve efficiency in cost reduction due to lower operating costs; for example, recent investments by Philips and other consumer electronic products in Singapore and Malaysia.

3. *Resource seeking.* Firms invest in countries to gain access to raw materials or other inputs; for example, investments by oil companies in the Middle East or textile companies in India and Pakistan.

Some investments may include more than one of the above elements, and some of the motives are specific. For example, in banking, a number of investments are made because banks follow their home-country clients into emerging markets. Firms in oligopolistic industries gain economies of scale and other advantages that enable them to be superior to local competitors in host countries.[2] Moreover, firms choose FDI when the transaction costs associated with other modes (such as licensing) are higher.[3]

For years the absence of strong local competitors in most emerging markets was one of the reasons that the FDI flow was predominantly from the industrialized countries of the North to the developing countries of the South. The import substitution and protectionist strategies of most emerging markets made FDI a more viable mode than trade to gain access to these markets. Now government-induced market imperfections are declining; there are some strong and competitive local firms that can prevent the entry of foreign firms. Moreover, since most of the countries are moving away from protectionist politics and are opening up their markets to all types of entry by foreign firms, the nature of the resource flow has changed. According to a UNCTAD study, most developing countries had already moved toward more hospitable and less restrictive policies toward FDI. However, in the last decade, macroeconomic determinants, rather than the microeconomic determinants mentioned above, have become more important: factors such as the investments or capital flow to countries where it can achieve highest returns, and the market size or potential for local sales and benefits which can be achieved through local sourcing.[4]

Moreover, in recent years cooperative strategies are considered more effective than competition to achieve efficiencies. Increasingly firms are looking for cooperation against competition to achieve a competitive advantage. As a result, the boundaries of firms have become blurred,[5] and cooperative strategies have become more and more common to achieve competitive gains.[6]

This is evident from the increasing number of alliances taking place in the business sector. The number of joint ventures and alliances increased tenfold in Europe during the period 1980–1985. This figure increased even more dramatically after 1988–1989, when the "Europe 1992" discussion gained momentum. Cooperation in some industries has become essential to their survival: industries such as services industries (including banks, airlines, and telecommunication), automobile manufactures, manufacturers of electronic equipment and components, computer peripherals manufacturers, software producers, and even universities and schools are most active in these cooperative strategies. Thus, throughout the 1980s and 1990s we have seen that the cooperative, rather than the traditional competitive, form of doing business has grown rapidly. This form continues to increase among firms of all sizes and industries. The cooperative strategies refer to a variety of interfirm agreements through which two or more firms exchange or share resources and capabilities. These arrangements range from informal occasional links to contacts so close that one can hardly see that the organizations involved are indeed separate. In extreme case, these alliances take the form of mergers and acquisitions. The degree of alliance has also led to low or high interdependence between the organizations involved. It is understood that if a partner could do the job alone, he would probably not agree to share ownership and control of his own activities with others. In other words, for this type of relationship there has to be mutual benefit. The parties would ideally have complementary resources, and there are benefits to be achieved by pooling these resources. On the other hand, each party to a collaborative agreement loses its right to dictate its own future and become dependent on the activities and decisions of the other parties to the relationship.

The term "strategic alliance" has only recently been used to describe collaborative arrangements. In fact, until the mid-1980s the term "joint venture" (JV) was used to cover almost all types of interfirm collaboration.[7] The idea of creating JVs to acquire complementary resources is not new. For example, for multinational enterprises (MNEs) from developed countries JVs are very attractive, as they can overcome the uncertainties and share the risk with a local partner who is familiar with and can handle these uncertainties. This is apparent from the number of JVs between Western firms and firms/organizations from Eastern Europe and China. However, the rate of failure in JVs is very high.[8] In spite of this, the number of alliances and JVs in international business relationships is increasing. The European companies are particularly keen on these relationships. The drive toward a single Europe, the deregulation of several industries, and the liberalization of a number of centrally planned economies are some of the reasons behind this trend. JVs signed with former Eastern bloc countries and China have increased tremendously. In 1994, alone 30,187 JV agreements were signed between firms from Western Europe and firms/organizations from the former Eastern bloc.[9]

The parties involved are, however, facing great problems in handling these relationships and interorganizational interdependencies. At present some evidence is available why two or more firms start a JV or another form of alliance and why firms use this type of arrangement as an entry strategy into foreign countries. Some evidence also exists as to why JVs and alliances fail; while the relations are cooperative, interests diverge and conflicts can easily arise.[10]

In this chapter the following issues are addressed:

1. What are the reasons and factors that are influencing global strategies of companies?
2. What are the advantages and disadvantages of cooperative competition?
3. What are the trends in Europe and elsewhere, and how are these trends influencing these cooperative strategies?
4. What are the factors that influence the success or failure of these relationships?

WHY COOPERATIVE STRATEGIES?

Privatization (the transfer of productive assets from public to private ownership) has been part of most structural adjustment policies since the 1980s. It has been undertaken to achieve a variety of objectives such as enhanced economic efficiency, reduction of financial deficits, and the reduction of the role of the state. If we summarize experiences with privatization strategies, we see that there is now a sufficient body of evidence to review the progress made and to assess what works and what does not. We end up with the cautionary point that privatization alone is unlikely to ease significantly the burden of the state-owned sector in many countries.

The emergence of China as a major player in the world economy has already had an impact equal to that of Japan in the earlier decades of the postwar world. China represents a non-uniform environment for the inward investor, and there are currently difficulties in the implementation and transparency of business law, contractual difficulties, regional differences, and uncertainties about the direction of future economic policies. These challenges need to be addressed by careful adaptation of company strategies.

There are several reasons why firms strive for cooperative strategies. According to some scholars, local government pressure, local facilities, and spreading of risks were major reasons for international alliances and JVs.[11] Others believe that local companies are drawn to a need for foreign capital, technology, and management and marketing know-how.[12] In general, the reason to form an alliance or a JV is to gain complementary resources from a JV partner, and an important characteristic of resource exchange is its dynamic nature. It is argued that JV partners' contributions are not a static bundle of skills or resources. These are subject to change and are dynamic in nature.[13] In spite of all these studies, the field of international alliances and JVs lacks a strong theoretical core and a framework that effectively integrates past research and serves as a springboard for launching new and profound research.

Other than these discussions at the firm and strategy levels, there are a number of developments in our environment that are forcing or facilitating these alliances and JVs. First, the increasing importance of internationalization, with ever-increasing competition, creates the need for teaming up. Second, the more the companies are internationalizing, the more they realize that "all business is local," and therefore they need to have local partners to handle local environments and cultural differences. This encourages cross-border alliances and JVs. Third, the changing nature of competition, rapid technological development, and the increased cost of research and development (R&D) are forcing companies to combine scarce resources. Fourth, the emergence of many new competitors in traditional businesses is forcing existing companies to develop and nurture strong relationships and networks to create barriers of entry for new competition. Finally, a shift from product to competence is forcing companies to go out and look for new and complementary knowledge and competence. As a result, while in the 1970s and 1980s we witnessed product- and market-driven alliances, in the 1990s we saw more knowledge- and competence-driven alliances.[14]

Today most of the worldwide activity in mergers and acquisitions involving cross-border companies is taking place in Europe and North America. Mergers between MCI and BT, and between Daimler Benz and Chrysler, are good examples. Some scholars believe that, on a global scale, European companies do not address the fundamental gap between themselves and their foreign competitors based on skills and competition. The managers, before making decisions on re-engineering, mergers, or acquisition, must first understand the dynamics of competition in their industry and relate their competitive position and its viability in the particular industry. Only then should they consider the issue of merger, acquisition or re-engineering, as different industries have different structures and behavior.

For example, the companies have to analyze whether the nature of their competition and their business is global, pan-European, or local, and how it would influence the attractiveness of a particular merger or alliance. In global business, an alliance with a partner from another region/market is most useful to improve skill and to get access to new markets and enjoy some economies of scale and efficiencies. In pan-European business, an alliance with a European partner is preferable, especially for companies that have a multiple-country presence. In this case, mergers and alliances can provide access to superior skills and economies of scale. In local businesses, however, companies should try to dominate their home market through mergers and acquisitions. In such cases, the companies should find a rich position to guard them against foreign competition.

ADVANTAGES AND DISADVANTAGES OF COOPERATIVE STRATEGIES

There are several advantages of cooperative strategies. The companies in most industries have realized that severe head-to-head competition exhausts them financially as well as managerially, and it negatively influences their innovative capabilities, whereas competition should in fact be encouraging innovations and efficiencies. The economies of scale, efficient use of each other's resources, and quick entry into new markets are some of the benefits that are widely discussed and established.

There are some studies that analyze different types of alliances and conclude which type of alliances are relatively advantageous. According to resource-based theory, the competitive advantage can be realized through a firm's own existing resources and core competencies, an assessment of their profit potential, and the selection of strategies based upon the opportunities created.[15] This theory suggests that a firm should not invest in a relationship that is not related to its own core competencies. It holds that alliances and strategies based upon existing core competencies could lead to sustainable advantages.

The key to organizational survival is the ability to acquire and maintain resources. The relationship between the firm and its environment is of utmost importance in this process. Thus, the only way firms can gain competitive advantage is by cooperating with key parts of their environment through strategic alliances. It is these key parts of the environment that can provide the firm with crucial resources complementary to its own resources. The degree of alliance depends upon the critical nature of resources that parties can exchange with each other. It will also dictate the extent of interdependencies between the firms. Alliances that are strategic should be competence/resource driven and should enhance the competitive advantage of the parties involved.[16]

Among the disadvantages, giving up autonomy over one's own strategic resources is considered the most crucial one. The greater the extent of cooperation, the more one has to sacrifice its autonomy and control over its resources. The alliance or partner becomes a co-owner of the crucial resources, and there is a risk that the other partner may use the resource or knowledge attained through the cooperation in a non-cooperative manner or outside the scope of this relationship. Moreover, the resource can now only be used jointly and not by one partner, even if he was the original owner of that resource. This is particularly problematic if the resource in question is the core of its technological know-how. In a market-oriented alliance, there is a risk that a firm might give access to its market at its own expense. Although the alliances are established to create mutual interdependencies, the disadvantages arise from changes in the strategic priorities and conditions for one partner or for both, changes that make the relationship less important.[17] It is therefore stressed that parties should contribute with complementary resources so that partners can benefit from each other.

It is quite difficult to keep the focus on external competition. The purpose of alliances is to create competitive advantage for the partners against other competitors. This can lead to internal problems regarding what is in joint interest and what is the interest of one of the parties. Who is responsible for what, and who will benefit from what? Whose clients are the new customers? All these issues might lead to the fact that more energy is spent on these internal issues than to the external competition.

Another disadvantage is that parties can very easily develop overly optimistic expectations from the alliance. There are a multitude of interests that work with and against each other. For example, the executives involved have their own ambitions and expectations; the firms involved have their own; and the relationship or alliance may have different joint ambitions and expectations. The executives are thus torn between all these sometimes conflicting interests. The time and resources they should spend on external competition and to achieve competitive advantage is now spent on the above-mentioned tussles. They are always afraid of being overdependent on the other firm or executives.

In addition to these disadvantages, alliances are vulnerable due to complexities such as task complexity; whether the alliance is for a specific task (e.g., marketing, R&D, etc.) or as an overall alliance; alliance complexity; the number of partners involved; the sharing of each other's crucial resources as well as decision making; and the cultural fit of the organizations involved. Different companies, depending upon their size, location, and management style, have different cultures. It is very difficult to comprehend each other's culture and even more difficult to force one company's culture on the other.[18]

THE IMPACT OF THE EUROPEAN UNION ON COOPERATIVE STRATEGIES

The European Union (EU) is not new; it has already existed for more than 40 years and has successfully bonded together fifteen countries in a single market and has achieved a closer voluntary union. In early 1992, after the signing of the Treaty of European Union in Maastricht, a framework was created to build a democratically elected European Parliament, a joint foreign and security policy, and a single currency. It forms a strong and united European front in an increasingly competitive world. The quest for a single currency has been a long-sought-after dream of big business in Europe. To businesspeople the carousel of ever-changing currency rates has been a big problem, and the benefits of an enormous market regulated by a single stable currency, as in the United States, are enormous. The single currency, controlled by European Central Bank, has price stability, limited budgetary deficits, and stable interest rates as its main objectives.

This means that states will be giving up their right to depreciate their currencies and in practice to set interest rates. As a consequence, a state will not be able to gain competitive advantage (for example, through devaluation) at the expense of other member-states. In the long run, all countries will achieve a low inflation rate and highly productive economies and will be able to influence collective policies by taking part in decision-making and policy matters.

The creation of the industrial world's largest domestic market, with close to 400 million affluent consumers, has in fact been achieved. European businesses now have access to a domestic market larger in size than that of their American and Japanese competitors. As a result, the volume of trade between European countries has increased. Until recently, around 30 papers and documents were needed for a laden lorry crossing EU borders. At present, only one document, the so-called "Single Administrative Document" is required, and in the future even that will no longer be necessary. Individuals are able to move freely, and there is a wider choice of goods in shops. The introduction of a single European currency, the Euro, has taken place, and a timetable has been agreed upon for the successive replacement of local/national currency. An elected European parliament and an European police force already exist.

THE IMPACT OF THE ASIAN CRISIS ON COOPERATIVE STRATEGIES

The rising investment that helped Asian economies to develop was predicted on the assumption of ever-rising exports. This became valid in countries like Japan, South Korea, and Taiwan, but not in most other Asian economies. For example, in Indonesia, the increasing imports of consumer products, such as fashion items and electronics, led to an increasing imbalance in exports and imports. The devaluation of the Chinese renminbi in 1994 and the Japanese yen in 1995 and 1997 were other factors that redirected the capital flow and helped these two economies to export more, while export growth in other Asian economies fell from 30 percent in early 1995 to zero in mid-1996. In an effort to develop their exports and capacity levels, companies from these countries dramatically increased their short-term bank loans, but due to a continuous stagnation in exports the present crisis became inevitable.[19] Due to a lack of regulating laws, supervisory mechanisms, and unplanned imbalance in savings and consumption, the crisis got out of hand.

As we know, the governments are not the only culprits. Both Thailand and Indonesia did not have deficit budgeting. In fact, both of these countries had surpluses in 1996, but there was a high level of foreign borrowings and current account deficit. Moreover, a high portion of these borrowings were going to finance consumption and property glut. In 1997, total foreign debts exceeded $100 billion in Indonesia.

While the crisis did not really come unexpectedly, its intensity was much greater than people could imagine. In 1994, during the Mexican economic crisis, a number of scholars warned that some of the Asian economies had the same symptoms. And in the early months of 1997, after the Thai crisis, South Korea, Indonesia, and Malaysia were particularly warned. When the crisis hit the two

Table 2.1
Asia's Shrinking Economics (GDP in billions of U.S. dollars)

Country	1996	1998	1998 (PPP*)
China	839	1,063	4,730
Hong Kong	154	188	190
Indonesia	226	51	1,020
Malaysia	92	71	240
Philippines	84	68	240
South Korea	485	272	660
Singapore	94	92	90
Taiwan	272	269	450
Thailand	186	97	530
Total	**2,432**	**2,171**	**8,150**

*PPP = Purchasing Power Parity.
Source: The Economist, February 7, 1998, p. 90.

worst economies, South Korea and Indonesia, these countries had to be saved by rescue packages of $57 billion and $43 billion, respectively. As a result of the crisis, the Asian economies are wasting away. Indonesia's GDP was $226 billion in 1996; in 1998, it was expected to be $51 billion if the exchange rate remained at early 1998 levels. The same goes for other Asian economies, as seen in Table 2.1.[20]

Although the exchange rates are undervalued and the relative purchasing power parity will give a different picture due to non-tradeable services such as housing and transportation, Table 2.1 shows that after the crisis most Asian economies were heavily undervalued. What is becoming more apparent now is that after about one year of the crisis, the Western economies are feeling the crunch. Not only the Japanese, European, and American banks faced heavy losses due to bad loans in Asia; other financial institutions also faced big problems. For example, J. P. Morgan has been involved in litigation over non-payment on derivative contracts to the value of $3.4 billion in South Korea alone. ABN-AMRO Bank's 7 percent risk-weighted assets, about $13 billion, are in the troubled Asian economies. The Japanese, German, and American banks are even more heavily involved.[21] In addition to losses by these financial institutions, the trade between Europe and America and the trade between Japan and America are facing problems due to the Asian crisis. These three powers are inducing each other to help the Asian economies out, as it is in their interest to improve the conditions in Asia. The G-7 meeting in February 1998, the Euro-Asia summit in April 1998, and the International Monetary Fund's (IMF) repeated concessions given to Indonesia are some examples of Western efforts to rescue Asia.

If we look at the industry level, some of the industries, such as the banking in Indonesia, have contributed to this crisis, while others have been hard hit by this crisis. Take, for example, the airline industry. Throughout the world this industry has an overcapacity and needs restructuring. For example, the European and American airlines are merging or entering into alliances with each other. Experts believe that by the year 2000, some 50 percent of the European airlines will disappear.

MULTINATIONALS VERSUS GOVERNMENTS

Many scholars have pointed to the development of the changing relationship between MNEs and governments and divide it into different eras. In general, they agree with Boddewyn's assessment that a period of conflict followed World War II, where less developed countries challenged MNEs that were investing for purposes sometimes felt to be inimical to the host country's chosen path.[22] From a date often fixed in the late 1970s, a shift occurred in which the relationship was not so conflictual but where governments were seen as a constraint on the activities of MNEs. The 1980s saw the building of cooperative relationships between MNEs and governments, and the key problem became the danger of oversubsidizing inward investment through excessive locational competition ("tournaments" for attracting FDI). Finally, the late 1990s and the Asian crisis, followed by a crisis in Brazil, have turned the wheel backwards. Many economies in Asia, such as Indonesia and India, are moving backwards to rather restrictive policies and an era of suspicion toward MNEs, governments, and investors from the West.

For countries such as Thailand, South Korea, and even Malaysia, conditions have improved. Thailand, the first country to plunge into the crisis, is perhaps also the first one to get out of it. The baht is rising, and so is the stock exchange. But the interest rate continues to cripple companies. Foreign investors have returned; ABN-AMRO bought interest into one of the important Thai banks, and George Soros provided a $650 million package for Nokorn Thai Strip Mill, an ultra-modern mill producing steel for export. Companies and banks are merging with each other to fight overcapacity and to achieve efficiencies. One example of some of the measures taken by the Thai government, in agreement with the IMF, was that in December 1997 it announced that 56 finance companies would be closed down. Their assests (about $20 billion) were to be segregated into the good and the bad, such as empty office blocks. The good assets were to be disposed as soon as possible, and the rest were to be eliminated by the end of 1998.

In Korea, the National Assembly passed eighteen financial reform bills, including one establishing a new supervisory agency. As in Thailand, commercial banks' bad loans (estimated at about $20 billion) were to be bought at a discount by an asset management corporation. As a result of such reforms, the confidence of foreign investors is coming back. In 1998, a group of 134 banks from 32 countries agreed to swap $22 billion in short-term loans to South Korean banks for a large credit guaranteed by the government. Also, in day-to-day life the confidence is coming back. The department stores are full with customers as shopkeepers are removing the signs "IMF Sale" and hotels are packed with businesspersons. Foreign firms are buying parts of Korean companies, as most foreign investors believe that President Kim Dae Jung is committed to reshaping the economy.[23]

There has also been a growth of the "New Mercantilism" where, through the rhetoric of competitiveness (as Krugman shows), "beggar-my-neighbor" policies are followed. Trade is described in terms of metaphors from warfare rather than being regarded as mutually beneficial. FDI is seen as a competitive weapon against other firms and, by curious identification, against other countries. The rhetoric of the governments of many merging states is among the most belligerent for development, not as an end in itself (to enrich the indigenous populace) but to pre-empt others in a race toward an indeterminate (or at least ill-defined) goal. The notion of "Partners in Development" looks like a relic of a previous era, not because of conflict between multinationals and individual countries, but because coalitions of MNEs and countries are seen as rivals.[24] At the company level, however, the economy needs a real restructuring in most industries. While in some industries the monopolies have to be broken, in others there are too many companies.

ARE COOPERATIVE STRATEGIES WORKING?

In Europe, we have a number of industries that have recently been deregulated or sectors that have been opened to new competition. In these industries (e.g., telecommunications and transportation), new competition coming from global competitors is creating dramatic new conditions that are difficult for newly liberalized companies to manage. Therefore, it is necessary for the companies to first understand their industry (its competition and structure) and then, within that context, to analyze their own competition position. Depending upon this analysis, the companies should choose different strategies.[25]

The question is: Are strategic alliances or mergers the right way to achieve competitive advantage? And what have we learned so far? Are strategic alliances working? By this time we have an abundance of examples available to be able to answer these questions. Almost all major corporations are involved or have been involved in mergers, acquisitions, and strategic alliances. In the last 10 years, IBM alone has joined in over 400 strategic alliances with various companies, including its perpetual rival, Apple. Big Blue has recently teamed up with Siemens and Toshiba to develop a new (costly) generation of DRAM computer chips. Other companies such as ABB, Nobel Industries, Saab, AT&T, Telia, PTT Netherlands, GE, Merck, Time Warner, Matsushita, Fujitsu, Fokker,

Procter & Gamble, and Philip Morris are some of the companies that have recently been involved in these activities. A number of studies conclude that more than 51 percent of strategic alliances are successful for both partners, and only 33 percent result in failure for both.[26]

SUCCESS FACTORS

The making of successful alliance strategies depends upon several factors. According to one opinion, cost cutting or saving cash alone is not enough to justify an alliance. The reason to enter an alliance is to gain access to a new market or a special expertise, or to gain competitive strength in a particular market. Both parties must have something to offer to each other.

The management of mergers, acquisitions, and alliances is complicated not just because it is difficult to manage a bigger company, but because there are so many "fuzzy" areas, such as personal ambitions and relationships between managers coming from different firms. We have witnessed a number of successful mergers and alliances. For example, Astra and Merck, where the relationship started simply with U.S. rights to its partner's new drugs, was later turned into a new corporation worth $500 million a year, with Merck selling 50 percent of its shares to Astra. Corning Glass, a $3 billion-a-year company, formed a joint venture with Dow Chemical and formed Dow Corning as a joint venture company which is now listed in the *Fortune* 500.

One key to success is to create some sort of equal partnership and a spirit of continuous advantage for both partners. Acting as equals does not mean that it is otherwise not possible to trust, or that partners have no desire to share, but to give each other respect. For example, Ford has bought 24 percent of Mazda and has formed a number of cooperative ventures as an equal. Mazda markets Ford products and smaller cars (e.g., Mercury Tracer) and Ford markets Mazda's light trucks as its Rangers. In other words, for the alliance to work efficiently, the companies should have a mentality of collaboration, not of acquisition and control.

The alliance among competitors and the economic value of a relationship is very crucial. This is illustrated by the alliance between Microsoft and Apple. Although Apple alleged in court that Microsoft Windows violates the rules of intellectual property and copyrights, the two companies have a successful alliance. Microsoft has even strengthened its alliance with Apple and supplies software applications for Macintosh computers, helping them to gain entrance to the business market.

The key to a successful relationship, according to Bleeke and Ernst, is a common objective and open communication. They also profess that a relationship starts slowly and takes years to establish. The most successful alliances are of a complementary nature, where one partner can provide what the other needs and needs what the other can provide. The alliance between Toshiba and Motorola is a good example of this complementarity. Toshiba contributed with expertise in DRAMs and access to the Japanese market; Motorola contributed with an expertise in microprocessors and access to the American market. According to the above-mentioned scholars, 75 percent of alliances securing at least two markets succeeded, while the figure was only 43 percent in the case of alliances that were focused on a single market.[27] One important issue is to be open to each other and to share not only the problem parts of your business, but also the successful parts. The companies have to open their books and let their networks talk to each other. If one company stays secretive, it would not encourage the other party to cooperate wholeheartedly.

In conclusion, it is fair to say that strategic alliances, JVs, mergers, or acquisitions are not easy to handle or manage because the nature of relationships is laden with conflicting or competitive interests. No matter how well prepared and structured, they are bound to get into trouble at some point. These troubles require more flexibility and better communication, and studies have revealed that eventually a majority of these ventures prove to be successful for both partners. We have also learned that depending upon the industry, strategic alliances, mergers, and acquisitions are necessary and are demanded by changing environments.

NOTES

1. Rich and Gumpert (1988); Kay (1991).
2. Buckley and Ghauri (1994).
3. Nooteboom (1993).
4. UNCTAD (1998).
5. Rich and Gumpert (1988); Kay (1991).
6. Janger (1980); Rich and Gumpert (1988).
7. Badarocco (1991).
8. Killing (1983); Nooteboom (1993).
9. Blodgett (1992); Buckley and Ghauri (1994); Ghauri (1995).
10. Beamish and Lane (1982); Cavusgil and Ghauri (1990).
11. Tomlinson (1970); Janger (1980).
12. Abdul (1979); Ahn (1980); Buckley and Ghauri (1993).
13. Bivens and Lovell (1966); Killing (1983); Connolly (1984); Harrigan (1986).
14. Badarocco (1991); Lorange and Roos (1992).
15. Grant (1991); Faulkner (1995).
16. Faulkner (1995).
17. Lorange and Roos (1992).
18. Hofstede (1991).
19. *Fortune* (1998).
20. *The Economist* (1997).
21. *Financial Times* (1998).
22. Boddewyn (1992).
23. *Business Week* (1998).
24. Krugman (1994).
25. Wright (1979).

26. Bleeke and Ernst (1993); Inkpen and Birkenshaw (1994); Faulkner (1995).
27. Bleeke and Ernst (1993); Geringer and Herbert (1989).

REFERENCES

Abdul, A. R. (1979). *The Mixed Enterprises in Malaysia: A Study of Joint Ventures between Malaysian Public Corporations and Foreign Enterprises*. Doctoral dissertation, Katholieke Universiteit te Leuven, no. 36.

Ahn, D. S. (1980). "Joint Ventures in the ASEAN Countries." *Entereconomics* (July–August): 193–198.

Badaracco, J. L., Jr. (1991). *The Knowledge Link: How Firms Compete through Strategic Alliances*. Boston: Harvard Business School Press.

Beamish, P. W. and H. W. Lane (1982). "Joint Venture Performance in Developing Countries." Paper presented at the ASAC Conference, Ottawa University.

Bivens, K. K. and E. B. Lovell (1996). *Joint Ventures with Foreign Partners*. New York: National Industrial Conference Board.

Bleeke, J. and D. Ernst (eds.) (1993). *Collaborating to Compete: Using Strategic Alliances and Acquisitions in the Global Market-place*. New York: John Wiley & Sons.

Blodgett, L. L. (1992). "Research Notes and Communication Factors in the Instability of International Joint Ventures: An Event History Analysis." *Strategic Management Journal*, 13: 475–481.

Boddewyn, J. J. (1992). "Political Behaviour Research." In P. J. Buckley (ed.), *New Directions in International Business*. Cheltenham, UK: Edward Elgar.

Buckley, P. J. and P. N. Ghauri (eds.) (1993). *The Internationalization of the Firm: A Reader*. London: Academic Press.

——— (1994). *The Economics of Change in East and Central Europe: Its Impact on International Business*. London: Academic Press.

Business Week (1998). "Korea Is Cheering Far Too Soon." April 6, p. 45.

Cavusgil, S. T. and P. N. Ghauri (1990). *Doing Business in Developing Countries: Entry and Negotiation Strategies*. London: Routledge.

Connolly, S. G. (1984). "Joint Ventures with Third World Multinationals: A New Form of Entry to International Markets." *Columbia Journal of World Business* (Summer): 18–22.

The Economist (1997). "A Survey of Indonesia." July 26.

Faulkner, D. (1995). *International Strategic Alliances: Co-operating to Compete*. London: McGraw-Hill.

Financial Times (1998). "Banks' Exposure Start Coming into Form." February 21, p. 27.

Fortune (1998). "Why Asia's Collapse Won't Kill the Economy." February 2, pp. 8–10.

Geringer, I. M. and C. Herbert (1989). "Control and Performance of International Joint Ventures." *Journal of International Business Studies*, 20: 235–254.

Ghauri, P. N. (1995). "Marketing to Eastern Europe." In M. Baker (ed.), *Marketing: Theory and Practice*. London: Macmillan, 379–389.

Grant, R. M. (1991). "The Resource-Based Theory of Competitive Advantage: Implications for Strategy Formulation." *California Management Review* (Spring): 114–135.

Harrigan, K. R. (1986). *Managing for Joint Venture Success*. Lexington, MA: Lexington Books.

Hofstede, G. H. (1991). *Cultures and Organizations: Software of the Mind*. New York: McGraw-Hill.

Inkpen, A. C. and J. Birkenshaw (1994). "International Joint Ventures and Performance: An Interorganisational Perspective." *International Business Review*, 3(3): 182–200.

Janger, A. (1980). *Organization of International Joint Ventures*. New York: Conference Board.

Kay, N. (1991). "Industrial Collaborative Activity and the Completion of the Internal Market." *Journal of Common Market Studies*, 24: 347–362.

Killing, J. P. (1983). *Strategies for Joint Venture Success*. Kent, UK: Croom Helm.

Krugman, P. (1994). "Does Third World Growth Hurt First World Prosperity?" *Harvard Business Review* (July–August): 113–121.

Lorange, P. and J. Roos (1992). *Strategic Alliances: Formation, Implementation and Evolution*, Cambridge, MA: Blackwell.

Nooteboom, B. (1993). "Relaties in industrie en huwelijk." *Economische Statistische Berichten*, 22(29): 1170–1175.

Rich, S. R. and D. E. Gumpert (1988). "What Is New in Super Conductivity Business." *New York Times*, January 24, p. F17.

Tomlinson, J.W.C. (1970). *The Joint Venture Process in International Business: India and Pakistan*. Cambridge, MA: MIT Press.

UNCTAD (1998). *World Development Report*. Geneva: UNCTAD.

Wright, R. W. (1979). "Joint Venture Problems in Japan." *Columbia Journal of World Business* (Spring): 25–31.

Chapter 3

Integrating Country of Origin into Global Marketing Strategy: A Review of U.S. Marking Statutes

Irvine Clarke III and Margaret Owens

INTRODUCTION

Marketers are cognizant that the country of origin affects consumers product evaluations (Bilkey and Ness 1982; Erickson et al. 1984; Han 1989; Han and Terpstra 1988; Johansson et al. 1985). Country-of-origin effects have been found for general products (Darling and Wood 1990; Howard 1989), specific categories of products (Cordell 1992; Hong and Wyer 1989, 1990; Roth and Romeo 1992), and even for certain brands (Chao 1993; Han and Terpstra 1988; Haubl 1996; Tse and Gorn 1993; Witt 1990). However, the continued globalization of markets has driven business into a worldwide search for low-cost, high-quality components and finished goods, often in countries that have not been historically associated with the manufacture of these types of products, confounding the use of country of origin in international product strategy development. Additionally, global sourcing typically requires that components of the product arrive from multiple countries, making it even more complex to identify any specific country of origin. Achieving the desired country-of-origin designation has become so perplexing that many marketing managers are ignoring this key component of global marketing strategy.

   Obtaining the proper country-of-origin marking for a product can have a profound impact on the success of countless international products. Substantial research has demonstrated that country of origin affects consumers' perceptions of product quality (Hong and Wyer 1989, 1990; Johansson et al. 1985; Johansson and Thorelli, 1985; Papadopoulos and Heslop 1993), brand image (Han and Terpstra 1988; McConnell 1967; Yaprak 1987), purchase decisions (Papadopoulos and Heslop 1993), and the consumer's propensity to use a product's "made in" label (Han and Terpstra 1988; Johansson et al., 1985; Tse and Gorn

1993). Similarly, consumers have shown a willingness to pay a premium for products originating from a desirable location (Bilkey and Nes 1982; Schooler and Wildt 1968). Additionally, tariff rates typically vary depending on the country marking of the product (Sturm 1976). Overall, both customer-perceived quality and market entry costs can be directly attributed to obtaining an advantageous country marking.

PURPOSE OF THE STUDY

One of the keys to international success is understanding and complying with country-of-origin marking regulations (Moore 1996). Since astute international marketers can use marking statutes to develop proactive strategies that provide the entire benefit of country of origin, an enhanced understanding of how to obtain the desired country-of-origin designation could acutely improve a marketer's ability in international strategy development. Yet, while the current literature clearly indicates that these markings have an impact on consumer product perceptions, there is little, if anything, that examines the actual legal issues involved in obtaining desired country-of-origin markings, thereby providing global marketing managers real action-oriented strategic choices. Further, international marketing texts stress the importance of understanding the political/legal environment of potential markets; however, once again, there is little that focuses on the legal identification of relevant statutes or precedents pertaining to the awarding of coveted "made in" labels. Therefore, it is the purpose of this chapter to review U.S. Civil Code regarding the designation of country of origin for products entering the United States and to provide global marketing managers' guidance in obtaining appropriate product markings. As the United States is the world's largest consumer market, and U.S. country-of-origin markings approach international procedure, this chapter will illustrate the four major legal tests for country marking and explain how to use each to obtain the optimal country-of-origin designation. These tests of transformation are providing a foundation for the WTO "Agreement of Rule of Origin," designed to create a global harmonization of marking regulations. As a legal heuristic for the tests of substantial transformation is developed, the marketer is released to use the tests strategically to assess country-of-origin markings for an optimal product configuration, thus integrating country-of-origin into global marketing strategy.

BACKGROUND

The requirement that imported goods be marked with the country of origin first appeared in the Tariff Act of 1890 and has been included in subsequent tariff acts. The purpose of the marking statute was to advise the ultimate purchaser in the United States of the foreign origin of goods. Congress had the power to impose this requirement on imported goods as an exercise of constitutional power over commerce with foreign nations (U.S. Const. Art. I, §8, cl. 3).[1]

The United States marking statutes provide that with certain exceptions, articles of foreign origin are to be marked with the country of origin in some manner. In general, the country-of-origin statute requires that every article or container of foreign origin imported into the United States be marked legibly, indelibly and permanently, to indicate to the ultimate purchaser the English name of the country where the product originated (Moore 1996). The country of origin is defined in the United States Code of Federal Regulations at 19 C.F.R. §134 1(b). This section provides:

(b) *Country of Origin.* "Country of origin" means the country of manufacture, production, or growth of any articles of foreign origin entering the United States. Further work or material added to an article in another country must effect a substantial transformation in order to render such other country the "country of origin" within the meaning of this part: however, for a good of a NAFTA country, the NAFTA Marking Rules will determine the country of origin.

The country of origin is determined by looking to the nature of the good being imported and the processes it had gone through and whether it has been substantially transformed.

TESTS OF TRANSFORMATION

When articles are processed in foreign countries before being imported to the United States, the country of origin for marking purposes will be the country where a substantial transformation or where the last substantial transformation has occurred. Federal courts have been asked to interpret the law on whether or not substantial transformation of imported articles has occurred for marking purposes. Cases decided by the federal courts have created four main tests to determine whether substantial transformation has occurred. They are the *name, character, and use test*, the *essence test*, the *value-added test*, and the *article of commerce test*. One or more of these tests may be used when making the decision about using foreign parts or assembly, depending on what outcome the decision maker is trying to achieve with a particular product, that is, enhanced marketability or increased profits. Table 3.1 provides an introduction to the application of each test.

Name, Character, and Use Test

The first and probably most used test is the *name, character, and use test.* This test states that an imported article is substantially transformed if it is transformed into a new and different article having a distinctive name, character, or use. The criteria of name, character, and use are methods used to determine if and when substantial transformation has occurred for the purpose of determining the country-of-origin marks to be placed on a product. It is necessary that the

Table 3.1
Tests of Transformation

Tests of Transformation	Application
Name, Character, Use Test	Fundamental characteristics are materially altered Technical process Major manufacturing process Skilled labor
Essence Test	Functionally necessary No separate commercial value Technical process Skilled labor Destruction with disassembly
Value Added Test	Cost of production—skilled labor/technical process Feature of consumer interest Combination vs. material alteration
Article of Commerce Test	Producer to consumer good Change in classification under tariff schedules Material alteration Technical process Skilled labor

fundamental characteristics of the product be changed or the characteristics or use be materially altered. An article must emerge from the manufacturing process with a name, character, and use differing from those of the original materials subjected to the process.

A simple example of what constitutes substantial transformation is the making of an imported wooden handle into a hairbrush. The manufacturer imports wooden handles from Japan, and the word "Japan" is marked on the handle; however, the marking is in a place where, when the bristles are attached by the manufacturer, the word "Japan" is obliterated. Customs wants the handles individually marked so that the ultimate retail consumer will know the handle was made in Japan. This factual situation brought forth the court case interpreting customs regulations and caused the Customs Service to formulate a standard to be followed when dealing with this issue. See *United States v. Gibson-Thomsen Co.*, 27 C.C.P.A. 267 (1940). In this situation the character and use of the imported product had changed from a wooden handle into a hairbrush with bristles used to brush human hair. The wooden handle lost its identity in the final product and was not required to have the word "Japan" on the handle.

A second example of this test deals with a manufacturer importing multiple parts that are subjected to varying degrees of processing to complete the finished product. Fluted drill blanks, jobber drill bits, taps, dies, and reamers are all imported from Taiwan for finishing and sale to the ultimate consumer. Each of the products goes through a different finishing process. The fluted drill blanks are modified in many different ways to create 200 different tools. In addition, they are pointed, heat treated, and put through a finishing process. The jobber drill bits are put through a finishing process, but no other steps are utilized in completing the product. Processing the taps requires the manufacturer to remove the point, change the threading, heat treat, and put an oxide coating on the finished product. The dies and reamers are heat treated and given an oxide treatment, but no other processes are performed to complete the product.

Although the products are from one foreign manufacturer, each of the products is looked at separately to determine whether it has been substantially transformed in the United States by the receiving manufacturer. In this example, it was determined that only the fluted drillbits and the taps were substantially transformed. The court determined that the processes used on these two products were somewhat complex and required technical skill to perform; thus, their physical character was changed. Neither of these products would have to have "Made in Taiwan" marked on it. The dies and reamers were determined not to be substantially transformed; therefore, they would have to be marked. Since these two products were not marked, they were seized because of the manufacturer's failure to comply with the marking statutes. See *Matter of Property Seized from ICS*, 163 F.R.D. 292 (E.D. Wis. 1995).

This final example is demonstrative of how important it is for the marketer to thoroughly evaluate the processes to be performed on the imported part. The expected increase in profits from using a foreign part was totally lost by the manufacturer, and most likely its entire profit was lost by the confiscation of two of the products as illegal contraband.

Essence Test

The second test is the *essence test*. This test stands for the proposition that the imported part is substantially transformed when it becomes an integral part of the new article with which it is combined. In other words, the imported part makes the final product what it is—it becomes the intrinsic nature of the final product. The imported part is considered integral if (1) it is functionally necessary to the new article, versus accessory; (2) if the imported part has no commercial value separate from the new article; (3) if the imported part becomes part of the new article by a process that requires some degree of skill; and (4) if removal of the imported part from the new article would destroy either the imported part or the new article. Court opinions take all of these into consideration, with no condition controlling.

An example of the essence test is as follows. In an attempt to reduce its manufacturing costs, a typewriter ribbon manufacturer decided to import the spool upon which it wound the typewriter ribbon. The spool was manufactured in a foreign country and imported into the United States, where the manufacturer wound the ribbon on the spool. Although the manufacturer wanted to save money on the production of the spool, he did not want to have to mark the spool itself with the name of the country where it was made. The ultimate consumer might not be inclined to purchase the product if the name of the producing country was marked on the spool. This is a situation where the essence test could be used to the advantage of the manufacturer because it could be shown that the spools were substantially transformed after importation to the United States into new articles with a distinctive use, the spool becoming an integral part of the new article. The empty spools were the vehicles to sell ribbon. The ribbon was the major feature of interest to the consumer. The ribbon was the essence of the finished product. See *Grafton Spools, Ltd. v. United States*, 45 Cust. Ct. 16, 223 C.D. 2190 (1960). Here, the manufacturer was able to achieve a significant savings on production costs and maintain the product's desired image in the mind of the retail consumer.

Marketers may find that using foreign labor to product part of a product could provide a competitive advantage by lowering costs and increasing the quality of the product. Before marketers advise a manufacturer to use foreign labor or foreign components, they should address the following questions: (1) Is the imported part functionally necessary to the new article or is it merely decorative or an accessory? (2) Does the imported part have any value apart from the new article? (3) Does it require some degree of technical skill or competence to combine the imported part with the new article? (4) If you removed the imported part from the new article, would the part or new article be destroyed? Each of these questions has to be considered, and none of them is sufficient by itself.

Value-Added Test

The third test is the *value-added test*. This test stands for the proposition that neither the imported part or the domestic part has a value standing on its own, however, when combined value is added to the final product. The value added is the desirability of the final product to the consumer because of the combining of the two parts without undergoing a substantial transformation. Manufacturers relying on this test should be concerned about what processes are being performed on the components of the final product. In determining the country of origin of a finished product, the courts have found the country of origin to be the country that incurred the greatest cost in producing a component of the finished product, reasoning that the part that cost the most to produce added the most value to the finished product.

A typical example is as follows. An American shoe manufacturer has the upper part of the shoe manufactured in foreign country "X." Country "X" incurs substantial cost in manufacturing the uppers. The uppers were imported into the United States, where the manufacturer attached the soles and then marked the shoes "Made in America"—another case gone wrong for the manufacturer. Here, the uppers were considered to be the essence of the shoes. The soles were not the major feature of interest to the consumer, nor did the soles add significant value to the ultimate product. Attachment of the uppers to the outsoles was "significantly less costly" than the process of manufacturing the uppers. The desirability of the final product to the consumer came from the shoe uppers rather than the soles. Unlike empty spools, the uppers were not merely vehicles to sell the soles. The uppers remained the major feature of interest to the consumer. See *Uniroyal, Inc. v. United States*, 542 F.Supp. 1026 (1982). In using this test, marketers should examine which part of the product attracts the consumer and which part is more costly to produce in attempting to obtain the desired country-of-origin effect. The result causes the manufacturer to have to remark the shoes with the proper country of origin, that is, "X," thereby decreasing significantly the manufacturer's profits.

Creative thinking aided in resolving this problem with future imports. The manufacturer and the Customs Service agreed on a formula for processing that would cause the shoes to be substantially transformed in the United States and thus be marked "Made in the U.S.A." The uppers would be imported with part of the heel cut out, thereby causing additional materials and a costly and complex operation to be performed to complete the shoe (Serko 1985). This is an example of how although initially a problem may arise it can be resolved through creative thinking. Marketers need to be aware of this for obtaining a desirable country-of-origin effect. If the target market prefers articles from a specific country "X," the final product must be combined so that country "X" contributes the part that is more costly to produce and is identified as the part that is the major feature of interest to the consumer.

Article of Commerce Test

The fourth test is the *article of commerce test*. This test examines whether a new article of commerce has emerged from operations performed on the imported article. The manufacturing of calculators, computers, and other technology has brought this test to the forefront. For example, a U.S. manufacturer imports a number of components from Taiwan that have been made from materials imported into Taiwan from several foreign countries and the United States. Final assembly of the product will be in the United States. The manufacturer wants Taiwan to be the country of origin so it may reap duty-free benefits as a beneficiary developing country (BDC) and ultimately pass on those benefits to the U.S. manufacturer.

Materials received in Taiwan are imported for use in the construction of integrated circuits (ICs) and photodiodes that will be used in the final product, a calculator. Silicone slices are imported into Taiwan that have to be further manufactured to produce chips. Lead frame strips, containing many connected frames, are imported into Taiwan from the U.S. manufacturer and eventually separated as parts of individual ICs. Gold wire is imported into Taiwan on spools and cut as it comes off the spool for wiring the chips to the lead frames. IC chips arrive in Taiwan from the U.S. manufacturer in unsevered slice form. The slice must then be scribed and broken up. Mold compounds, black for the ICs and transparent for the photodiodes, are utilized to encapsulate the IC chips. All of the component parts are then imported into the United States for final assembly by the manufacturer into the final product. Under this scenario, the imported parts underwent further operations in Taiwan to become a new article of commerce. The operations performed to create the final new article of commerce required a number of employees who had to be technically trained in numerous skills to cause the completed article to function. See *Texas Instruments, Inc. v. United States*, 681 F.2d 778 (1982). With continuing advances in technology, this test will be important to marketers now and in the future.

This test actually stands for the proposition that the product is being transformed from a producer's good to a retail consumer's good. In other words, the producer is using the product to make its final product. The producer's good is an item that is not used by nor capable of use by the retail consumer. A consumer good is one which has value and use to the consumer. ICs and photodiodes have no use to the consumer separate and apart from the calculator.

COUNTRY-OF-ORIGIN CRITERIA

The country of origin of an article, considered to be a new and different article of commerce, will be determined using two main criteria. The first criterion is: Where was the article transformed from a "producer good" to a "consumer good"? The second criterion is: Have the operations underlying the asserted transformation effected a change in the classification of the merchandise under the Tariff Schedules of the United States? A marketing manager would need to ask these questions when attempting to determine what the country of origin would be of the imported article and the impact of that country of origin on positioning decisions for the item.

Figure 3.1 shows how alteration criteria may be used as guidelines in relation to the four main tests when attempting to determine where substantial transformation has occurred.

A component is *functionally necessary* when it is required in the finished product to operate or run or is the vehicle to make the finished product usable. *Integral* means that the part becomes part of the finished product such that removal of the part would destroy both the part and the finished product. The degree of labor/technology used in the transformation will also play a determining factor in the transformation decision.

In an effort to assist marketing managers in their assessment of the transformation tests, and demonstrate an application of the tests, Table 3.2 set forth various products and demonstrates under which test the product might fall for country-of-origin marking requirements.[2]

A manufacturer or marketer should look carefully at the processes being used and/or what effect the foreign part will have on the ultimate product being made. Each situation will call for a different analysis, and it is important that the

Figure 3.1
Alternative Approaches to Country-of-Origin Test

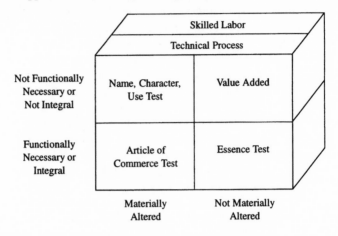

manufacturer or marketer look at the current law relating to country-of-origin marking requirements. In addition, there may be special trade agreements in effect, countries designated as beneficiary developing countries, and duty-free rules relating to countries that are insular possessions of the United States.[3]

CUSTOMS CONSIDERATIONS

An important aspect of country-of-origin markings is the accompanying customs duty considerations, which can certainly affect the profitability and market acceptance of products. Most customs duties are based on a percentage of the value of the imported merchandise. Therefore, the value of the goods may be a major factor in the amount of duties assessed (Sturm 1976). The importer may be concerned with country of origin as it may have a direct impact on the cost of his goods. If an importer or marketer is not concerned with what country of origin is marked on the product but is interested in using foreign labor or foreign components to lower cost and increase profitability, then he should consider obtaining those items from countries that have special consideration. For example, the United States Generalized System of Preference (GSP) allows duty-free entry for certain eligible products from a country designated as a BDC. This allows manufactured or semi-manufactured goods to enter the country duty free or with tariff preferences.

In addition, there are countries that have special trade agreements such as the North American Free Trade Agreement (NAFTA) and insular possessions of the United States that can export to the United States duty free if certain rules of origin are satisfied. Also certain countries have quotas that they are allowed to export to the United States, and the importer or marketer may want to use one of these countries for manufacturing or processing articles if one country has

Table 3.2
Country-of-Origin Tests Applied by U.S. Customs Service

Product	Name, Character, and Use Test	Value Added Test	Article of Commerce Test	Essence Test
Adhesives	X			
Air conditioning equipment		X		
Apparel			X	X
Automotive			X	X
Brooms	X			
Brushes	X			
Building materials	X			
Canned fish/seafood	X		X	
Canned, prepared specialty foods	X	X	X	
Clocks	X			X
Computer equipment	X		X	
Cured fish/seafood	X		X	
Dies, jigs, tools	X			
Dolls, cloth	X			
Electrical appliances	X		X	
Electrical components	X		X	
Fabricated metal products				X
Farm machinery			X	X
Fasteners, buttons, needles, pins	X		X	
Footwear		X		
Frozen foods	X			
Fruit juices, vegetables	X			
Furniture	X			
Garden machinery			X	X
Glass products	X			
Hand tools	X			
Hardware	X			
Heating equipment		X		
Household appliances	X		X	
Household audio equipment	X		X	
Household video equipment	X		X	
Industrial machinery			X	X
Leather and leather products		X		
Minerals	X			
Ores	X			
Orthopedic prosthetic supplies		X	X	
Plate making, porcelain	X			
Plated ware, silverware	X			
Processed specialty foods	X	X	X	
Radio equipment	X		X	
Refrigerator equipment		X		
Rubber and misc. plastic products	X			
Sewing needlework goods	X	X		
Sports, recreational goods				X
Stone, clay, concrete products	X			
Stuffed toys	X			
Surgical and medical instruments	X		X	
Toys	X			X
TV equipment	X		X	
Watches	X			X

different or lower quotas. Finally, there is a J-List contained in the customs regulations that lists articles exempted from individual markings. A manufacturer or importer may be able to obtain some cost benefit by using articles from this list.

The Customs Service can be a beneficial source of information if the importer or marketer is unsure about his particular product. Upon request, Customs will generally issue a ruling when a request is submitted in accordance with regulations and in the interest of sound administration of customs. A request may be submitted to an area or district office, a national import specialist (NIS) in New York, or headquarters. On receipt of an application, a local import specialist reviews the request for sufficiency and other details. The local import specialist records a local decision and forwards the application to the Customs Service's New York region. A binding ruling known as "30 day request" will be processed. If Customs Headquarters has to be involved, a target turnaround is 120 days. If later revocation, correction, or other adverse change is necessary, Customs will not apply the ruling for up to 90 days if the recipient can show it relied on the original ruling to its detriment. Requests to reconsider rulings are directed to the director of commercial rulings division in Washington, DC. Customs will issue administrative rulings on petitions under 19 U.S.C. §1516. No third person should rely absolutely on a ruling letter or assume the ruling will apply to any transaction other than the kind described in the letter. An importer who receives an adverse ruling from the Customs Service can seek judicial review of the decision by filing an administrative action in federal court.

Additionally, an importer may obtain a one-time waiver of the marking of imported articles that are economically prohibitive to mark relative to their value. This would be conditioned on the importer advising the foreign supplier that future shipments must be properly marked. Also there can be special agreements with Customs on a formula to meet import requirements. When unintentional and unusual marking problems arise, it is possible to negotiate a practical solution with Customs, including one-time waivers or make special arrangements such as special labels.

On occasion, Customs may publish an interim regulation that does not constitute a "major rule"; however, it may have a major impact on an importer who does not know. Customs may assess a liquidated damages claim based on the interim regulation. An importer may have obtained a ruling prior to the interim regulation, and if so, the assessment may be mitigated where it can be shown that he relied on the ruling. Customs takes the position that it is not required to notify importers of the revocation of rulings that have been issued by it.

There are civil and criminal penalties for violations of the country-of-origin marking requirement. These include attempting to import merchandise with false documents. In addition, liquidated damages can be paid on merchandise properly marked outside the marking period. Customs has mitigation guidelines in connection with marking violations based on appraised value of merchandise and number of violations (Serko 1991).

PRACTICAL STRATEGIC ISSUES

By understanding how country-of-origin markings are prescribed, the potential customs considerations, and the tests that ordain application, marketers can begin to devise "transformation strategies" that blend the advantages of global sourcing with the desired country of origin to achieve maximum benefit.

If an importer or marketer wishes to obtain a specific country-of-origin effect for imported articles, one or more of the four tests may assist in determining how to proceed. The first and most important point to consider is the type of product being marketed. From these four tests, the courts will be guided to a determination of the country of origin based on the processes the articles have undergone en route to the United States and the use of the products in the United States.

For example, an importer or marketer of household audio or video equipment would look at what foreign components and/or labor is needed to manufacture the product. In addition, it would be necessary to look at the potential consumer market and make a determination regarding the consumer's perception about foreign products versus domestic products. Once these two decisions are made and depending upon what is shown by the research, the marketer should choose to have the imported article undergo its last substantial transformation, where the fundamental characteristics of the product will be materially altered, where the product will be transformed from a producer's good to a consumer good, or where the components will become integral to the final product.

Once the country of origin for marking purposes has been chosen, if the imported product will require some type of manufacturing process, the importer or marketer may also want to consider employing some skilled labor in the chosen country and/or some recognized technical process as well to perform the work, as the courts appear to add some weight for this when determining country of origin. The same analysis would be made for any type of product, and the ultimate marketing decision would be made on the results of the analysis. The questions to be asked are:

1. What is the product being marketed?
2. Who are the potential consumers, and what are their beliefs or perceptions about foreign products versus domestic products?
3. What is the preferred country of origin for the product?
4. How can the product be manufactured to obtain the desired country-of-origin effect?

The integration of manufacturing and sourcing decisions into a coordinated global strategy involves a practical understanding of the relevant marking statutes. As shown earlier, if the article loses its identity and becomes a new article, the *name, character, and use test* would apply. The marketer can have the product emerge from the preferred country of origin with an altered identity such that it has a new name, character, or use.

Pursuant to the *essence test*, the importer or marketer should choose to have the components become an integral part of the product being imported in the desired country of origin. The components of the imported product will be considered integral if they are functionally necessary to the new product, if the components have no commercial value apart from the new product, if the components become part of the new product by a process that requires come degree of skill, and if removal of the components from the new product would destroy the component or the new product. The importer or marketer should be able to meet all of these conditions when choosing the country of origin for a product, as no condition is sufficient by itself.

If an importer or marketer should have products that would fall under the category of the *value-added test*, the country of origin would be the country that produces the component of major interest to the consumer and the most costly to produce. The marketer desiring to have the final product marked with a specific country of origin should have the part that is attractive to the consumer and most costly to produce manufactured in the desired country of origin.

In order to obtain the desired country-of-origin effect pursuant to the *article of commerce test*, the product must be transformed from a producer's good into a retail consumer's good in the specific country desired to the country of origin. The importer or marketer needs to consider two criteria: (1) where the article was transformed from a "producer's good" to a "consumer's good" and (2) whether the operations underlying the asserted transformation effected a change in the classification of the merchandise under the Tariff Schedules of the United States. The answer to these two questions needs to be the specific country or origin desired by the importer pursuant to the *article of commerce test*.

As illustrated in Table 3.2, products may benefit from more than a single test. Although the components being used or the processes to which the product is being subjected may not fulfill the requirements of one test, they may very well fulfill another.

CONCLUSIONS

Country-of-origin markings as they would apply to products, or even components, can be an effective strategic tool for global marketers. When assessing a foreign market as a new product outlet, a company should consider the information conveyed through country-of-origin markings to the target markets in that country. Markings should be carefully assessed for the potential information they provide to prospective buyers as well as the political considerations that might apply (e.g., taxes, tariffs, and quotas). One concern would be to see which approach is acceptable in the greatest number of potential target markets to use as a base for strategic marking decisions. Once the decision is made, the specific tests of transformations discussed in this paper can be used to facilitate the favored country-of-origin markings.

It is the purpose of this chapter to discuss the specific legal statutes employed by the U.S. government that affect country-of-origin markings. Global marketers would be well advised to understand the marking statutes in any of the countries in which they plan to sell their products.[4] However, developing WTO rules will embody an international trade classification-based methodology based on the longstanding doctrine of "substantial transformation," which will harmonize the rules for all member countries, making these tests ever more important to the global marketer (Clawson 1996).

Marketers should remember that if an imported article is subjected to a process in the United States that results in a substantial transformation, the imported article will generally be considered to be made in the United States. Conversely, if the manufacturing process in the United States is minor, leaving the identity of the imported article intact, the country of origin generally must appear on the product. The marketing of the product and potential import tariffs may be dependent on what marking requirements, if any, are placed on the final product. The federal courts look at each product; however, the four tests previously described have emerged as the main tests used in determining country of origin.

By understanding the regulations that stipulate country-of-origin markings, marketers will have greater ability to achieve the desired country-of-origin designations for products. This enhanced knowledge will increase the flexibility of marketers to balance global sourcing opportunities, customs disparities, and consumer perceptions. The four tests of transformation, discussed in this chapter, offer marketers the tools required to direct their product's transformation, enhancing the opportunity for achieving the benefits of country of origin. Global strategy development will be improved as marketers take a proactive role in the transformation of their products to achieve a desirable country-of-origin marking.

NOTES

1. The current marking statute, found at 19 United States Code §1304, provides for marking imports with the country of origin, with certain exceptions. Regulations implementing the country of origin marking requirements can be found at 19 Code of Federal Regulations §134 *et seq.*

2. Current federal case law, customs court rulings, international court rulings, and the Code of Federal Regulations have been relied upon in preparation of Table 3.2.

3. Table 3.2 illustrates what tests the courts have used in their analysis of the various products being substantially transformed. These classifications are for illustration only and should not be relied upon by manufacturers or marketers in making their decision about the use of foreign labor or foreign parts in the manufacture of their particular product. Merchandise not directly covered by the table may be classified by similitude to one of the articles shown. Table 3.2 and the respective tests should provide importers or marketers with an initial starting point for determining under which test their particular product will likely fit.

4. It should be noted here that this chapter was written from the perspective of the U.S. Marking Statutes. Each country may have its own way of dealing with country-of-origin markings, and the international strategic marketer should be cognizant of marking regulations in all possible foreign target markets.

REFERENCES

19 C.F.R. §12.130(c)(1) (1996).

19 C.F.R. §177.21–177.31 (1996).

19 C.F.R. §102 et seq.

19 U.S.C. §1304.

19 C.F.R. §134 et seq.

Anheuser-Busch Brewing Association v. United States, 207 U.S. 556, 28 S. Ct. 204, 52 L.Ed. 336 (1908).

Belcrest Linens v. United States, 741 F.2d 1368 (Fed. Ct. 1984).

Bilkey, Warren J. and Erik Ness (1982). "Country-of-Origin Effects on Product Evaluations." *Journal of International Business Studies,* 8(1) (Spring/Summer): 89–99.

Chao, P. (1993). "Partitioning Country of Origin Effects: Consumer Evaluations of a Hybrid Product." *Journal of International Business Studies,* 24(2): 291–306.

Clawson, James B. (1996). " 'Made in USA' Policy Comments." FTC File No. P894219.

Cordell, Victor V. (1992). "Effects of Consumer Preferences for Foreign Sourced Products." *Journal of International Business Studies,* 23(2): 251–269.

Darling, John R. and Van R. Wood (1990). "A Longitudinal Study Comparing Perceptions of U.S. and Japanese Consumer Products in a Third Neutral Country: Finland 1975 to 1985." *Journal of International Business Studies,* 21(3): 427–450.

Dellums v. U.S. Nuclear Regulatory Com'n, 863 F.2d 968 (D.C. Cir. 1988).

The Diamond Match Co. v. United States, 49 C.C.P.A. 52, C.A.D. 796 (1962).

Erickson, Gary M., Johnny K. Johansson, and Paul Chao (1984). "Image Variables in Multi-Attribute Product Evaluations: Country-of-Origin Effects." *Journal of Consumer Research,* 11 (September): 694–699.

Ferrostall Metals Corp. v. United States, 664 F. Supp. 53 (CIT 1987).

Friedlander & Co., Inc. v. United States, 27 C.C.P.A. 297, C.A.D. 104 (1940).

Globemaster, Inc. v. United States, 68 Cust. Ct. 77, 340 F.Supp. 974 (1972).

Grafton Spools, Ltd. v. United States, 45 Cust. Ct. 16, 223 C.D. 2190 (1960).

Han, C. M. (1989). "Country Image: Halo or Summary Construct?" *Journal of Marketing Research,* 26 (May): 222–229.

Han, C. M. and Vern Terpstra (1988). "Country-of-Origin Effects for Uni-National and Bi-National Products." *Journal of International Business Studies,* 19 (Summer): 235–254.

Haubl, Gerald (1996). "A Cross-National Investigation of the Effects of Country of Origin and Brand Name on the Evaluation of a New Car." *International Marketing Review,* 13(5): 76–97.

Hong, Sung-Tai and Robert S. Wyer, Jr. (1989). "Effects of Country-of-Origin and Product-Attribute Information on Product Evaluation: An Information Processing Perspective." *Journal of Consumer Research,* 16 (September): 175–187.

———— (1990). "Determinants of Product Evaluation: Effects of the Time Interval Between Knowledge of a Product's Country-of-Origin and Information About Its Specific Attributes." *Journal of Consumer Research,* 17 (December): 277–288.

Howard, D. G. (1989). "Understanding How American Consumers Formulate Their Attitudes About Foreign Products." *Journal of International Consumer Marketing*, 2(2): 7–24.

Johansson, Johnny K., Susan P. Douglas, and Ikujiro Nonaka (1985). "Assessing the Impact of Country of Origin on Product Evaluations: A New Methodological Perspective." *Journal of Marketing Research*, 22 (November): 388–396.

Johansson, Johnny K. and Hans B. Thorelli (1985). "International Product Positioning." *Journal of International Business Studies* (Fall): 57–75.

Koru North America v. United States, 702 F.Supp. 279 (CIT 1988).

Madison Galleries, Ltd. v. United States, 870 F.2d 627 (Fed. Cir. 1989).

Mast Industries, Inc. v. Regan, 596 F.Supp. 1567 (1984).

Matter of Property Seized from ICS, 163 F.R.D. 292 (E. D.Wis. 1995).

McConnell, J. Douglas (1967). *A Behavior Study of the Development and Persistence of Brand Loyalty for a Consumer Product*. Ph.D. dissertation, Stanford University.

Moore, Thomas P. (1996). "Problems with Country-of-Origin Marking." *Logistics Management*, 35(11) (November): 78.

National Juice Products Ass'n v. United States, 10 CIT 48, 628 F.Supp 978 (1986).

Norcal/Crosetti Foods, Inc. v. United States, 731 F. Supp. 510 (CIT 1990).

Pabrini, Inc. v. United States, 630 F.Supp. 360 (CIT 1986).

Papadopoulos, Nicolas and Louise A. Heslop (1993). *Product-Country Images: Impact and Role in International Marketing*. New York: Haworth Press.

Roth, Martin S. and Jean B. Romeo (1992). "Matching Product Category and Country Image Perceptions: A Framework for Managing Country-of-Origin Effects." *Journal of International Business Studies*, 23(3): 477–497.

Schooler, Robert D. and Albert R. Wildt (1968). "Elasticity of Product Bias."*Journal of Marketing Research*, 5 (February): 78–81.

Serko, David (1985). *Import Practice Customs International Trade Law*. New York: Practicing Law Institute.

——— (1991). *Import Practice Customs International Trade Law*, 2nd ed. New York: Practicing Law Institute.

Sturm, Ruth F. (1976). *A Manual of Customs Law*. New York: American Importers Association.

Superior Wire v. United States, 764 F.Supp. 427 (CIT 1987).

Target Sportswear, Inc. v. United States, 70 F.3d 604 (Fed. Cir. 1995).

Texas Instruments Inc. v. United States, 681 F.2d 778 (1982).

Torrington Co. v. United States, 764 F.2d 1563 (Fed. Cir. 1985).

Tse, David K. and Gerald J. Gorn (1993). "An Experiment on the Salience of Country-of-Origin in the Era of Global Brands." *Journal of International Marketing*, 1(1): 57–76.

U.S. Constitution, Art. I, §8, Cl.3.

Uniroyal, Inc. v. United States, 542 F.Supp. 1026 (1982).

United States v. Gibson-Thomsen Co., 27 C.C.P.A. 267, C.A.D. 98 (1940).

United States v. Murray, 621 F.2d 1163 (1st Cir.), *cert. denied*, 449 U.S. 837, 101 S.Ct. 112, 66 L.Ed.2d 44 (1980).

United States v. 100 Pieces, more or less, Style 200, Artificial Knees, 283 F.Supp. 309 (C.D. Cal. 1968).

Witt, J. A. (1990). "An Empirical Study of the Combined Effects of Country-of-Origin,

Brand, and Store on Consumer Perceived Risk." Doctoral dissertation, University of Arkansas.

Yaprak, Attila (1987). "The Country of Origin Paradigm in Cross-National Consumer Behavior: The State of the Art." In K. Bahn and M. Sirgy (eds.), *Third World Marketing Congress*. Barcelona, Spain: Academy of Marketing Science, International Conference Series.

Yuri Fashions Co. v. United States, 10 CIT 189, 632 F.Supp. 41 (1986), *aff'd* 804 F.2 1246 (Fed. Cir. 1986).

Chapter 4

Macrosegmentation Schemes for the Emerging Eastern European and Former Soviet Country Markets

Angela D'Auria Stanton and C. P. Rao

INTRODUCTION

What a difference a decade makes. Ten years ago Eastern Europe and the Soviet Union were "behind the iron curtain." Today, the countries comprising this region are transforming its basic economic and ideological underpinnings. Eastern Europe and the countries of the former Soviet Republic (now referred to as the Commonwealth of Independent States) are in the arduous process of establishing market economies. With a total population of 415 million[1] and a gross national product of approximately $4 trillion (Brady 1990), many U.S. corporations view this region as the opportunity of the decade for market expansion and growth.

Unfortunately, it is difficult to view these former communist countries as a single market. Although a regional orientation would make it easier for corporations to enter this market, it is at best, unrealistic. The countries in this region are at varying stages of market development. Czechoslovakia, Hungary, and Poland, for example, have made the biggest inroads at moving toward an open market economy. One year after the fall of the Berlin Wall, approximately 10,000 joint ventures had been set up in these countries (Jain 1993). Their other Eastern European neighbors, however, have not been so fortunate. Yugoslavia has been torn apart by ethnic wars, while Romania and Bulgaria still lack the infrastructure that a post-communist existence requires.

The countries comprising the Commonwealth of Independent States (CIS) are also in divergently different positions. Russia, the largest of the CIS nations, is trying to quickly immerse itself in a market economy orientation through extensive reform. Georgia and Armenia, although politically unstable, are expected to align themselves closely to Russia in terms of economic reform.

The Baltic States (Estonia, Latvia, and Lithuania), although small in terms of land mass and population, have a geographical advantage based on their proximity to both Europe and Russia. Additionally, these countries have a highly trained and low-paid workforce, making it an attractive area for production facilities (Hofheinz 1991). The southernmost countries of Azerbaijan, Uzbekistan, Turkmenistan, Kyrgyzstan, and Tajikistan have made trade alliances with their Muslim neighbors, Iran, Turkey, and Pakistan, and have entered the Islamic common market.[2] Kazakhastan appears to be forming its own allegiances with the West and may move toward a market economy sooner than many of the CIS nations due to its wealth of oil reserves (Rao 1992). Finally, the outlook for Moldova (formerly Moldavia), the Ukraine, and Belarus is undefined (Jain 1993). These countries, like Romania and Bulgaria, are only at the earliest stages of developing an infrastructure sufficient to support a market economy.

The changing face of Eastern Europe and the former Soviet republics provides multinational corporations (MNCs) with a plethora of opportunities and challenges. The emergence of this region, coupled with intensifying competition and saturated markets worldwide, has been met with an onslaught of MNCs attempting to make their stake here. Developing a successful marketing strategy, however, will not be an easy task. Success in Eastern Europe and the Commonwealth of Independent States will depend, in part, upon the abilities of firms to group these markets into viable segments.

MARKET SEGMENTATION

Small and large companies have made great strides toward adopting the marketing concept and becoming market-oriented (Lichtenthal and Wilson 1992). A marketing orientation is based on a customer-driven focus. During the past decade marketers have seen the "renaissance of market segmentation" (Weinstein 1994, p. 2). First recognized by Wendell Smith in the mid-1950s, segmentation has evolved from an academic concept into a viable "real world" marketing strategy (Smith 1956). Market segmentation, according to Smith, is "based upon developments on the demand side of the market and represents a rational and more precise adjustment of product and marketing effort to consumer or user requirements" (Smith 1956, p. 6). More simply, the main purpose of segmentation is to develop an effective marketing strategy based on the identification of relatively homogeneous groups of consumers that show similar consumption patterns. This concept of segmentation has been almost as universally accepted as the marketing concept itself (Haley 1968). The problem with segmenting markets has always been, however, in how it should it be done, especially when looking at international markets. Although domestic segmentation strategies have received a great deal of attention, research contributions in international market segmentation have been relatively sparse (Douglas and Craig 1992). This concept is further compounded when the international market to be segmented is an emergent one, as is the case with Eastern Europe and the former Soviet countries.

Two primary schemes have been historically incorporated by firms when segmenting markets: macrosegmentation and microsegmentation. Additionally, a relatively new hybrid-type concept, intermarket segmentation, has also been proposed by academicians as a viable framework for segmenting internationally. The type of segmentation scheme employed is a reflection of a country's marketing infrastructure and sophistication. When a country is beginning its marketing journey, typically, little empirical research has been conducted on the consumers in that market. Thus, macrosegmentation schemes are generally the best initial portrayal. As marketing activities increase and more information is available on a country's preferences, needs, and attitudes, marketers tend to delve into the finer, more refined segments produced through microsegmentation. Intermarket segmentation is an extension of the microsegmentation philosophy. With this approach, homogeneous segments that transcend national boundaries or strategically equivalent segments (SES) are the optimal goal (Kale and Sudharshan 1987; Jain 1989). Because the countries in Eastern Europe and the former Soviet countries are only in the early stages of converting their economies and developing their market structures, and as little information is available on consumers in these countries, the only viable segmentation alternative for marketers at this time is macrosegmentation.

MACROSEGMENTATION

Macrosegmentation, also referred to as country segmentation, typically involves grouping countries based on geographic, religious, economic, demographic, and cultural factors. A review of the international market segmentation literature by Baalbaki and Malhorta (1993) showed a consistent trend toward using these types of environmental variables in grouping markets. Many researchers have proposed that firms rely on country segmentation when moving into new markets (Helson et al. 1993; Johansson and Moinpour 1977; Jain 1993; Downham 1986; Toyne and Walters 1993). As Sethi (1971, p. 348) stated: "Developing a successful strategy for global marketing depends to a large extent upon a firm's ability to segment its world markets so that uniform sets of marketing decisions can be applied to a group of countries." Various macrosegmentation criteria and their applicability to the markets of Eastern Europe and the former Soviet Republic follow.

Geographic Market Segmentation

Geographic market segmentation is one of the most commonly used approaches in an initial segmentation framework (Weinstein 1994). It is a logical starting point because the information is readily available at a low cost. Additionally, the rise in regional marketing lends itself to using geography as a basis

Table 4.1
Geographic Market Segmentation

Regional Market Segment 1: European Segment	Regional Market Segment 2: Asian Segment
Eastern Europe	Kazakhstan
Baltic Republics	Uzbekistan
European Russia	Turkmenistan
Belarus	Tajikistan
Moldova	Kyrgyzstan
Ukraine	Russia (Siberia)
Georgia	
Armenia	
Azerbaijan	
Population: 300 million (approx.)	**Population: 60 million (approx.)**

(Weinstein 1994). In most instances this has been done to make managing a global corporation easier. Typically, corporations operating worldwide have a Western European region, an Asia-Pacific region, a Central/South American region, a North American region, and a Middle East/African region. Each of these areas will then have a regional headquarters from which decisions can be made and disseminated. Another way in which geography has been used to cluster groups of countries has been in the development of trading blocks such as the European Economic Community (EEC) and the North American Free Trade Agreement (NAFTA). These types of country groupings appeal to corporations in that the barriers or non-barriers to entry within the trade blocks will be the same for all of the countries in the block. This can help a multinational firm target specific strategies toward the grouping. The problem with this geographic orientation is that one cannot assume that all countries within a particular geographic grouping have the same wants, needs, and desires.

If the nations of Eastern Europe and the Commonwealth of Independent States were segmented geographically, the possible solution posited in Table 4.1 might be appropriate (Rao 1992). The Ural Mountains were used as a dividing line in this scheme. It is not unusual in a geographic segmentation scheme for a land mass such as mountains or water to be used for a point of departure.

The advantage of this alternative is that it divides the market into only two segments, which will enable multinational corporations to market only two different regionalized products (Rao 1992). Further, a geographical market division strategy enhances the "place" component of the marketing mix by making it easier for companies to distribute their products in these regions.

There are three primary disadvantages to this alternative. The first is the variety of cultures and languages, especially within the European Segment. This will make delivering a single product or message difficult. Second, there is a huge disparity between the sizes of the segments. As can be seen in Table 4.1, the European Segment has five times the population of the Asian Segment. Although the Asian Segment is much larger in terms of land area, much of this land is barren and unpopulated. In this scheme, multinational corporations may vie for the larger European Segment and ignore the smaller Asian Segment. Finally, several of the countries in the European Segment, specifically Azerbaijan, Armenia, and Georgia, are politically unstable. This makes it inherently riskier for a multinational corporation to enter these markets. This creates a dilemma, however, in that specifically avoiding certain countries within a segment may damage the stability and ultimately the viability of the entire segment itself.

Currently, Eastern European countries have close ties to the former Soviet republics. This will change, however. As time passes, the economies of the Eastern European countries will develop and prosper. With prosperity will come a stronger alliance with Western Europe, and ties with the Soviet republics will diminish. Furthermore, the European Soviet republics have strong economic and political ties with the Asian Soviet republics. Separating these markets may result in increased fragmentation. Thus, segmenting based on geography appears to be a questionable alternative.

Religious Market Segmentation

Another variable that can be used in segmenting the emerging Eastern European and former Soviet markets is religion. Although these countries had no "official" religion while under communist rule, religious beliefs were still prevalent throughout the region. There are two primary religious orientations in this region: Christian and Muslim. Additionally, religious orientation tends to be predominant within a country's borders. Table 4.2 depicts a possible religious market segmentation scheme.

The advantage of this alternative is that it divides this emerging market into only two different segments. This, in turn, will enable U.S. corporations to focus their marketing activities on only two market segments, as opposed to many smaller fragmented markets.

There are, however, many disadvantages to this alternative. First, many of the countries in each segment are not in close geographic proximity. This will make it more difficult for multinational corporations to market their products, especially from the distribution aspect. Additionally, Armenia and Georgia, unlike the remainder of the new states located in the Christian market, are considered politically unstable and are far less developed than the other Christian countries. Thus, it will be more difficult to create the infrastructure necessary to conduct successful marketing activities.

The Christian market has a population of 352 million and a GNP of approx-

Table 4.2
Religious Market Segmentation

Christian Market Segment	Muslim Market Segment
Eastern Europe	Kazakhstan
Baltic Republics	Azerbaijan
Russia	Uzbekistan
Belarus	Tajikistan
Moldova	Kyrgyzstan
Ukraine	
Georgia	
Armenia	
Population: 352 million (approx.)	**Population: 51 million (approx.)**
GNP: U.S.$3.251 trillion (approx.)	**GNP: U.S.$200 billion (approx.)**

imately $3.251 trillion, while the Muslim markets have a combined population of 51 million and a GNP of approximately $200 billion. Due to the size disparity between the Christian and Muslim markets, this type of segmentation scheme may cause U.S. companies to focus their activities on the larger Christian market and ignore the Muslim countries.

Neglecting the Asian segment because it is smaller, however, would be a mistake for multinational corporations. Many of the Muslim nations of the former Soviet Union—Kazakhstan, Tajikistan, Uzbekistan, and Kyrgyzstan—have already entered the Islamic Common Market. Thus, although these countries seem like a smaller market opportunity by themselves, they certainly exert a more powerful presence as a part of this trading alliance. Additionally, one of the Muslim countries, Kazakhstan, has one of the largest oil reserves in the world, supplying over 39 percent of the oil demands of the CIS. This country is politically moderate and is in the process of developing strong ties with the West. Kazakhstan holds promise for U.S. oil companies, and neglect of this country represents a significant opportunity cost.

Economic/Cultural Market Segmentation

Another possible segmentation scheme for the nations of the Commonwealth of Independent States and Eastern Europe is based on similarities of culture and economy. This segmentation scheme is illustrated in Table 4.3.

There are many advantages to this segmentation scheme. The Eastern European countries in segment 1 are well on the way to developing market economies. The Baltic republics have kept their European culture and religious

Table 4.3
Economic/Cultural Market Segmentation

Economic/Cultural Segment 1	Economic/Cultural Segment 2	Economic/Cultural Segment 3
Eastern Europe	Belarus	Armenia
Baltic Republics	Ukraine	Azerbaijan
	Russia	Georgia
	Kazakhstan	Turkmenistan
	Moldova	Uzbekistan
		Tajikistan
		Kyrgyzstan
Population: 123 million	Population: 236.4 million	Population: 43.5 million

identity. Thus, these countries are easily integrated into the Eastern European market segment. Although the Baltic republics have not progressed economically as quickly as their Eastern European neighbors, all indicators seem to show that the Baltics will continue to move forward. In addition, their geographic proximity to Eastern Europe will facilitate marketing efforts. The five Slavic former Soviet republics in market segment 2 are politically stable countries that have close cultural ties with each other. Additionally, these Slavic countries are far more economically developed than many of the other former Soviet republics. Hence, they appear more likely to function effectively as one economic unit.

The third market segment consists of a combination of politically unstable countries that also suffer from cultural and economic instability. Although it may be advisable for U.S. corporations to avoid this segment, it should be noted that purposefully ignoring this market may lead to further instability and may also jeopardize the stability of the former Soviet republics in the second segment.

Portfolio Segmentation

Portfolio models, such as the Boston Consulting Group (BCG) matrix and the General Electric (GE) Multifactor Portfolio Model, have been used extensively in marketing. These models have been used from a strategic perspective to help companies

understand the economics of their businesses better, to improve the quality of their plans, to have better communication between business and corporate management, to pinpoint information gaps and important issues, and to eliminate weaker businesses and strengthen their investment in more promising businesses. (Kotler 1991, p. 44)

Portfolio models, typically two-dimensional in their orientation, evaluate two attributes (e.g., market attractiveness, competition, etc.) in a matrix format.

This methodology was employed by Kraljic in analyzing the chance of success of the Eastern European market countries (1990). Kraljic evaluated countries in this region on two attributes: economic development potential and readiness and ability to change. In analyzing a country's economic development potential, Kraljic took into account the country's infrastructure, natural resources, skills, industry structure, foreign debt, and exports in convertible currency (1990). A country's readiness and ability to change was a combination of each nation's scope of and experience with reforms, national homogeneity, quality of leadership, traditions, and commitment (Kraljic 1990).

This type of approach can also be applied as a macro country segmentation scheme. In Figure 3.2, four target segments seem to evolve. The first segment, consisting of Romania and Bulgaria, was evaluated by Kraljic as low in both economic development potential and readiness and ability to change (1990). Additional countries, not listed in the original Kraljic model, that would also seem to belong in this segment are Armenia, Georgia, Azerbaijan, Turkmenistan, Uzbekistan, and Tajikistan. It should be noted that in Kraljic's original analysis the former Soviet Union was treated as one country since it did not disband until 1991. The second segment consists of Russia, Belarus, the Ukraine, Kazakhstan, and Moldavia. This segment reflects countries with a high economic development potential but a low readiness and ability to change. Russia's inclusion in this segment may seem odd to some because this placement implies that the country has not initiated appropriate reforms. Although Russia has made radical reforms, it was placed in this segment because of the diversity of the populace and the country's somewhat unstable leadership. The third segment in this arrangement consists of countries that have low economic development potential but a high readiness and ability to change. Countries included in this segment are Poland and the Baltic republics. Poland's inclusion in this segment is due primarily to its small base of natural resources. The fourth and final segment includes Hungary and the former Czechoslovakia. These two nations have been the most successful to date and exude high degrees of both economic potential and the readiness and the ability to change.

Although this segmentation scheme appears to be intuitively pleasing, it should be noted that it is highly subjective. Furthermore, each of the countries in a particular segment cannot necessarily be approached in the same way. In this model two or more countries may end up in the same segment based on greatly different underlying ratings and weights.

Rationale for Macrosegmentation Schemes

The country segmentation approach in Eastern Europe and the former Soviet countries is intuitively pleasing for several reasons. First, this macro level of segmentation can be done with data that are currently available. In newly developing markets it is often difficult to collect primary data from representative samples of the population, partly because of regional domestic instabilities and partly because of the diversity in culture throughout the region (Naor 1994). Marketing research efforts typically do not evolve until a country's marketing infrastructure has been developed. Thus, as stated by Naor (1994), "efforts to obtain market data would clearly have to precede efforts to obtain marketing data." In the case of Eastern Europe and the Commonwealth of Independent States, this will require a great deal of time and resources, since their previously closed economies required little in the way of marketing (Naor 1994).

Another benefit of an initial country segmentation approach is that multinational companies can borrow from their earlier experiences in entering new markets (Jain 1993). This concept of "cross-fertilization" is at the core of a successful global marketing program (Helsen et al. 1993). A firm's "experience factor" in entering new markets is a definite competitive advantage. Previous experience in employing macrosegmentation approaches with such country variables as GNP, geographic proximity, and political ideology provide the firm with a knowledge of what may work in a given situation.

Finally, there is a long tradition of using a priori approaches as a basis for segmentation (Haley 1968; Green 1977; Wind 1978). Country segmentation provides corporations with a starting point in that it identifies established groupings about which something is known or can be inferred, relative to various characteristics (e.g., demographic or socioeconomic characteristics) (Frank 1968).

This very conventional approach, however, is not without its drawbacks. A country segmentation approach assumes, as stated previously, that all people within a given country or group of countries are homogeneous. This is, at best, an unrealistic view of the world. This approach neglects the fact that markets transcend geopolitical boundaries.

CONCLUSION

The Commonwealth of Independent States and Eastern Europe, with a total population of 410 million and a gross national product of almost $4 trillion, is a market that rivals those of the United States and the European Community. Multinational corporations should look to these emerging markets as an opportunity for continued growth. Although the region's marketing infrastructure is far from complete, it is vital that U.S. companies begin gaining market strongholds before their global competitors. As companies move into this region they must find some way of segmenting this vast and varied market.

Segmentation in these markets, however, is difficult because of the limited amount of data available for segmenting these markets systematically at both macro and micro levels. Although several segmentation schemes are proposed in the marketing literature, in view of the paucity of information about these markets, macro level country segmentation schemes are better suited at this time. These macrosegmentation schemes have the potential to provide a useful basis for segmentation these former communist country markets and thereby assist firms in their marketing strategy decision-making process. Shama (1992) believes that the countries in Eastern Europe and the former Soviet Union should be looked at separately. He states that although the "countries have many things in common, they are also dissimilar in many ways" (Shama 1992, p. 58). This rationale has also been suggested by Ettenson (1993) and by Kaynak and Samli (1986). Kaynak and Samli (1986) specifically note that corporations should assess the relative speed of socioeconomic, technological, and marketing progress in a given country market. With this support in mind, the initial country segmentation proposed based on economic/cultural conditions or using the extended version of Kralgic's (1990) portfolio model seems appropriate at this stage in the region's development. Both approaches seem to provide a starting point from which further segmentation in the Eastern Bloc, focusing more on the microsegmentation orientation of consumer needs, attitudes, and behaviors, can be based. Segmentation strategies will gain increasing prominence in this region as it is revealed that the countries will transform into free economies at different rates and that consumers' wants, needs, and desires are heterogeneous. Country segmentation, however, provides the necessary impetus for U.S. firms to begin market development of this emerging economic giant.

NOTES

1. *The 1992 Almanac* (Boston: Houghton Mifflin, 1991).
2. *Wall Street Journal*, February 18, 1992, p. 1.

REFERENCES

Baalbaki, Imad B. and Naresh K. Malhotra (1993). "Marketing Management Bases for International Market Segmentation: An Alternate Look at the Standization/Customization Debate." *International Marketing Review*, 10(1): 19–44.

Brady, Rose (1990). "Moscow Clearing the Runway." *Business Week*, September 17, p. 16.

Dalgic, Tevfik (1992). "Euromarketing: Charting the Map for Globalization." *International Marketing Review*, 9(5): 31–42.

Douglas, Susan P. and C. Samuel Craig (1992). "Advances in International Marketing." *International Journal of Research in Marketing* (December): 291–318.

Downham, J. (1986). "International Market Research." In R. M. Worcester (ed.), *Consumer Market Research*, 3rd ed. Amsterdam: Elsevier Science Publishers, pp. 629–654.

Ettenson, Richard (1993). "Brand Name and Country of Origin Effects in the Emerging Market Economies of Russia, Poland and Hungary." *International Marketing Review*, 10(5): 14–36.

Frank, Ronald E. (1968). "Market Segmentation Research: Findings and Implications." In Frank M. Bass, Charles W. King, and Edgar A. Pessemier (eds.), *The Appli-*

cation of the Sciences to Marketing Management. New York: John Wiley & Sons, pp. 39–68.

Green, Paul E. (1977). "A New Approach to Market Segmentation." *Business Horizons* (February): 61–73.

Haley, Russell I. (1968). "Benefit Segmentation: A Decision-Oriented Research Tool." *Journal of Marketing* (July): 30–35.

Helson, Kristiaan, Kamel Jedidi, and Wayne S. DeSarbo (1993). "A New Approach to Country Segmentation Utilizing Multinational Diffusion Patterns." *Journal of Marketing* (October): 60–71.

Hofheinz, Paul (1991). "Opportunity in the Baltics." *Fortune*, October 21, p. 68.

Jain, Subhash (1993). *International Marketing Management*, 4th ed. Belmont, CA: Wadsworth Publishing Company.

Johansson, J. K. and R. Moinpour (1977). "Objective and Perceived Similarity of Pacific Rim Countries." *Columbia Journal of World Business* (Winter): 65–76.

Kale, H. and D. Sudharshan (1987). "A Strategic Approach to International Segmentation." *International Marketing Review* (Summer): 60–71.

Kaynak, Erdener and A. Coskun Samli (1986). "Eastern European Marketing Systems and Western Marketing Research Voids: A Research Agenda." *Journal of Business Research*, 14: 109–116.

Kraljic, Peter (1990). "The Economic Gap Separating East and West."*Columbia Journal of World Business*, 24(4): 14–19.

Lichtenthal, J. David and David T. Wilson (1992). "Becoming Market Oriented." *Journal of Business Research*, 24: 191–207.

Naor, Jacob (1994). "Marketing Under Newly-Emerging East European and Soviet Conditions—Some Thoughts on What Needs to Be Done." In Peter J. Buckley and Pervez N. Ghauri (eds.), *The Economics of Change in East and Central Europe*. London: Academic Press, pp. 343–354.

Rao, C. P. (1992). "Eastern European and Soviet Countries: Should U.S. Companies Expand into Unchartered Waters?" Unpublished White Paper.

Sethi, S. P. (1971). "Comparative Cluster Analysis for World Markets." *Journal of Marketing Research* (August): 348–354.

Shama, Avraham (1992). "Transforming the Consumer in Russia and Eastern Europe." *International Marketing Review*, 9(5): 43–59.

Smith, Wendell R. (1956). "Product Differentiation and Market Segmentation as Alternative Marketing Strategies." *Journal of Marketing* (July): 3–8.

Toyne, B. and P. G. Walters (1993). *Global Marketing Management: A Strategic Perspective*. Boston: Allyn and Bacon.

Weinstein, Art (1994). *Market Segmentation*, rev. ed. Chicago: Probus Publishing Company.

Wind, Yoram (1978). "Issues and Advances in Segmentation Research." *Journal of Marketing Research* (August): 317–337.

Part II

Micromanagement Issues

Chapter 5

A Resource-Based Model of the Internationalization Process of the Firm

D. Deo Sharma

INTRODUCTION

Studies of internationalization have achieved considerable prominence in international business (IB) research. On a basis of these studies, behaviorally based process models have been developed to explain the internationalization process of firms: for example, Bilkey and Tesar (1977), Cavusgil (1980), Johanson and Vahlne (1977, 1990), and Reid (1981). These models emphasize the role of experiential knowledge in the internationalization of firms. The internationalization process is also gradual. A number of empirical studies followed, which lent support to the above description (Davidson 1983; Erramilli and Rao 1993; Johanson and Weidershiem-Paul 1975; Kogut and Singh 1988). These studies have been criticized on various counts. Commenting on one of the process models, namely, the u-model, Andersen (1993), for example, claims that it is unlikely that experience alone can explain the internationalization of firms. Moreover, a number of other empirical studies failed to support these models. For example, Calof and Beamish (1995) found that in only 52 percent of the cases could a change in the existing foreign market entry mode be explained by a change in the experiential knowledge possessed by the firm. Sharma (1983) and Sharma and Johanson (1987) have observed in separate studies that the market entry mode adopted by the studied firms did not change over time. There was no gradual internationalization. Sharma (1992) noted that hotel firms concentrate their market entry to a limited number of countries. In each country, hotel firms operate a number of premises and simultaneously use a number of market entry modes. Others report either no or a negative relationship between experience and the firm's choice of foreign market entry mode (Shetty 1979; Stopford and Wells 1972; Davidson and McFetridge 1985; Daniel et al. 1976). This review of the literature indicates that other variables apart from experiential knowledge can explain the internationalization process of firms.

Further, the experienced-based internationalization process models make two assumptions. First, that the resources needed to proceed with internationalization are available within the firm. Second, that the resources available within the firm can readily be transferred across countries. Both these assumptions need questioning.

In this chapter it is asserted that resources[1] within a firm exert an independent impact on its internationalization process. To improve our understanding of the internationalization process of firms we need to pay more attention to the resources that firms own. This is the purpose of the present chapter. A model will be developed for the internationalization process of firms and of the dynamics of this process based on the resources owned by firms. It is emphasized that firms internationalize on a basis of their own unique collection of resources. There are two reasons for this emphasis on resources. First, in at least one of the internationalization process models, namely, the original u-model (Johanson and Vahlne 1977), the resources of the firm were explicitly included under the heading "resource commitment." But, in subsequent theoretical and empirical research, this concept has received little explicit attention. Second, as we have noted, some of the empirical evidence shows that a firms resources are important in explaining internationalization. What, then, is the nature of the resources that firms commit in the course of their internationalization process? And how do these influence the course of the process—that is, the choice of country market, the choice of entry mode, and the related dynamic?

The chapter is based on three theoretical schools, drawing from the literature on resource-based strategy (Barney 1986a, 1991, 1992; Collis 1994; Hansen and Wernerfelt 1989; Lippman and Rumelt 1982; Senge 1992; Wernerfelt 1984), the theory of the growth of the firm (Penrose 1966), and behavioral organization theory (Cyert and March 1963). Firms are regarded as a collection of resources. My view is similar to that expressed in IB literature, in which horizontal foreign direct investment (FDI) is seen as an extension of the capabilities of the firm across borders (Kogut 1983, 1993). It will be argued that for the purpose of explaining the internationalization of firms, it is appropriate to unbundle the resources. Resources differ in nature, which affects the internationalization process of firms. A differentiation in the nature of the resources allows for a loose coupling in the course of the internationalization process. In so doing I am suggesting a divorce between the legal or visible foreign market entry mode and the "real" foreign market entry mode of a firm. I argue that whereas the visible manifestations of foreign market entry change now and then, the real market entry mode is being modified all the time.

In the following pages, resources will be discussed, after which the resource-based model will be presented. The chapter closes with some concluding remarks.

RESOURCE COMMITMENT IN THE INTERNATIONALIZATION PROCESS

Resources are defined here as the stocks of available factors that are owned or controlled by the firm. Resources consist of assets, organizational processes, and attributes of the firm. All these have accumulated in the course of time-bound historical processes. It should be pointed out that the nature and the quality of the organizational resources are an outcome of the firm as a whole system. Resources are important because of their value-generating abilities.

Firms internationalize and commit a package of (1) tangible and (2) non-tangible resources abroad. Tangible resources such as capital are required to pay for supplies. Non-tangible resources include non–human-related resources such as patents, trademarks, copyrights and registered designs, trade secrets, data base, trust, goodwill, trade name, credibility, reputation, image, and the firm's relationships. In addition there is know-how about suppliers and organizations, about culture and organizational and managerial practices, and about routines and human resources. An important factor is the uniqueness, or the niche, that the firms attain by combining their tangible and non-tangible resources. As resources are heterogeneous (Alchian and Demsetz 1972), there are various ways for firms to achieve uniqueness in the market vis-à-vis customers, competitors, and suppliers.

Characteristics of the Tangible Resources

In the ownership-based foreign market entry modes, the foreign firm contributes tangible resources such as capital. Two aspects are important: (1) the speed with which tangible resources can be transferred abroad and (2) the scope of the market served. Tangible resources such as capital are highly mobile across national borders. Mobility refers to the ease with which resources of a firm are transferred in-house by the same firm without a loss in its commercial value. The use of such a tangible resources in one place precludes its use in another. The alternative cost for the use of tangible resources is high, which also implies that unless the investing firm is acquiring an existing operation there will be a period of gestation before it earns any returns. For these reasons a firm aiming for rapid internationalization or hoping to serve a large number of foreign markets may find the ownership-based route to internationalization problematic and slow. The scarcity of financial resources, for example, can restrict a firm's entry into a foreign market. Further, the investment of tangible resources is permanent and difficult to terminate because of local regulations, for instance, or the adverse reaction of the local environment. Finally, disposing of an established business can lead to substantial losses. Tangible resources such as equipment are also indivisible.

Characteristics of the Non-tangible Resources

The non-tangible resources such as reputation, goodwill, image, organizational routines, and brand name can be used in two or more locations at the same time, and at little extra cost. The alternative cost of this use is small. Once non-tangible resources have been developed, there are economies of scale in their use. Only marginal additional investment is required. Nevertheless, these resources are only imperfectly mobile across national borders (this issue will be discussed later). Human resources do not lend themselves to multi-site use, however. In this respect human resources can be classified into two groups. The first consists of skilled and top-level managerial people who articulate the strategies and who support the productive capacity of other resources (Wright and Snell 1991), and it is a source of advantage (Lado and Wilson 1994). The supply of this resource cannot be quickly increased; the managerial resources available within a firm at any given time are limited (Hambrick 1987). Managerial resources are only imperfectly mobile across countries. Recruiting managers on the local labor market is problematic, and additional resources are then required to infuse new recruits with the firm's organizational values and norms. The second human resource group consists of lower-level personnel, who are available in abundance.

A further characteristic of several non-tangible resources such as administrative routines and human resources is that over time there is a learning effect. Firms learn how to generate savings in their use of these resources. As firms learn how to use their non-tangible resources, these become more economic and rational (Penrose 1966). Firms are streamlining their organizational structure and their decision-making processes to replace the use of skilled manpower. In effect, firms will always at any time be in possession of unused non-tangible resources or they will be in the process of creating extra resources. Indeed, an increasing use of some of the non-tangible resources, such as image and reputation, may even improve the future value of these resources (Prahalad and Hamel 1990). Increased use of non-tangible resources results in a history- or path-dependent accumulation of reputation, goodwill, and credibility (Barney 1986a), and it demands sustained effort and investment on the part of the firm. Non-use of these resources leads to decay and erosion in their value (Reed and DeFillippi 1990). It is only when a firm has been operating in a market for years and has consistently kept its promises that it develops such resources as trust and credibility.

The use of non-tangible resources across countries is restricted for two reasons, namely, because such resources are non-tradable and are either quasi-mobile or immobile. The trust and goodwill of an established dealer, for example, cannot be bought. Non-tradability arises for a number of reasons, including market failure (Barney 1986a), specialization in use or location (Klein, Crawford, and Alchian 1978), or sunk costs (Caves 1984). Mobility is restricted due to organizational culture or because of organizational routines (Nelson and

Winter 1982) or the firm's reputation (Weigelt and Camerer 1988) among suppliers (Porter 1980) and customers (Klien and Lefler 1981). Mobility is also restricted because various factors make the duplication and transferability of non-tangible resources across firms difficult. Examples of such factors are path-dependency (Barney 1991); team production (Teece 1982) and socially complex production (Amit and Schoemaker 1993); tacit, non-codifiable, and implicit knowledge and skills (Polanyi 1967); causal ambiguity (Lippman and Rumelt 1982); and high transaction costs (Chatterjee and Wernefelt 1991).

For these reasons non-tangible resources are either fully or partially firm-specific and have no other use outside the firm. These specificities may be based on site, physical assets, dedicated assets, or human assets (Williamson 1985). Imitation is difficult and imperfect (Arthur et al. 1987). Intangibility concerns the difficulty in replicating the resources possessed by a firm by other firms without reducing its value. Not all resources are imitable. Mansfield (1985) and Levin and associates (1987) show that tangible resources such as product and production processes are relatively easy to imitate. The imitation of organizational culture, organizational principles, and organizational routines, on the other hand, is problematic (Daft 1978; Damanpour and Evans 1984). These resources are accumulated internally and are valuable and usable within "specific" and supportive social and technical infrastructure. They are a source of firm-specific heterogeneity. They are also a source of rigidity and inertia in the firm (Lieberman and Montegomery 1988). Because of the path-dependency of non-tangible resources, a firm's ability to exploit opportunities is constrained in both time and space. On these resources the future activities of the firm are built and undertaken. It is argued here that the availability of the non-tangible resources is what projects the direction and determines the speed of a firm's internationalization process. In the context of the internationalization process of firms these non-tangible resources may consist of (1) internationally trained manpower and other management resources; (2) internationally active buyers, suppliers, and the other actors among whom the firm enjoys a good reputation, goodwill, and trust; and (3) an established brand name.

The non-tangible resources of a firm are not fixed. As we noted, extra and unused resources are always available, or are in the process of being generated. The very "abundance" of non-tangible resources, on the other hand, triggers the idea of internationalization and may encourage a firm to improve its use of these resources by entering foreign markets. The existence of the unused non-tangible resources puts pressure on the firm to internationalize. It may be difficult for legal or other reasons to lay skilled people off, or it may be believed that those who are currently underutilized may be needed in the firm at a later stage. In such a situation a firm may seek entry to a foreign market, or it may accept an offer from an external party to participate in an international venture. In either case, the extended use of the non-tangible resources will generate extra value but cost the firm little extra. It is thus claimed here that unused or underutilized resources are a precondition for initiating an internationalization process in a firm. Unused or underutilized resources can be defined as "excess factor services over and above what is needed to meet managers' requirements for organizational slack" (Teece 1982, p. 58). They also create a dynamic in the internationalization process and in the selection of the mode for foreign entry. It should also be noted that the use of the non-tangible resources is limited as regards geographical area as well as in its purpose or scope. This is true even within one and the same firm. The speed with which firms internationalize and from which country the process starts are thus determined by the availability of these partially transferable, inimitable or semi-imitable, and path-dependent non-tangible resources. I suggest that the availability of non-tangible resources is both a constraint and a source of support in the internationalization process of the firm. The preceding description implies that the transfer of tangible and of non-tangible resources across countries can be decoupled. The decoupling of the two types of resources is always possible in all industries. As we shall see in the following discussion, this decoupling has implications for the firm's internationalization process.

A RESOURCE-BASED MODEL

Firms start operations in the domestic market, and their first accumulated resources are in that market. The model states that an internationalization process is caused by the underutilized resources in a firm. These resources can be used to generate value for the firm. But the transferability and mobility of the domestically based resources abroad is restricted in time and space. The process of going abroad is slow and gradual one. As a firm internationalizes, it accumulates resources from the foreign markets and combines them with its own. In this process a dynamic evolves. Three dynamic processes are important, namely, the internal education effect, the rationalization effect, and the quality-improvement effect. Through these processes the resource base of the firm is altered. Some resources are enhanced and others are not. Thus, in the process of internationalization, firms, on the one hand, exploit their own resource base to generate value. On the other hand, firms also enhance their resource base. The value of the current resources is improved through new combinations. The new combinations supply resources for future internationalization. We see the internationalization process of firms as a continuing process of resource creation, resource accumulation, and its subsequent exploitation by the firm. A disruption in the resource creation-accumulation-exploitation process in a firm will terminate its internationalization process. In this process a decoupling of the real and the legal market entry modes develops. The model is thus divided into an operation prior to foreign market entry, the initial entry into foreign markets, and the dynamics of the process.

Operations Prior to Foreign Market Entry

Firms start their operations in the domestic market. By combining tangible and non-tangible resources, firms develop a unique position vis-à-vis their competitors and satisfy the demands of their clients. The "uniqueness" achieved by a firm is contingent on attributes of its environment. At any given moment and on the basis of the natural resources then available, man created and over time accumulated assets; some may be induced by government policies (Teece 1981). Three environmental attributes are important. First is the level of incomes and their distribution among buyers. This affects the quality and quantity of the service and product sold by a firm. Second is the concentration of clients, which affects the distribution of sales and service outlets. Third is the mode of sales. This affects the number of outlets and the delivery process. Environmental conditions like income level affect the technology and production processes chosen by the firm. The production technology in turn affect the firm's administrative structure and routines, marketing, the after-sales service offered, and the distribution channels used by the firm. Government policies endow firms with an "induced" competitive advantage (Scott and Lodge 1985). As firms interact with clients and competitors in the domestic market, tangible and non-tangible resources accumulate. The first development of a unique configuration of tangible and non-tangible resources manifests itself in the products and services, the mode of market operation, the way distribution channels are managed, organizational routines, processes, decision-making procedures, goodwill, reputation, and credibility—all in response to the values, norms, and resource endowments of the domestic market (Pavitt 1988). Dunning (1986), Ergas (1984), and Franko (1976) have shown that the advantages generated by TNCs reflect the resource endowments markets, cultures, and the institutional setup in the domestic market. At this point firms are interacting with the domestic environment and are procuring their resources from the domestic market. These are accumulated in the non-tangible resources of the firms. The domestically based uniqueness and the company-specific advantages are utilized in going abroad.

Initial Internationalization

The resources accumulated by a firm in the domestic market project the trajectory for the future development of the firm. Going abroad is an aspect of the firm's domestic operations (Kogut 1991a, 1991b; Linder 1961). As unused or underutilized resources accumulate, they put pressure on the firms to grow (Penrose 1966). Internationalization provides one growth outlet, and it is an aspect of the growth of the firm. If the domestic market is already saturated, going abroad is the only option left. At the initial foreign market entry, the manner in which the firm interacts with its foreign clients is the same as the one it uses in the domestic market. Firms continue to rely upon their current managerial practices and their current administrative structures and routines for collecting and interpreting information, for interacting with clients and suppliers, and for supplying after-sales service and managing locally recruited labor. As excess resources appear, these then put pressure on the firm to improve the way it uses them to create value. Decisions are made as problems or opportunities arise. Firms facing such an opportunity or problem engage in sequential decision making, examining only a limited number of options (Cyert and March 1963). When problems and/or opportunities are discovered, the search for solutions is based on the current stock of resources and their configuration. The search for solutions is located in the vicinity of the problem area, and the first option is to try to apply already tested and proven solutions. In the initial internationalization process the tested and proven solutions originate in the resources that the firms has collected in the domestic market.

As the current stock of resources of a firm is history-dependent, the alternatives that have been successfully applied in the past are examined. The current stock of resources is suitable for managing such problems and opportunities as lie in the vicinity of any problems and opportunities that the firm has faced in the past. The firm possesses the resources to manage these problems and opportunities. It is difficult to be innovative, as the current stock of non-tangible resources, such as the firm's routines, administrative structures, and its managerial practices, is unable to catch and interpret appropriately novel signals from the environment. Based on the current stock of resource endowments firms face different sets of "options," and the uncertainty to which they are exposed and the way they evaluate the (identical) options supplied by the environment will all vary. Many "options" are impossible for certain firms because they do not match the current stock of non-tangible resources of that firm, that is, its reputation and its goodwill with its suppliers and buyers. Firms also abstain from innovating because it could disrupt their current organization (Hannan and Freeman 1977). This happens even if the firms are familiar with the market (Abernathy and Utterback 1978).

Due to the specific ways in which the current stock of non-tangible resources is used, these resources determine the speed with which the internationalization process of a firm will proceed. The internationalization process is slow and gradual. The process is slow because many non-tangible resources are only imperfectly mobile across international borders; they are specialized both in use and in location (Klein, Crawford, and Alchian 1978). A firm's reputation and the loyalty of its suppliers and buyers and the goodwill it enjoys in the domestic market, for example, cannot be easily transferred abroad. Similarly, the organizational culture of a firm develops in response to environmental conditions in the domestic market and are only imperfectly applicable or transferable to other countries (Hofstede 1984). The path-dependency and team-production of non-tangible resources generate similar rigidities (Diericks and Cool 1989). The greater the difference between the domestic and the foreign markets, the more difficult, time-consuming, and resource-consuming the transfer of non-tangible resources will be. A firm's resources are thus both a source of support and a source of constraint upon the future course of the firm's internationalization process.

Building up reputation, developing credibility, establishing a brand name, and developing a network of reliable dealers abroad are all—as in the domestic market—path-dependent processes. The only way to develop these resources is through being active abroad. The process is different for each market. In order to internationalize, the foreign firm must develop a local client base and a local supplier base and must win the loyalty of both. It takes time to develop a reputation in a foreign market and to develop organizational structures, routines, and processes to meet the needs of this market. At first, for example, the skilled manpower for managing the foreign market is lacking. It is hardly wise or feasible to transfer a large number of skilled managers abroad to organize international operations. Operations abroad allow firms to uncover the limits of their own resource base. It tells the firm on what resources to build their operations in that specific market and where the need is for complementary resources. Firms can of course hire from outside managers who have worked in a particular market. There are difficulties in sending abroad managers hired from the market, since they will be unaware of the unique combination of non-tangible resources in the particular firm. Hiring is also problematic when the path-dependent, non-tangible resources such as organizational routines, culture, and the image have to be transferred across national boundaries. The international transfer of other non-tangible resources also has its problems since these resources will have been developed locally in active cooperation and interaction with local buyers, suppliers, and other environmental actors. Such resource-based rigidities explain why the internationalization process is a slow and gradual one.

By operating abroad, supplying goods and services, and fulfilling their promises, firms develop market-specific non-tangible resources. As these resources accumulate, their wider use to create value for the firm is motivated. There is "always" an excess supply, either perceived or real, and consequently an increase and greater dynamic in the resource commitment of the firm in that specific market.

Discovering Foreign Market Opportunities

In the initial internationalization process the discovering of opportunities abroad is a reactive process. Domestic firms lack knowledge of the resources in the foreign markets and of the opportunities and risks of going abroad. Firms also lack the managerial and other non-tangible resources needed for combining external resources with the resources possessed by the firm. The current stock of non-tangible resources in a firm in the shape of organizational routines and managerial practices fails to catch novel signals from outside. The process of combining the internal resources of the firm with the external resources is initiated by external actors with whom the firm has had exchanges in the past. The external actors are familiar with the current stock of resources of the firm concerned—that it can be trusted, that it enjoys a good reputation and has generated goodwill. Examples of such external actors could be an internationally active client or an internationally operating supplier who have done business with the firm in the past and are familiar with its resources. The same external agents connect the resources of the firm with resources that are available in the environment. They act as "internalized agents" at the boundaries of the firm. They fulfill two functions: they act as attention arousers and as bridge-builders between the foreign-going firm and the actors in the foreign environment. As attention arousers, external actors supply information and direct the attention of firms to the opportunities and problems that prevail abroad. This may make the internationalizing firm more receptive to foreign markets. As bridge-builders, external actors connect the resources of the foreign-going firms with the resources of actors in the foreign markets. In its simplest form, bridge-builders may provide information to the internationalizing firm on specific buyers and sellers and their needs. The bridge-builders may also award the first foreign assignment to the foreign-going firm. Tesar (1975) and Bell (1995), for example, noted that other firms were the most important factor in initiating exporting.

Country Market and Market Entry Mode Selection

To answer the question of why firms enter a particular country market, the crucial aspect is the compatibility between the firm's current stock of resources and the resources needed for successful entry into a foreign market. The compatibility between the two improves as firms enter country markets that are similar to their domestic market. Similarity in surrounding support infrastructure and social context improves the chances of a successful transfer (Cantwell 1991). Entry into similar markets is the first step, because it facilitates the transfer abroad of firm-specific non-tangible resources. As the non-tangible resources are location specific, there is a greater probability of a successful transfer of non-tangible resources across countries, if the foreign market is identical or very similar to the domestic market in terms of consumer choice, legal systems, and political institutions. These similarities between markets help the entering firm to understand the underlying causal relations in event on the market, among the market actors, and in the institutional environments. There will be few problems arising from causal ambiguity, and uncertainty is reduced. Similarities in market and institutional conditions between the domestic and the foreign markets also make it more likely that the firm's resources are usable abroad. The firm can thus rely upon its current management and marketing practices in the foreign market. The more dissimilar the foreign market and the domestic market, the less useful will the domestic-market–based non-tangible resources be in the internationalization process. Dissimilarity implies that foreign market is idiosyncratic, and the effects of locations specificity are high. The difficulties in transferring the firms specific resources will increase, and the likelihood of a failure is high. For this reason the internationalization processes of firms start with countries that are similar to the domestic market of the firm. That firms start their internalization process with the countries of this kind is supported by many studies (Johanson and Wiedersheim-Paul 1975; Kogut and Singh 1988). For similar reasons, firms find it difficult to enter new and unrelated business areas in foreign markets. The new and unrelated business areas are far away from the current stock of resources of firms.

The internationalization process of the firm starts with the commitment of such resources as are readily transferable across borders. Apart from capital these include equipment and products. The tangible resources such as product and production technology are imitable and readily transferable across borders (Hayes and Wheelwright 1984). Initially small numbers of export orders are handled by the firm from its domestic market. Foreign market entry in related product areas through exporting is favored because a number of resources, such as equipment, are indivisible. The firm has already installed production capacity in the domestic market. Foreign market entry into related product areas allows more efficient use of the excess resources. The same is unlikely to happen if the foreign market entry is made in unrelated product markets (Mahoney and Pandian 1992). Entry into similar markets that have the "same" per capita income, for example, provides the benefit that firms need not innovate. In the initial foreign market entry, the firm uses its current excess production capacity and other resources to generate value, and the foreign firm invests only limited amounts of tangible and non-tangible resources in the foreign market. The domestic-market–based managerial practices and administrative structures are used to serve foreign markets. As interaction with the foreign market intensifies, the firm's manpower base gets better at handling foreign markets. Similarly, organizational structures, routines, and processes evolve, specifically to deal with the foreign markets. Finally, the firm establishes a loyal local client base. Goodwill and reputation are established, although because of path-dependency this takes time. The process is gradual, but continuous. On the other hand, several non-tangible resources are non-tradable and inimitable, and the firm cannot acquire them from others, for instance, by imitating competitors or by purchasing them in the market. Firms find it difficult, for example, to implement organizational practices with which they are unfamiliar (Bartlett and Ghoshal 1989). This determines the speed at which firms can internationalize. The internationalization process is slow, as the internationalization patterns observed by Cavusgil (1980) and Johanson and Wiedersheim-Paul (1975) confirm.

In many situations, however, a firm's non-tangible resources can be easily transferred across countries, in which case the internationalization process can proceed rapidly. This can happen, for instance, when the foreign-going firm follows established clients abroad, as confirmed by research (Ball and Tschoegl 1982; Brimmer and Dahl 1975; Goldberg and Johnson 1990; Sagari 1982; Sharma and Johanson 1987; Weinstein 1977). The prior business relationship in the domestic market implies that the firm has already established goodwill and reputation and that it has committed other non-tangible resources to managing the clients and suppliers. As the buyer firms go abroad, the foreign-going firm follows. The problems and the search for solutions are limited. In the course of the internationalization process there is no change in the manner in which the foreign-going firm conducts its business. By following established clients abroad, the firm will find itself operating in more or less the same environment as in the domestic market and can easily transfer a significant stock of its current non-tangible resources from the domestic to the foreign market. There is no need to go abroad slowly. Last, if the firm is internationalizing by way of acquisition, it needs "only" to transfer capital resources abroad. Transferring capital resources abroad is not particularly problematic. In such situations, too, the internationalization process can be rapid.

Dynamics in the Internationalization Process

Through their active presence in the market, firms accumulate resources for managing operations and develop organizational structures and routines for combining their own resources with those of the local environment. The crucial point is that, as regards the amount of non-tangible resources invested abroad, there may be hardly any difference between ownership, joint ventures, or contracts as the mode for internationalization. The amount of resources invested abroad is contingent upon what resources the firm needs to commit in order to conduct business, to keep up relations with specific buyers and sellers, and to maintain its reputation and goodwill in the market, rather than on the formal shape of the internationalization process. The capacity to learn about the resources available in foreign markets is contingent upon the structure and configuration of the nontangible resources. Exporting allows firms to interact with clients, agents, and competitors. Firms are forced to meet the needs of their clients and partners. Resources such as reputation, goodwill, and credibility are invested and accumulated. Through contractual relationships firms develop channels for communicating with a market. In international management contracts, for example, firms deploy their own skilled staff abroad to operate a local firm and to make their marketing, production, and procurement decisions on behalf of the local firm. They also install administrative and marketing routines. These allow as much investment in and accumulation of location-specific resources as do the ownership-based market entry modes. In a study of management contracts entered into by a cement firm, Sharma (1993) reported that the firm placed executives in all the high positions in the local firm. They also installed all the administrative and marketing routines. The management contract allowed the cement firm to operate abroad for decades. The expatriates were in continuous interaction with the local lawmakers, clients, and suppliers, and the cement firm invested as well as accumulated non-tangible resources such as reputation and goodwill in the market. The existing store of a firm's market-specific resources, primarily non-tangible in nature, in combination with its unused or underutilized resources, forms the base for future resource-commitment decisions. A dynamic through three parallel processes evolves, namely, the internal educational effect, the rationalization effect, and the service quality effect.

Internal Education Effect

The internal education effect originates in three ways. The first is through the training of employees. Through foreign operations the human resources of the firm acquire training in managing such operations. There is a change in the composition of the human resources and in their orientation. Staff engaged in overseas operations discover opportunities and risks and learn to combine the internal resources of the firm with those of the foreign locality in order to exploit the opportunities further. Firms are transformed into loosely coupled systems (Weick 1979). Managers in a foreign location are familiar with local resources and promote additional tangible and non-tangible resource commitment on the part of the firm. Their commitment to a particular market deepens. Second, attitudes and visions change. As firms engage in international operations and achieve or expect to achieve success in them, a favorable attitude toward international operations evolves. The strategic vision of the firm changes. This change in strategic vision forms a cognitive map that shapes the underlying logic for mobilizing, combining, and developing resources within the firm. An escalation in the commitment to the foreign market results. For this to happen, success in terms of earning profits is not essential. With the initial internationalization, firms and individuals commit resources in the form of reputation and goodwill, time, and self-identities; the commitment then escalates (Brockner 1992; Staw 1981), due either to future expectations (Vroom 1964) or to the self-justifying behavior of the decision makers (Festinger 1957). A success, however, provides an additional impetus to internationalization.

Third, there are structural and configurational changes. The locally specific investment of resources gives rise to a gradually increasing international structural and decision-making orientation in the firm. Foreign clients and competitors enter the decision-making processes. Processes evolve by way of structural changes to solve particular problems or to exploit particular opportunities. The resource base and structure become more conductive to international operations. Gradually an international division or a specific position will emerge to promote international operations.

Rationalization Effect

The second dynamic process that triggers behavioral change is via the rationalization effect, that is, the resources employed by firms are rationalized. As firms operate abroad they achieve longer production runs and develop more rationalized decision-making routines and more effective administrative systems, to substitute for the use of skilled manpower (Porter 1985). The use of case-to-case decision making is replaced by general routines. International operations expand, which in turn triggers and justifies the investments of resources in technical development and computerization. The rationalized administrative structure is connected with two effects. First, the monitoring capability of the firm is improved (Rubin 1978). The firm comes to possess better resources for judging and evaluating local partners and clients and for selecting sites. Second, skilled manpower resources are replaced by machinery and structural improvements in the firm. Efficiency is enhanced, and skilled manpower is released and replenished. Hotel chains, for example, have computerized their booking systems. Now clients can book rooms in any hotel in the chain from a single location. Previously bookings were arranged by each hotel separately, which was manpower intensive. All this results in saving resources and cutting costs, which improves the competitiveness of the firm abroad. This justifies the strategy pursued by the firm. The existence of unused resources puts pressure on the firm to expand its foreign operations.

Quality Improvement Effect

Last, we have the quality improvement effect. The market demands new and better products and services, something that happens for two reasons. First, competitors improve the quality of their product, service, and/or delivery system. Internationalization brings real or potential competitors into the decision making. This affects the behavior and orientation of the firm, as competitors offer a credible alternative to the buyers. The environment and the context within which a firm operates are altered. Second, due to their internal drive based on their non-tangible resources and to a desire to maintain and develop goodwill and reputation with existing clients, firms invest in improving the quality of their products (Sapiro 1983). This is effected on the basis of a firm's current stock of resources. By going abroad, firms avail themselves of "new" resources from the foreign market and combine these with their current stock of resources. Firms either launch improved products or reposition their established products. Either way, performance, goodwill, and reputation will be enhanced as a result of product development and improved quality control procedures.

Patterns of Entry Mode Dynamics

The three forces just described either change or reinforce a firm's level of resource commitment in a particular foreign market. With increasing resource commitment firms acquire a better position for entering other foreign markets. An internationally oriented staff, organizational structure, and procedures, together with the existence of unused or underused resources, puts pressure on management to commit additional resources to foreign markets. A dynamic develops, which can assume two different shapes. According to the first, the firm follows the steps delineated in the "stage" models, moving from exporting to the ownership-based foreign market entry mode (Bilkey and Tesar 1977; Johanson and Wiedersheim-Paul 1975). The firm gradually invests more resources in the same market. This pattern is possible in industries where the production and consumption stages can be separated from each other. Since non-tangible resources are either immobile or semi-mobile and semi-transferable, an outright transfer across borders is not feasible. The process is gradual.

In the service industries such as the hotel industry, another pattern can be observed, namely, that the mode of foreign market entry adopted by a firm remains unchanged over time (Dunning and McQueen 1982; Sharma 1991). Hotel chains such as Hilton International and Hyatt International have always entered foreign markets by way of management contracts. There has been no change in the choice of foreign market entry mode. Irrespective of the mode selected, the firm reduces risks, interacts with clients, and the local legal and political environment; demonstrates its offerings in the foreign market; and controls the service outlet. In these respects the ownership and the contract-based foreign market entry modes could be said to be identical. However, "no change" in the foreign market entry mode is not the same as the absence of any dynamic. The dynamic can be seen as additional resources are committed to an existing foreign market by expanding the firm's facilities there. The outfit abroad seeks additional resource commitment on the part of the home firm in its particular region or country. As a result of the education, rationalization, and quality improvement effects, firm adds more operations in the same country and occasionally in the same city. The emerging expansion pattern reveals the companies deepening their engagement in a particular market without changing their entry mode. The dynamic consists in geographical expansion without any change in entry mode. Firms do not move from contract arrangements or exporting to an ownership-based mode of entry. Such a transformation would not be accompanied by any marked improvement in the position of the firm, in control, or in the ability to detect problems and opportunities abroad. For these purposes contract-based foreign market entry modes are just as effective as the ownership-based entry modes. Thus, Litteljohan and Ruper (1991) report that in the hotel industry contractual arrangements give the operator enough control over the decision making in the local firms. But the contract-based foreign market entry modes economize on the use of capital resources and increase the speed of the internationalization process.

This observation, that the entry mode remains unchanged throughout many foreign market entries, emphasizes the importance of the "how we do it" approach and of the effect of the history of the firm. As we have noted, a foreign outfit with subsequent location-specific commitments makes heavy demands on resources. It affects the non-tangible resources that will develop in the firm for interacting with clients, partners, and competitors. Gradually, these all become the administrative history of the firm, and there evolves a belief that "this is how things work." Such a firm will then stick to its tried and tested foreign market entry mode. Teece (1976) discovered that prior know-how of transfer through a partner improves the inclination of subsequent know-how transfer through similar mechanisms. In a situation where each foreign outfit is exposed to a very different sort of environment, it is difficult to evolve a legal entry mode that responds to the needs and the demands of each separate environment. The choice of a foreign market entry mode is based on simplicity. The same legal entry mode is used repeatedly, irrespective of the specific environment of the firm. Growing resources commitments may or may not alter the legal shape of the foreign market entry mode, but the "real" foreign market entry mode keeps on changing, depending on the resources commitment by the firm in each separate market.

Legal versus Real Foreign Market Entry Modes

As a result of accumulating location-specific resources, the organization of the firm becomes loosely coupled. Two types of loose coupling can be identified, the spatial and the functional kind.

Spatial Loose Coupling

Spatial loose coupling refers to domestic and foreign operations. This type of loose coupling evolves as foreign outfit expand their operations and develop an independent resource base. The outfit independently attracts resources from the environment to expand its own operations. For example, the outfit may be able to procure financial resources from the local capital market. In the course of internationalization there will be a change in the context of the foreign outfit. At the beginning of the process, relations between the foreign outfit and foreign clients are dyadic. The number of foreign clients is limited and their needs fairly simple. Occasional visits and reporting are enough for the parent firm to keep a track of this dyadic relationship (Forsgen 1989). Gradually, the nature of the relationship between the foreign outfit and the local environment evolves into a complicated web of relations, which are difficult to keep a track of. A political coalition emerges (Pfeffer 1978), and the outfit's power base is enhanced. As the foreign outfit becomes enmeshed in the local environment and evolves an independent context, the parent firm is unable to keep a track of the entire web of relationships in which the foreign outfit is now engaged. The foreign outfit will seek and obtain resources and will become an "autonomous" unit (Ghoshal and Bartlett 1993; Forsgren et al. 1995) and will emerge as powerful center. This enhanced power base is used by the outfit to attract more resources from the common pool of resources of the group, perhaps to acquire a world product mandate (Poynter and Rugman 1982) or to become a global leader (Bartlett and Ghoshal 1986). All this changes the resource commitment and foreign market entry mode in a particular market.

Functional Loose Coupling

Functional loose coupling refers to the different specialties within the firm, which occurs between the levels at which the entry strategy is formulated and the level at which it is implemented. The formulation level is dominated by those belonging to the legal and financial affairs departments and their concern is with the institutional and the regulatory requirements to which firms are exposed. Entry mode decisions at this level are a reflection of such requirements, and those involved have to decide on the legal shape of the foreign market entry mode. At this level the effects of a change in the resources of the firm and the subsequent international orientation are "not considered." The changes that do occur reflect changes in the institutional environment, such as changes in the financial market or in government policies. Commitment decisions at this level concern the investment of primarily the capital resources.

The implementation level is dominated by those in the operational departments such as marketing, procurement, and production. The people at this level are in day-to-day contact with local clients and partners and thus learn to work with local customers, partners, and competitors. They invest resources in adapting to the needs of their counterparts (Hallen, Johansson, and Sayeed 1991). These investments in specific resources allow firms to benefit from mutual dependence (Zajac and Olsen 1993), mutual orientation (Dyer 1996), and mutual trust (Madhok 1995). Changes at the implementation level reflect changes in the basic business conditions within which the firms operate, the manner in which business is conducted and resources are exchanged, and the way in which clients and suppliers are managed. Commitment at this level concerns primarily nontangible resources such as the image and reputation of the firm, its goodwill, and its credibility. These commitments by firms are an investment at safeguarding the future business transaction with a specific partner. These form the firm-specific advantage of multinational firms. Consequently, one cannot assume that wholly owned subsidiaries are more efficient, as asserted by Davidson and McFetridge 1985). Collaborative arrangements could be equally value-generating for the internationalizing firm. Efficiency of the foreign operations is derived from commitment of resources rather than by its legal form. Exchange is guided by trust and a cooperative attitude, resulting in flexibility (Beamish and Banks 1987).

Because of the loose coupling between the formulation and the implementation level, the visible or legal forms that market entry assumes will be different from the "real" market entry modes. The visible market entry mode may remain the same across countries. The real market entry mode changes to suit the needs of the business. Because of decoupling, the legal and the real market entry modes can move independently of each other. One may change, while the other remains the same for all countries.

FINAL REMARKS

Behaviorally based internationalization process studies have been familiar for some time and have contributed a lot to our understanding of the internationalization process of firms. But these studies pay little explicit attention to the resource aspects of a firm's internationalization process. The present study aims to take the earlier studies a step further. It has been argued here that the internationalization process and the associated dynamics exhibit greater variety than is indicated in experience-based behavioral models, which depends upon the resource base of the firms concerned. This is not the same as to deny the contribution made by the experience/knowledge–based internationalization process models. This chapter makes a point that firms with different qualities and types of resources may vary in their internationalization process. As a consequence, firms of different size will internationalize in different ways. Similarly, as the resources of firms are path-dependent, firms from different countries may vary in their real internationalization process. On both these issues we need more research.

A more fundamental point has also been made, namely, that internationalization concerns the creation and utilization of resources and that in the process of internationalization a firm's resource base plays an independent part and creates an independent dynamic. The current resource base of a firm is both a source of support and a source of constraint when it comes to internationalization. The process of transferring non-tangible resources across countries is slow and gradual, which means that the internationalization process is frequently a slow and gradual one. However, if the firm only needs to transfer tangible resources, the process could be speeded up. This change in emphasis will enable researchers to integrate contract-based foreign market entry modes more effectively into their work. As more firms rely on contract-based arrangements in their internationalization processes, such a change in emphasis becomes desirable. It would not be far-fetched to say that after long years of international operations a firm may become internationally oriented, developing non-tangible resources that may allow it to relinquish the ownership of foreign production units. These may operate in the international market through an international buyer and supplier network connected by contracts.

NOTE

1. Throughout this chapter, the terms *resources* and *capabilities* are used interchangeably.

REFERENCES

Abernathy, W. J. and J. M. Utterback (1978). "Patterns of Industrial Innovation." *Technology Review* (June/July): 41–47.

Alchian, A. and H. Demsetz (1972). "Production, Information Costs, and Economic Organization." *American Economic Review*, 62: 777–794.

Amit, R. and P.J.H. Schoemaker (1993). "Strategic Assets and Organizational Rent." *Strategic Management Journal*, 14: 33–46.

Andersen, O. (1993). "On the Internationalization Process of Firms: A Critical Analysis." *Journal of International Business Studies*, 24: 209–232.

Authur, W. S., Y. Ermoliev, and Y. M. Kanivski, (1987). "Path Dependent Processes and the Emergence of Macro Structure." *European Journal of Operations Research*, 30: 294–303.

Ball, C. and A. E. Tschoegl (1982). "The Decision to Establish a Foreign Bank Branch or Subsidiary." *Journal of Financial and Qualitative Analysis*, 14 (September): 411–424.

Barney, J. B. (1986a). "Strategic Factor Markets: Expectations, Luck, and Business Strategy." *Management Science*, 32: 1231–1241.

——— (1986b). "Organizational Culture: Can It Be a Source of Sustained Competitive Advantage?" *Academy of Management Review*, 11: 656–665.

—— (1991). "Firm Resources and Sustained Competitive Advantage." *Journal of Management*, 17: 99–120.

—— (1992). "Integrating Organizational Behavior and Strategy Formulation Research: A Resource Based Analysis." In P. Srivastava and A.H.J. Dutton (eds.), *Advances in Strategic Management*, Vol. 8. Greenwich, CT: JAI Press, pp. 39–62.

Bartlett, C. and S. Ghoshal (1986). "Tap Your Subsidiaries for Global Reach." *Harvard Business Review*, 64(6): 87–94.

—— (1989). *Managing Across Borders: The Transnational Solution*. Boston: Harvard University Press.

Beamish, Paul (1985). *Joint Venture Performance in Developing Countries*. Doctoral dissertation, University of Ontario, London, Ontario.

Beamish, Paul and John C. Banks (1987). "Equity Joint Ventures and the Theory of the Multinational Enterprise." *Journal of International Business Studies*, 18(2): 1–16.

Bell, J. (1995). "The Internationalization of Small Computer Software-Firms. A Further Challenge to 'Stage' Theories." *European Journal of Marketing*, 29(8): 60–75.

Bilkey, W. and G. Tesar (1977). "The Export Behavior of Smaller Wisconsin Manufacturing Firms." *Journal of International Business Studies*, 9: 93–98.

Boorstin, D. J. (1984). *The Image: A Guide to Pseudo Events in America*. Magnolia, MA: Peter Smith.

Brimmer, A. and F. Dahl (1975). "Growth of American International Banking: Implications for Public Policy." *Journal of Finance*, 30(2): 341–363.

Brockner, J. (1992). "The Escalation of Commitment to a Failing Course of Action: Towards Theoretical Progress." *Academy of Management Review*, 17: 39–61.

Calof, J. L. and P. W. Beamish (1995). "Adapting to Foreign Markets: Explaining Internationalization." *International Business Review*, 4(2): 115–131.

Cantwell, J. (1991). "The Theory of Technological Competence and Its Application to International Production." In D. McFetridge (ed.), *Foreign Investment, Technology and Economic Growth*. Calgary: University of Calgary Press, pp. 33–67.

Caves, R. (1984). "Economic Analysis and the Quest for Competitive Advantage." *American Economic Review*, 74(2): 127–132.

Cavusgil, T. S. (1980). "On the Internationalisation Process of Firms." *European Research*, 8: 273–281.

Chatterjee, S. and B. Wernefelt (1991). "The Link Between Resources and Type of Diversification: Theory and Evidence." *Strategic Management Journal*, 12: 33–48.

Collis, D. J. (1994). "How Valuable Are Organizational Capabilities?" *Strategic Management Journal*, 15: 143–152.

Cyert, R. M. and J. G. March (1963). *A Behavioral Theory of the Firm*. Englewood Cliffs, NJ: Prentice Hall.

Daft, R. L. (1978). "A Dual-Core Model of Organizational Innovation." *Academy of Management Journal*, 21: 193–210.

Damanpour, F. and W. M. Evans. (1984). "Organizational Innovation and Performance: The Problem of Organizational Lag." *Administrative Science Quarterly*, 29: 392–409.

Daniel, J. D., E. W. Orgam, and L. H. Radebough (1976). *International Business: Environments and Operations*. Reading, MA: Addison-Wesley.

Davidson, W. H. (1976). "Patterns of Factor Saving Innovation in the Industrialized World." *European Economic Review*, 8: 207–217.

Davidson, W. H. (1983). "Market Similarity and Market Selection: Implications for International Marketing Strategy." *Journal of Business Research*, 11: 439–456.

Davidson, W. H. and D. G. McFetridge (1985). "Key Characteristics in the Choice of International Technology Transfer Mode." *Journal of International Business Studies*, 11: 439–456.

DChericks, I. and K. Cool (1989). "Asset Stock Accumulation and Sustainability of Competitive Advantage." *Management Science*, 35: 1504–1511.

Dunning, J. (1986). *Japanese Participation in British Industry: Trojan Horse or Catalyst for Growth?* Dover, NH: Croom Helm.

Dunning, J. H. and M. McQueen (1982). "Multinational Corporations in the International Hotel Industry." *Annals of Tourism Research*, 9: 69–90.

Dyer, J. H. (1996). "Does Governance Matter? Keiretsu Alliance and Asset Specificity as Sources of Japanese Competitive Advantage." *Organizational Science*.

Ergas, H. (1984). *Why Do Some Countries Innovate More than Others?* Brussels: Center for European Policy Studies.

Erramilli, M. K. and C. P. Rao (1993). "Service Firms' International Entry Mode Choice: A Modified Transaction-Cost Analysis Approach." *Journal of Marketing*, 57: 19–38.

Festinger, L. (1957). *A Theory of Cognitive Dissonance*. Evanston, IL: Row & Peterson.

Forsgren, M. (1989). *Managing the Internationalization Process*. London: Routledge.

Forsgren, M., U. Holm, and J. Johanson (1995). "Division Headquarters Go Abroad: A Step in the Internationalization of the Multinational Corporations." *Journal of Management Studies*, 32(4): 475–491.

Franko, L. G. (1976). *The European Multinationals: A Renewed Challenge to America and British Big Business*. Stamford, CT: Greylock Publishing.

Ghoshal, S. and C. Bartlett (1993). "The Multinational Corporation as an Interorganizational Network." In S. Ghoshal and E. Westney (eds.), *Organization Theory and the Multinational Corporation*. New York: St. Martin's Press, 77–104.

Goldberg, L. G. and D. Johnson (1990). "The Determinants of U.S. Banking Activities Abroad." *Journal of International Money and Finance*, 9 (June): 123–137.

Håkansson, H. (1989). *Corporate Technological Behavior*. London: Routledge.

Hallen, L., J. Johanson, and N. Sayeed (1991). "Interfirm Adaptation in Business Relationships." *Journal of Marketing*, 55 (April): 29–37.

Hambrick, D. (1987). "Top Management Team: Key to Strategic Success." *California Management Review*, 30: 88–108.

Hannan, M. J. and J. H. Freeman (1977). "The Population Ecology of Organizations." *American Journal of Sociology*, 82: 929–964.

Hansen, G. and B. Wernerfelt (1989). "Determinants of Firm Performance: The Relative Importance of Economic and Organizational Factors." *Strategic Management Journal*, 10: 399–411.

Hayes, R. H. and S. Wheelwright (1984). *Restoring Our Competitive Edge*. New York: Wiley.

Hofstede, G. (1984). *Cultures and Consequences*. San Francisco: Sage.

Johanson, J. and J-E. Vahlne (1977). "The Internationalisation Process of the Firm: A Model of Knowledge Development and Increasing Foreign Commitment." *Journal of International Business Studies*, 8: 23–32.

——— (1990). "The Mechanism of Internationalisation." *International Marketing Review*, 7: 11–24.

Johanson, J. and F. Wiederheim-Paul (1975). "The Internationalisation of the Firm: Four Swedish Cases." *Journal of Management Studies*, 12: 305–322.

Klein, B., R. Crawford, and A. Alchian (1978). "Vertical Integration, Appropriate Rents, and the Competitive Contracting Process." *Journal of Law and Economics*, 21: 297–326.

Klein, B. and K. Lefler (1981). "The Role of Price in Guaranteeing Quality." *Journal of Political Economy*, 89: 615–641.

Kogut, B. (1983). "Foreign Direct Investment as a Sequential Process." In C. P. Kindelberger and D. Audretsch (eds.), *The Multinational Corporation in the 1980s*. Cambridge, MA: Harvard Business School Press, pp. 35–56.

——— (1991a). "Country Capabilities and the Permeability of Borders." *Strategic Management Journal*, 12: 33–47.

——— (1991b). "Joint Ventures and Option to Expand and Acquire." *Management Science*, 37: 19–33.

——— (1993). "Learning, or the Importance of Being Inert: Country Imprinting and International Competition." In S. Ghoshal and E. Westney (eds.), *Organization Theory and the Multinational Corporation*. New York: St. Martin's Press, pp. 136–154.

Kogut, B. and H. Singh (1988). "The Effects of National Culture on the Choice of Entry Mode." *Journal of International Business Studies*, 19(3): 411–432.

Lado, A. A. and M. C. Wilson (1994). "Human Resources Systems and Sustained Competitive Advantage." *Academy of Management Review*, 19: 699–727.

Lado, A. A., N. G. Boyd, and P. M. Wright. (1992). "A Competence Based Model of Sustainable Competitive Advantage: Towards a Conceptual Integration." *Journal of Management*, 18: 77–91.

Levin, R., A. Klevorick, and S. Winter (1987). "Appropriating the Returns from Industrial Research and Development." *Brookings Papers on Economic Activity*, 3: 783–820.

Lieberman, M. and D. B. Montegomery (1988). "First Mover Advantages." *Strategic Management Journal*, 9: 41–58.

Linder, S. B. (1961). *An Essay on Trade and Transformation*. New York: Wiley.

Lippman, S. and R. Rumelt (1982). "Uncertain Imitability: An Analysis of Interfirm Differences in Efficiency Under Competition." *Bell Journal of Economics*, 13: 418–438.

Littlejohan, D. and A. Ruper (1991). "Changes in International Hotel Companies' Strategies." In R. Teare and A. Boer (eds.), *Strategic Hospitality Management*. London: Cassell, pp. 194–212.

Madhok, Anoop (1995). "Revisiting Multinational Firms' Tolerance for Joint Ventures: A Trust-Based Approach." *Journal of International Business Studies*, 26: 117–137.

Mahoney, J. T. and R. J. Pandian (1992). "The Resource-Based View Within the Conversation of Strategic Management." *Strategic Management Journal*, 13: 363–380.

Mansfield, E. M. (1985). "How Rapidly Does New Industrial Technology Leak Out?" *Journal of Industrial Economics*, 35: 217–223.

Nelson, R. and S. Winter (1982). *An Evolutionary Theory of Economic Exchange*. Cambridge, MA: Harvard University Press.

Pavitt, K. (1988). "International Patterns of Technological Accumulation." In N. Hood and J. E. Vahlne (eds.), *Strategies in Global Competition*. London: Croom Helm.

Penrose, E. T. (1966). *The Theory of the Growth of the Firm.* London: Basil Blackwell.

Pfeffer, J. (1978). *Organizational Design.* Chicago: AHM Publishing Co.

Polanyi, M., (1967). *The Tacit Dimension.* Garden City, NY: Anchor.

Porter, M. (1980). *Competitive Strategy.* New York: Free Press.

——— (1985). *Competitive Advantage.* New York: Free Press.

Poynter, T. A. and A. Rugman (1982). "World Product Mandate: How Will Multinational Respond?" *Business Quarterly,* 47(3): 54–61.

Prahalad, C. V. and G. Hamel (1990). "The Core Competencies of Corporations." *Harvard Business Review,* 68(3): 79–91.

Reed, R. and R. J. DeFillipi (1990). "Causal Ambiguity, Barriers to Imitation, and Sustainable Competitive Advantage." *Academy of Management Review,* 15: 88–102.

Reid, S. 1981. "The Decision Maker and Export Entry and Expansion." *Journal of International Business Research,* 12: 101–112.

Rubin, P. (1978). "The Theory of the Firm and the Structure of Franchising Contract." *Journal of Law and Economics,* 21: 223–234.

Sagari, S. B. (1982). "United States Foreign Direct Investment in the Banking Industry." *Transnational Corporations,* 1(3): 93–123.

Sapiro, C. (1983). "Premium for High Quality as Returns to Reputation." *Quarterly Journal of Economics,* 97: 20–35.

Scott, B. R. and G. R. Lodge (eds.) (1985). *US Competitiveness in the World Economy.* Boston: Harvard University Press.

Senge, P. M. (1992). *The Fifth Discipline: Art of Practice of the Learning Organization.* New York: Doubleday Currency.

Sharma, D. D. (1983). *Swedish Firms and Management Contracts.* Uppsala: Almqvist and Wiksell.

——— (1991). *The International Operations of Professional Firms.* Lund, Sweden: Studentlitteratur.

——— (1992). *Foreign Market Entry Mode Selection: The Case of the Swedish Hotel Chain.* Paper presented at the Academy of Marketing Science Annual Conference, San Diego, April.

——— (1993). *Contract Strategies in Hotel Industry: The Swedish Hotel Firms Abroad.* Paper presented at the Annual Academy of Marketing Science Conference, Miami, 26–29 May.

Sharma, D. D. and J. Johanson (1987). "Technical Consultancy in Internationalisation." *International Marketing Review,* 4: 20–29.

Shetty, Y. K. (1979). "Managing the Multinational Corporation: European and American Styles." *Management International Review,* 19(3): 39–48.

Staw, B. M. (1981). "The Escalation of Commitment to a Course of Action." *Academy of Management Review,* 6: 577–587.

Stopford, J. and L. Wells (1992). *Managing the Multinational Enterprise.* New York: Basic Books.

Teece, D. J. (1976). *The Multinational Corporation and the Resource Cost of International Technology Transfer.* Cambridge, MA: Ballinger.

——— (1981). "The Multinational Enterprise: Market Failure and Market Power Considerations." *Sloan Management Review,* 22: 3–17.

——— (1982). "Towards an Economic Theory of the Multiproduct Firm." *Journal of Economic Behavior and Organization,* 3: 39–63.

——— (1987). *The Competitive Challenge: Strategies for Industrial Innovation and Renewal.* Cambridge MA: Ballinger.

Tesar, G. (1975). *Empirical Study of Export Operations Among Small and Medium-Sized Manufacturing Firms.* Doctoral dissertation, University of Wisconsin, Madison.

Vernon, R. (1966). "International Investment and International Trade in Product Cycle." *Quarterly Journal of Economics,* 80: 190–207.

Vroom, V. (1964). *Work and Motivation.* New York: Wiley.

Weick, K. (1979). *The Social Psychology of Organizing.* Reading MA: Addison-Wesley.

Weigelt, K. and C. Camerer (1988). "Reputation and Corporate Strategy." *Strategic Management Journal,* 9: 443–454.

Weinstein, A. K. (1977). "Foreign Investment by Service Firms: The Case of Multinational Advertising Agencies." *Journal of International Business Studies,* 8(1): 83–91.

Welch, L. and A. Pacifico (1990). "Management Contracts: A Role in Internationalization?" *International Marketing Review,* 7: 64–74.

Wernerfelt, B. (1984). "A Resource Based View of the Firm." *Strategic Management Journal,* 5 (2): 171–180.

Williamson, O. (1985). *The Economic Institutions of Capitalism.* New York: Free Press.

Winter, S. (1987). "Knowledge and Competence as Strategic Assets." In D. J. Teece (ed.), *The Competitive Challenge: Strategies for Industrial Innovation and Renewal.* Cambridge, MA: Ballinger, pp. 159–184.

Wright, P. M. and S. A. Snell (1991). "Towards an Integrative View of Human Resource Management." *Human Resource Management Review,* 1: 203–225.

Zajac, E. and C. P. Olsen (1993). "From Transaction Costs to Transaction Value Analysis: Implications for the Study of Interorganizational Analysis." *Journal of Management Studies,* 30: 131–145.

Chapter 6

The Interface between Global Sourcing and Marketing

C. P. Rao and Jerome Witt

INTRODUCTION

In the 1960s, the multinational firm was a uniquely American phenomenon. The awesome strengths of U.S. multinationals were so overwhelming that Europeans, for example, were seriously concerned with American dominance in their domestic markets. The 1970s and 1980s saw the development of multinational firms originating in Europe, Japan, and a number of newly industrialized countries (NICs), which ended fears of American dominance. The development of multinationals on a global scale created a new competitive environment while, at the same time, traditional trade barriers began to crumble. These developments mandated the globalization of corporate strategies. In the new era of global competition, some authors argued that the well-managed contemporary company should emphasize globally standardized products that are advanced, functional, reliable, better quality, and lower priced rather than market-customized products for each national market. The manifestation of this widely held position forces the issue of global sourcing to the forefront.

Sourcing strategy generally refers to identifying which production units will serve which particular markets and how components will be supplied for production. In the past a polycentric approach, by which operations were organized on a country-by-country basis, was the modus operandi for many multinationals. Currently, the extensive geographical expansion of multinational firms has led to growing realization of the competitive advantage gained from coordinating and integrating operations across national boundaries. Consequently, the development of global marketing in synchronization with cross-national sourcing strategies is a major concern. Sourcing strategies are, however, multidimensional and include such factors as production locations, phases of production, internal versus external components sourcing, and internal versus external assembly.

Intra-firm trade by multinational firms has steadily increased in strategic response to the challenges of global competition. A useful framework to describe these cross-national business practices as they relate to sourcing strategies is the International Product Cycle (IPC) model. This model provides a compelling description of dynamic patterns in international trade of manufactured products and direct investment as a product advances through its life cycle. According to the IPC model, changes in inputs and product characteristics toward standardization over time determine an optimal production location at any particular phase of the product's life cycle.

There are, however, key deficiencies relating to the model's failure to explain the operational interdependence among affiliates of multinational firms. Since the pace of new product introduction abroad has accelerated, innovational lead time has shortened. As a result, the competitive advantage has migrated from the original innovator to the follower firms. This migration is not only a function of changing factor costs and demand patters, but also a function of change in the innovator's behavior. If the innovator fails to maintain the original advantage by, say, pursuing a global strategy of market dominance, a follower firm might gain the advantage. As a consequence, a follower firm might, by identifying and successfully implementing an appropriate sourcing strategy, overcome the innovator's preemptive move.

It is also possible that knowledge of the IPC model and its characteristic pattern can actually lead international managers to alter predicted outcomes. Shrewd competitors "ride over an international product cycle." Unfortunately, the IPC model does not view the multinational firm as an aggressive player. Conversely, the realities of the marketplace have shown that some multinational firms have set dual goals of establishing a global sourcing systems and serving multiple global markets and are proactively driving the manufacturing and marketing experience curves.

The challenge of any sourcing strategy is to materialize the value that will meet the customer's needs. This requires decisions such as whether to make or buy and, more specifically, where to make or buy. The objective of this decision making should be to achieve the quality-cost combination that maximizes both customer benefits and company profits.

Today, sourcing is the why, what, where, and how of supplying the targeted customer. A global marketing plan requires a global sourcing plan, the objective of which is to supply the customer with the highest quality at the lowest possible cost. The global approach to sourcing should take into account all of the variables that impact on the company's long-run ability to create and deliver value to its customers.

THE GLOBAL SOURCING CHALLENGE

The decision to make or buy is arguably the most fundamental component of manufacturing strategy. Should a firm be vertically integrated or should it assign the manufacturing components to capable suppliers and perform an assembly

role? Averaged across all U.S. manufacturing establishments, the costs of purchased inputs amount to about 53 percent of sales revenues, while labor costs
amount to only 10 percent. Despite this, many manufacturers, obsessed with
labor issues, elect to allocate their overhead based on labor savings alone. While
human resources are key issues to any firm, the emphasis placed on the labor
component of cost is often disproportionate.

Since purchased inputs are such a large portion of total product cost, the
importance of the make-or-buy decision cannot be overstated. Gains to be made
by addressing purchasing issues are far greater than those to be derived from
attacking labor costs. Beyond static cost issues, however, there are longer-
term strategic considerations intertwined with the make-or-buy decision that
are of even greater importance. Traditionally, the most widely recognized benefit of global sourcing has been lower costs. Factors such as less expensive labor and lower land and facility costs have enticed companies to seek foreign
suppliers. However, lower cost is no longer the only benefit offered by global
sourcing. For many firms, the payoffs are increasingly coming from four other
factors.

1. *Availability.* Some firms source globally primarily to strengthen the reliability of their
   supply. They look to worldwide markets to supplement their domestic sources or to
   meet an increase in product demand. Flexibility in the course of today's dynamic and
   turbulent environment provides companies with an additional motive to ensure availability.

2. *Uniqueness.* In some cases a company may not be able to get the materials it needs
   from domestic sources. This may result in a situation where an industry requires
   technical specifications or capabilities that cannot be sourced domestically.

3. *Quality.* Quality is rapidly developing as a key lure for overseas purchases. This may
   be driven by technological superiority not available within domestic boundaries.

4. *Sustainable Competitive Advantage.* In a bid to gain an edge over its rivals, companies
   are using three avenues to secure a lasting competitive advantage. First, companies
   may seek to gain *technical supremacy* by obtaining sourcing access to innovative
   technology developed overseas, thus locking out competitors from this technology
   base. This practice is frequently pursued within the electronics and other high-tech
   industries. The second strategy is in the *penetration of markets.* Sourcing from a
   particular market may provide a company with a means of entry into a promising
   new market. This is often the case in those markets that are in the process of liberalizing their economies. Third, global sourcing can provide *speed and flexibility,*
   which are increasingly important competitive advantages in the international arena.
   By establishing a solid global sourcing program, these important advantages can be
   captured and sustained.

Global sourcing is, therefore, a general strategic orientation toward international supply markets. The first step to this should be a systematic extension of
sourcing activities to foreign markets, possibly worldwide (a strategy of "going
international"). Analogous to a move from export activities to direct investments,

foreign sourcing should be characterized by an increase in intensity. A procurement infrastructure should be established with buying offices, trading companies, logistic facilities, and information systems. Beyond immediate supply goals, the firm should pursue a number of other goals such as research in technology, influence on the structure of competition, support of marketing activities, and spreading financial risk.

In summary, global sourcing can be a critical feature in several competitive strategies such as:

1. Supporting a global strategy by realizing economies of scale through "material inputs."

2. Supporting a multinational strategy by developing potentials for differentiation and by taking an active role in influencing quality standards.

3. Supporting regionally limited strategies with respect to a general improvement of input-output relations and preparing for export activities by building a strategic bridgeheads in target markets.

GLOBAL SOURCING STRATEGY PERSPECTIVES

Shifting from a purely domestic oriented procurement policy toward a global sourcing needs a radical change in perspective. This may be described as shifting from domestically based purchasing operations to globally based supply management strategies. The traditional notion is that the purpose of effective procurement is to make sure that well-defined demands for materials are properly met. The proposed globally oriented strategic "supply management" assumes that procurement policy can and must make primary contributions to a company's success. In this context global sourcing as a procurement strategy is characterized by two features:

1. Operating in international markets, which means systematically extending procurement policy toward sources in worldwide markets; and

2. Strategic orientation, an overall sourcing orientation aimed at securing the company's potentials for competitive success.

In the evolution of such strategy, Arnold (1989) identified four distinct procurement policy development stages. These stages are briefly described below:

1. *The Traditional Procurement Policy.* In this stage the role and horizons of procurement policy are narrowly defined. The space horizon is limited to domestic sources. The time horizon is short-term operations based. The procurement function is narrowly defined as consisting of purely operative function whose major purpose is to facilitate other functions, especially the production function. There is no attempt to delineate the strategic role of procurement in the overall strategy development and implementation process of the business unit.

2. *International Purchasing*. In the second phase the space horizons of procurement policy are expanded to non-domestic sources of supply. The major goal is to supply the company's material demands at the lowest possible costs. The primary focus will therefore be on systematic investigation of foreign sources of supply for the following reasons: (a) attainment of price or cost advantages, (b) quality of purchased goods, and (c) service, delivery, and availability considerations. The strategic role of sourcing in the overall strategic management of the business unit is not clearly delineated. The drive for cost efficiency, involvement in overseas markets, and competitive sourcing practices may motivate the international purchasing phase.

3. *Strategic Procurement Policy*. In this approach procurement policy becomes an integral part of the overall business unit strategies. The procurement strategies are integrated with other business unit strategies, and the former's potential to significantly contribute to gaining sustainable competitive advantage is formally recognized. As the procurement policy gains strategic significance the need for global sourcing becomes all the more important. It is only through increased global sourcing activities the strategic role of procurement policy becomes feasible.

4. *Global Sourcing Strategy*. This is the final phase in the evolution of global sourcing strategy. This final phase requires the transfer of the strategic procurement tasks to the framework of international transactions and operates on a worldwide level. It is seen as a partial corporate strategy aimed at the worldwide utilization of material resources. The global sourcing strategy gets a boost from global marketing strategies. Corporations with extensive overseas operations are more likely to reach this final global sourcing strategy level than corporations with limited or no overseas marketing operations. The global marketing sourcing strategies work together in a mutually reinforcing manner. The corporate experience in developing and implementing global marketing strategies will greatly facilitate the development and implementation of global sourcing strategies. This is due to the fact that what is learned in marketing function becomes relevant for engaging in global sourcing activity. The world-mindedness, overseas market environmental knowledge, and cross-cultural negotiation skills gained in overseas marketing become effective tools for engaging in global sourcing. In a sense, global marketing and sourcing become mutually reinforcing types of phenomena.

Global sourcing strategy requires the following types of organizational characteristics:

1. *Corporate Size*. In this regard, a certain potential in resources is essential, with special techniques of management and organization as well as marketing knowledge and investment capital. For example, it is common with multinational corporations to maintain procurement offices in key centers of worldwide procurement environment such as Singapore. These international procurement offices (IPOs) develop the necessary expertise to source for their corporate worldwide production and marketing systems. These IPOs have to develop the necessary organization and coordination skills, which ensure smooth flow of material to their corporate production and marketing systems.

2. *Problem Awareness.* The management's adoption of a particular strategic orientation is of crucial importance. Global sourcing has to be embedded into the corporate philosophy and must be made with explicit guidelines for management decisions.

3. *Staff.* Sophisticated global sourcing strategies can be developed and effectively implemented only with properly qualified and experienced personnel. As this is a newly emerging strategic orientation, it is not always easy to find qualified and experienced personnel who can understand the intricacies and complexities of global sourcing. The extensive literature in international marketing is full of instances of the pitfalls one experiences in doing business in foreign environments.

The same problems to some extent apply to the global sourcing context.

ALTERNATIVE GLOBAL SOURCING STRATEGIES

The purchasing function in many United States–based firms traditionally has maintained adversarial relationships with suppliers. As world markets become increasingly competitive, firms have discovered that close partnership relationships with important suppliers can produce managerial, technological, and financial benefits. The Japanese practice of single sourcing—with the close relationship it forges between buyer and seller—has been used as a model by an increasing number of U.S. firms seeking to reduce and better manage their supplier bases.

A dilemma has evolved in considering the merits of a single versus a multiple sourcing strategy. In the past, the U.S. sourcing/contracting behavior has centered around multiple sourcing. The belief held by the majority of professional buyers was that for buyers to have only one source of supply for materials was a risk incurred only through incompetence or corruption. Indeed, single sourcing was regarded as a symptom of possible purchasing failure. However, the picture is strikingly different today. In recent years purchasing habits have changed and have succumbed to the attractions of single sourcing. The main driving force behind this switch in purchasing practices has been the result of efforts to match the performance of Japanese competitors.

Between the 1960s and the 1980s, the average cost of purchasing materials for U.S. industries increased by 10 percent, to raise total operating costs by over 60 percent. For this reason, efforts have centered on minimizing the price of purchased goods to increase their competitiveness. This approach hinged on three activities:

1. Buyer relies on a large number of players who can be played off against each other to gain price concessions and ensure supply continuity.

2. The buyer allocates amounts to suppliers to keep them in line, that is, to maintain and influence their business activities.

3. The buyer is characterized by an arms-length posture, using only short-term contracts.

While the preceding approach often results in a lower purchase price, it assumes that there are no differences in suppliers' abilities to provide different competitively advantaged products (technology gains, innovations). Such behavior has little incentive to foster long-term coordination and cooperation between buyers and suppliers.

Two caricatures of global sourcing strategies have evolved over preceding decades with respect to purchasing sourcing behavior. One, which may be called the "Western" strategy, involved typically a policy of short-term contracting with a number of different sources. The other, which may be called the "Japanese/Eastern" strategy, is characterized by single sources, long-term contracts, and cooperative relationship.

The polarization of choice evolved the debate by organizations over what is optimum choice behavior. Organizations employing strategies at opposite ends of the spectrum hold the idea that their strategic selection holds the best opportunities. The change from multiple to single sourcing is a major step with obvious risks for the personal reputations of those making the decision.

Both the single and multiple sourcing strategies have their pros and cons. In the context of global sourcing, such polarized thinking of single versus multiple sourcing may be counterproductive. Some authors, like some procurement experts, contend that this dichotomization of global sourcing strategies into Western multiple and Japanese single sourcing is an oversimplification of the reality of global sourcing strategies. The choice of optimum global sourcing strategy seems to depend on both the external global procurement environment and internal corporate circumstances. As the global production system constantly shifts from one part of the world to the other, corporations are forced to maintain the existing sources and at the same time to cultivate new sources that prove to be more advantageous in the near future. Similarly, a variety of corporate internal considerations, such as size, management structure, stage of development, market position, and the relative importance of supply materials, influence the choice of appropriate global sourcing strategy.

Irrespective of the type of global sourcing strategy (single, multiple, or a combination) opted for by the company, there is growing evidence to indicate that purchasing partnerships become the future modus operandi of global sourcing. As companies look more frequently to the purchasing function to help them meet their cost and quality goals, the possibility of forming partnerships with suppliers has become an area of great interest to many firms.

A purchasing partnership is defined here as "an agreement between a buyer and a supplier that involves a commitment over an extended time period, and includes the sharing of information along with a sharing of the risks and rewards of the relationship" (Sperkman 1988). Thus, a supplier partnership differs from a traditional supplier relationship in that it involves an inherent trust, as well as a mutual commitment and sharing. Establishment and maintenance of purchasing partnerships in a global sourcing context become more complex than when such partnerships are sought in the home country context. The cultural and business practice differences between the U.S. companies and the overseas suppliers creat a host of problems that need to be foreseen and the necessary precautions taken to make sure that purchasing partnerships with foreign vendors prove to be effective means for deriving all the benefits claimed from such partnerships. Again, the experiences in international marketing and the literature on strategic alliances can provide useful guidelines for formulating a systematic approach to the development and management of global sourcing partnerships.

CONCLUSIONS

It is widely recognized that the expansion of European and Japanese firms in U.S. production through direct investment has been staggering, while that of the U.S. firms' direct investment abroad has slowed since the 1970s. Now that many European and Japanese multinational firms have affiliates established in many parts of the world, they have become capable of tapping various resources on a global scale, if they opt to do so. Global strategy mandates that the affiliates of the multinational firm become part of a system in manufacturing, marketing, sourcing, and financial management rather than operating independently of others.

As the lowering of trade barriers eases the flow of goods worldwide, business survival increasingly hinges on a company's ability to compete globally even if its operations are limited to domestic markets. Competitors from overseas are targeting previously secure domestic markets, while competitors at home are using overseas sources of supply as a basis for cost reduction and product and service innovation. Global sourcing, therefore, is rapidly becoming a prerequisite to competing in today's marketplace.

On the other hand, global sourcing strategy has been conceived of as a set of alternative ways of serving foreign markets. In fact, many firms simultaneously use a mix of multiple sourcing strategies and single sourcing strategies in marketing their products in the United States. The question, then, is no longer whether to go global—virtually all companies will be tapping resources globally within five years—but how to capture the strategic benefits of global sourcing while minimizing the costs and risks.

Costs are no longer the only benefit of global sourcing. Other benefits like availability, uniqueness of raw materials, and quality are becoming increasingly important. Besides, obtaining high product quality, improved product availability, and lower costs could enable the companies to continue their leading edge or to sustain their competitive advantage. In addition, the benefits that could be obtained from forming global purchasing partnerships with suppliers all over the world will prove to be invaluable. In pursuing such benefits of global sourcing strategies, the sourcing strategies can learn many lessons from the rich experiences of the global marketing stategists. The types of problems and challenges typically faced by the global sourcing strategist are very similar to the experiences of global marketing strategists. Hence, by interfacing the global marketing and sourcing strategies many U.S. business organizations stand to gain immense benefits.

It is obvious that the benefits of global sourcing are too attractive to ignore. To compete effectively in the global marketplace of the 1990s, U.S. manufacturers/marketers must be supportive of the viability that the global sourcing strategies could bring. They have to make a commitment, especially from the top management, to examine total costs including indirect costs, to develop trust and respect toward overseas suppliers, to use technologies to enhance control, and to develop ways to handle business risks.

Moreover, to enhance this effectiveness, both the manufacturers and suppliers must tear down the orthodox practices of the past and create more innovative operating partnerships. It's time now for us to begin "tying the knot" with the overseas suppliers.

REFERENCES

Arnold, Ulli (1989). "Global Sourcing—An Indispensable Element in Worldwide Competition." *Management International Review*, 29(4): 15–27.

Carter, Joseph R. and Ram Narasimhan. (1990). "Purchasing in the International Marketplace: Implications for Operations." *Journal of Purchasing and Materials Management*, 26(3): 2–11.

Ellaram, Lisa M. (1990). "The Supplier Selection Decision in Strategic Partnerships." *Journal of Purchasing and Materials Management*, 26(4): 8–14.

―――― (1991). "A Managerial Quideline for the Development and Implementation of Purchasing Partnerships." *International Journal of Purchasing and Materials Management*, 27(3): 28–38.

Fagan, Mark L. (1991). "A Guide to Global Sourcing." *Journal of Business Strategy* 12 (3): 21–25.

Hanafee, P. (1984). "The Role of Purchasing and Materials Management in International Trade." *Journal of Purchasing and Materials Management*, 20: 7–13.

Hefler, K. F. (1981). "Global Sourcing: Offshore Investment Strategy for the 1980s." *The Journal of Business Strategy*, 2(1): 7–12.

Kotabe, Masaki and Glenn S. Omura, (1989). "Sourcing Strategies of European and Japanese Multinationals: A Comparison." *Journal of International Business Studies*, 20(1): 113–130.

McClenahen, John S. (1990). "Sources of Frustration: Combining Global Sourcing with Just-in-Time Manufacturing Is a Tough Task." *Industry Week*, 239(19): 74–81.

Min, Hokey and William P. Galle (1991). "International Purchasing Strategies of Multinational U.S. Firms." *International Journal of Purchasing and Materials Management*, 27(3): 9–18.

Monczka, Robert M. and Robert J. Trend. (1991). "Global Sourcing: A Development Approach." *International Journal of Purchasing and Materials Management*, 27 (2): 2–8.

Morgan, James P. (1991). "Purchasing 2000: When Sourcing Begins to Drive Corporate Strategy." *Purchasing*, 110(1): 122–129.

Presutti, William D., Jr. (1992). "The Single Source Issue: U.S. and Japanese Sourcing

Strategies." *International Journal of Purchasing and Materials Management*, 28 (1): 2–8.

Robert, E. (1988). "Strategic Supplier Selection: Understanding Long Term Buyer Relationships." *Business Horizons*, 34 (July–August): 75–81.

Schoenberger, Richard J. (1986). *World Class Manufacturing*. New York: Free Press.

Seshadri, Sudhindra and Kalyan Chatterjee (1991). "Multiple Source Procurement Competitions." *Marketing Science*, 10(3): 246–263.

Sperkman, R. (1988). "Strategic Supplier Selection: Understanding Long Buyer Relationship." *Business Horizons*, 34 (July–August): 65–72.

Trelven, Mark and Sharon B. Schweikhart (1988). "A Risk/Benefit Analysis of Sourcing Strategies: Single vs. Multiple Sourcing." *Journal of Operations Management*, 7 (4): 93–113.

Welch, James A. and P. Ranganath Nayak (1992). "Strategic Sourcing: A Progressive Approach to the Make-or-Buy Decision." *Academy of Management Executives*, 6 (1): 23–30.

Chapter 7

International Sourcing: Entering and Exiting Different Networks

Per Servais[*]

INTRODUCTION

The latest decade has presented an increasing amount of research on the internationalization of firms (Johanson and Vahlne 1990). One prominent representative of this development is the Uppsala internationalization model, which sees the internationalization of the firm as a process in which the firm gradually increases its international involvement and engagement. The model stresses objective knowledge, which can be taught, and experimental learning through "learning by doing." The model implies that market commitment and expansion develop in small steps. The model sets out to explain two patterns in the internationalization process of the firm: (1) The firm engages in a specific country as a development of the establishment chains. (2) The firm enters new markets with successively greater psychic distance, that is, start internationalization by going to the markets most easily understood by them.

As such, this internationalization model explicitly deals with export engagements. Johanson and Vahlne (1990) exemplify the model by using the term stages: "at the start no regular export activities are performed, then export takes place via independent representatives, later through a sales subsidiary, and eventually manufacturing may follow" (p. 13). Implicitly, this model may be applied to several function areas of the firm, not just marketing. The internationalization of other function areas like finance, management, and procurement may partly or fully follow the pivot point in the Uppsala internationalization model; hence, the internationalization process of the firm could be described as the gradual acquisition of knowledge about and the successive commitment to foreign markets. This chapter focuses on the internationalization of the procurement activities of the firm, but in the light of the internationalization model of the outward-bound activities described and seen from the procuring firm's perspective.

INTERNATIONAL PROCUREMENT

Hallén (1982) carried out a study of international purchasing[1] in which he examined the market conditions, the attitude toward procuring from abroad, and the ability to conduct international purchasing influence on the extent of international purchasing in industrial firms. He concludes that the number of potential domestic suppliers is often limited in small countries, and in the cases analyzed no domestic suppliers are available at all. In general, buyers have a more positive attitude toward their own domestic suppliers than toward foreign suppliers. This is reflected in the buyer-seller relationships in the manner that the domestic suppliers are almost always used, but frequently together with foreign suppliers. In this study, however, international purchases are not viewed as an internationalization process, nor are international purchases regarded as a "failure" or imperfection in the internationalization of the selling firms.

In a conceptual article, Monczka and Trent (1991) view foreign purchases as an internationalization process. The point of departure is quite the same as in the Uppsala internationalization model, however, focusing on foreign purchases. In the article the prime motivation for conducting foreign purchases is that the firms pursue international sourcing as a reaction to increased worldwide competition, in search of benefits such as cost reduction, quality improvement, increased exposure to worldwide technology, and delivery and reliability improvements (the motivations will be dealt with later). As the firm develops international experience, an internationalization process takes place. Monczka and Trent (1991) describe this process in four phases:

- Phase 1: Domestic Purchasing only.
- Phase 2: Experimental Foreign Purchasing.
- Phase 3: International Purchasing.
- Phase 4: Global Sourcing.

In Phase 1, firms are not engaged in direct foreign purchases, either because they do not perceive any incitements to do so or because they lack the expertise to conduct foreign purchases. Domestic suppliers provide the firms with all needed items: however, this does not imply that goods from abroad are not used, but all transactions and interactions are carried out through domestic suppliers. Hence, these purchases are not perceived by the procuring firms as foreign purchases. Monczka & Trent (1991) claim that most firms in the 1960s and 1970s operated in this stage, owing to the fact that worldwide competition pressures were not as significant as today and that the firms could still operate successfully in this phase.

A firm progresses to phase 2 because it, as Monczka and Trent (1991) express it, "is confronted with a requirement for which no suitable domestic suppliers exist or because competitors are gaining an advantage due to foreign purchases" (p. 4). As in the Uppsala internationalization model, triggering events may occur, "forcing" the firm into an internationalization process. These triggering events on the supply market could be supply disruptions by domestic suppliers or a declining domestic supply base, but they could also be a result of general dissatisfaction with the offers presented by "local" suppliers. The main feature in this phase is that foreign purchases are carried out on an ad hoc basis and that the knowledge about and the experience with foreign purchases are quite limited.

Phase 3 represents the international procurement stage, in which markets are viewed by the firms from a worldwide perspective. Firms shift from phase 2 to phase 3 because they realize significant performance improvements derived from foreign sourcing and experience success with foreign procurement. "Discussion of proactive international sourcing strategies does not occur until a firm reaches this point in the evolutionary process" (Monczka and Trent 1991, p. 4). In this phase firms systematically search foreign markets for potential suppliers.

The development from phase 1 to phase 3 resembles the development in export operation forms. In the case of export, the firm sets out with indirect export and ends up establishing its own sales subsidiaries abroad. In the case of foreign purchases the firm is, at first, only involved in indirect import activities; later on, the firm may be involved in direct import activities, that is, purchasing directly from the foreign producer; it is also possible that the firm sets up its own foreign purchasing offices abroad or uses the sales subsidiaries as "remote" purchasing departments.

With regard to phase 4, firms realize great benefits through the integration and coordination of procurement activities on a global basis. In this phase the requirements for managing the sourcing process are great; hence, firms must possess the required information systems, personal capabilities, and coordination and organizational mechanisms. These problems are more or less identical with the problems connected to the final stage of the Uppsala internationalization model regarding the manufacturing units abroad. Davis and associates (1974) have analyzed factors affecting the choice of global versus local suppliers in domestic-minded, venture-minded, and international-minded firms. They conclude that irrespective of the type of firm, management preference for global sourcing and centralized supplier selection must be tempered by conditions pushing the individual units toward local suppliers and decentralized decision making.

The Uppsala internationalization model has been supported by various empirical studies, such as Cavusgil (1984) and Strandskov (1987), with minor adjustments. Especially the first steps in the internationalization model seem to be well covered; however, the later phases in the model have been criticized (Hedlund and Kverneland 1985). With regard to the internationalization of purchasing activities most studies focus upon the motivations or reasons for conducting international purchases, but no attempt has been made to study this internation-

Figure 7.1
Possible Motives for International Purchases

	Internal	**External**
Proactive	• Lower prices • Improved quality • Exposure to new technology • Attitude	• Foreign market possibilities
Reactive	• Risk reduction in purchase	• Offers from foreign suppliers • Declining domestic supplier competition

alization process empirically; furthermore, the possible consequences to the firm of a de-internationalization have not been discussed.

In a study based on interviews conducted in 26 large American firms Monczka and Giunipero (1984) focused on the reasons why the firm purchases from foreign suppliers and why the firm originally began to purchase abroad. The reasons for starting were as follows (in order of priority):

• Foreign firms could offer a lower price than domestic suppliers (including costs).
• The firm is international and has an international attitude.
• Products from foreign firms are the only ones available on the market.
• Products from foreign firms are of a better quality.
• The technology required is available only from foreign firms.
• To conduct counter-trade.

Beside these arguments the firms also emphasized the large number of supplier alternatives, enhanced competition among suppliers and exposure to world market technology.

The results of Monczka and Giunipero's (1984) study are supported by a study by Carter and Narasimhan (1990) on 80 large American firms. In order of priority the firms stated lower product price, improved product quality, better production flexibility, and access to new technology as the prime reasons for conducting international purchasing. The most recent study by Min and Galle (1991) on 800 American firms seems to support the pattern even though the price factor is not so evident in this study. Compared with some of the findings in the export behavior literature (Strandskov 1987), the following motives for international purchasing can be elaborated (see Figure 7.1).

The proactive internal motives have already been commented on. It should, however, be stressed that the lower price could stem not only from lower production costs abroad but also from activities in the procuring firm decoupling some of the members in the chain and purchasing directly from the foreign producer, thus increasing profits for some of the members. Through a market analysis of the supplier, the procuring firm identifies potential suppliers on a worldwide basis. Distances (both physical and mental) have, however, turned out to be a barrier to frictionless transactions; hence, market analysis in a traditional sense is not likely to be conducted on a large scale.

Coincidental offers from a foreign supplier may lead to the first foreign purchase, similar to the first export order in the export behavior literature. The procuring firm may also be dissatisfied with the offers given by suppliers on the domestic market, leading to a search for new suppliers on an international basis. In some cases there might be no potential suppliers on the home market, leading to a search elsewhere. A traditional argument in the management literature encourages firms to spread their investments on different objects. In the case of purchases the argument would be to spread purchases on different suppliers in different countries (multiple sourcing). This seems, however, not always to be the case. Gadde and Håkansson (1993) stress the point that resources could be better used in establishing close buyer-seller relationships (single sourcing). Another issue is the willingness by the procuring firm to conduct foreign purchases. Some empirical research (Monczka and Giunipero 1984) stresses some of the obstacles in undertaking international purchasing (distances, language, cultural differences). In general, most empirical research has neglected the buyer-seller perspective and has not elaborated on issues such as which purchases are most likely to be internationalized. This issue will be elaborated further.

CLASSIFICATION OF BUYING SITUATIONS

Within traditional industrial buying-behavior models, international purchases have to a great extent been neglected. Furthermore, the commonly used classification framework of "buying classes" has been criticized for not including the dimension of the perceived importance of the purchase (Hill and Hillier 1977). Hence, the key question to Möller and Laaksonen (1986) is the development of a portfolio of supplier relationships with varying interaction modes. This strategic task comprises several sub-problems, such as being able to evaluate which interaction modes are "optimum" under given conditions. As Cunningham (1982) states, an overall strategic view of the range of purchasing activities from the buyer's perspective has been neglected, and purchasing is not confined to isolated decisions and short-term operational episodes. Möller and Laaksonen (1986) point out that suppliers can:

• Influence the economic efficiency of a firm (e.g., reducing stockholding).
• Influence the competitiveness of a firm (e.g., improving quality).

• Influence the adaptability of a firm (e.g., giving a firm access to resources held by a supplier and the usage of such resources with regard to its own customers).

In order to achieve this influence, the supplier may play different roles vis-à-vis the buying firm. More specifically, a supplier can offer various benefits to the customer (Gadde and Håkansson 1993). Development benefits are benefits achieved when letting the supplier conduct the R&D tasks. Rationalization benefits are benefits resulting from lower production costs obtained when buying from a supplier instead of producing yourself. Structural benefits are benefits achieved through appropriate relationships to suppliers.

The pivot point is in which situations certain types of relationships are likely to develop. Traditionally, the products are seen as a key factor when analyzing different situations, but major problems have occurred as many product classifications are not unequivocal. Uncertainty does have a large impact on the perception of different situations. Uncertainty has also been used as a tool for purchase classification (Håkansson and Wootz 1975). They argue that the perceived buying uncertainty is a function of (1) the buying problem or situation characteristics, (2) decision-maker(s) characteristics, and (3) contextual characteristics. Möller and Laaksonen (1986) suggest that experience level and purchase frequency are added. According to Möller and Laaksonen (1986) the uncertainty dimension can be separated into need uncertainty, technical uncertainty, market uncertainty, acceptance uncertainty, and transaction uncertainty. These different uncertainties call upon different actions or behavior on the part of the purchaser. For example, in the case of high transaction uncertainty the purchaser will contact more suppliers and in the case of high need uncertainty, familiar suppliers will be preferred (Håkansson et al. 1977).

Möller and Laaksonen (1986) warn that previous attempts to explain organizational buying behavior through the perception risk tool has had poor results due to, among other factors, the complexity or multidimensionality of the term. They claim: "Most of the other classifications are either too restricted (product type, usage, standardization) or suggested for other purposes. . . . or they may be too difficult to operationalize . . . to provide basis for buying classification" (p. 178).

Möller and Laaksonen (1986) isolate the key problem in defining buying situations as the use of either too simplistic or too complex approaches. Rather than suggesting one specific dimension, they suggest five product-related basic dimensions (importance, complexity, familiarity, innovativeness, and frequency) and three buyer-seller interaction–related dimensions (familiarity, dependence, and depth of interaction). In an empirical study McQuiston (1989) finds support for importance, complexity, and newness as classification dimensions.

In this chapter the perceived complexity and the perceived importance of a purchase are chosen as the two dimensions classifying purchase situations. These are subdivided into economic importance, end-product importance, production importance, and importance for the firm-specific advantage, as well as into func-

Figure 7.2
Different Buying Situations

	Sourcing Management	**Supplier Management**
High Perceived Complexity	*Situation*: Only a few potential suppliers with the wanted skills and of bottleneck products. Focus on the market and technological development.	*Situation*: A few suppliers of strategic items. Focus on R&D in close cooperation with supplier and/or integrated production.
	Performance Criteria: Supply reliability and dependence.	*Performance Criteria*: Mutual benefits in relation to FSA.
	Decision Level: Centralized.	*Decision Level*: Centralized.
	Sourcing: Mainly single sourcing.	*Sourcing*: Single.
	Relationships: Dependent relationships with some coordination.	*Relationships*: Partnership based on interdependent relationships.
	Purchasing Management	**Materials Management**
Low Perceived Complexity	*Situation*: many potential suppliers of standardized goods.	*Situation*: Some potential suppliers of leverage items.
	Performance Criteria: Low direct cost and standard transfer. Focus on functional efficiency.	*Performance Criteria*: Low indirect cost and specialized transfer. Focus on delivery security and supply base.
	Sourcing: Multiple among preferred local suppliers.	*Sourcing*: Parallel sourcing.
	Decision Level: Decentralized.	*Decision Level*: Decentralized with central coordination.
	Relationship: Arm's-length independent relationships with ad hoc suppliers.	*Relationship*: Some collaboration through independent relationships.
	Low Perceived Importance	**High Perceived Importance**

tional complexity, usage complexity, specification complexity, and commercial complexity. Based on this, Figure 7.2 can be established.

It should be noted that the dimensions are relative and difficult to measure quantitatively. In the case of a buying situation, like the "purchasing management" type, the buying firm would not value such purchases very highly and the firm would use as few resources as possible on the procurement process, delegating most of the obligations to a lower level in the organization. The firm relies on the market to sort out the "unable" supplier and will not perceive any incitements to search for suppliers abroad, but mainly use suppliers in the local community.

In buying situations perceived by the firm to have a fairly high degree of importance, but not complicated, such as large quantities or frequency (materials management), the firm searches for a supplier with either a large assortment or the ability to supply the wanted quantities on acceptable terms. The firm is interested in enhancing the competition among the suppliers, emphasizing "arm's-length" relationships and avoiding too great dependency on a particular supplier. The firm is, however, also interested in having a close market contact, enabling the firm to be "updated" with the development and, if necessary, to shift between preferred suppliers.

In both situations the firm focuses on the commercial and transactional aspects of the purchase emphasizing the costs connected with the purchase, thus stimulating the firm to avoid expensive chain members and dealing directly with the producer. Contrary to the former buying situation, where the firm was reluctant to go abroad, the firm in the latter situation is very eager to have more attractive offers to choose among.

Modern production plants are often highly specialized and sophisticated, making them sensitive to disturbances; security and accuracy are often critical aspects in buying situations of the sourcing type. This security may be obtained through long-term contracts or the use of parallel suppliers in order to stabilize the dependence. Hallén (1982) showed in his study that one of the reasons for having foreign suppliers was to have a sort of "portfolio" of suppliers (foreign and domestic) to draw upon. The specialization may, however, have the effect that only few suppliers (specialists) are available and they may not be located on the home market.

In many situations the procuring firm is highly dependent on resources outside its own organization. The firm may be interested in adapting its products or production to other firms and in entering more cooperative relationships, such as common research and development, information systems or "just-in-time" deliveries. In order to establish these interdependent relationships, frequent contacts are needed. In the case of internationally inexperienced procuring firms, the creation of close buyer-seller relations with a foreign supplier can be difficult owing to the physical and mental distances between the parties, let alone the cultural differences.

In the two latter buying situations, one might expect the decisions related to the relationships not to be confined to one individual in each organization, but to "teamwork" in both organizations.

The perception of the buying situation as displayed in Figure 7.2 will, however, change over time. A purchase that is perceived by the buying firm at a given time to be very complicated may, due to learning, later be perceived as rather simple. Another purchase may be perceived as very important to the firm but over time lose its importance, for example, to the end-product.

IMPLICATIONS

The Uppsala internationalization model foresees that firms will gradually increase their knowledge about and experience with foreign markets. In the case of international purchases one might expect the firm to begin searching for potential foreign suppliers in buying situations like the "rationalization type," since in this situation, there might be immediate economic benefits to the procuring firm. Whether this move is proactive or reactive depends on the experience the firm has gained in the internationalization of other areas, such as export or "triggering events" like a sudden offer from a foreign supplier. In this case the low degree of perceived complexity may not be an obstacle to conduct a search for and negotiations with potential suppliers, but it is reasonable to expect, according to the Uppsala internationalization model, that the search will be conducted in countries close to the country of the procuring firm.

Later, when the firm has gained experience with the latter type of purchases, chances are that it will proceed to purchases in the "security type" buying situation. In this situation purchases are perceived important enough to contain an incitement to search for suppliers abroad, yet this type of purchase demands a certain degree of experience with foreign markets to be conducted successfully. On the other hand, the lack of potential suppliers on the home market may "force" the procuring firm to conduct a search internationally. Chances that purchases in the "economizing type" buying situation are internationalized are quite small, owing to lack of incitements and the resources the firm is willing to spend in connection with this type of purchase.

When the firm has gained greater experience, especially in connection with the handling of cultural differences, it is willing to consider foreign suppliers (partners) in buying situations like the development type. Since this type of relationship combines the building of mutual trust and knowledge with a high degree of commitment to the relationship, these relationships tend to be quite stable, yet dynamic.

The procuring firm is, however, weaved into a network of business relationships comprising different firms. This implies that the actors in a network are more or less active and that the establishing of new relationships and the development in old ones are the results of the ongoing interaction between the parties. Johanson and Vahlne (1990) argue that entering a new network demands both motivation and resources and may require several firms to make adaptations. The internationalization (entering foreign networks) may be initiated by other firms within the network in a specific country. However, the network in a country may extend beyond the country's borders, and the extension of this network may have strong implications for the internationalization of the individual firm. Johanson and Vahlne (1990) note that "in relation to the internationalization of the firm the network view argues that the internationalizing firm is initially engaged in a network which is primarily domestic" (p. 19). Like in the case of exportation, international procurement means that the firm develops business relationships in foreign country networks. That can be achieved through:

• The establishment of relationships in foreign networks new to the firm (international extension).
• Development of relationships in those networks (penetration).
• Connecting networks in different countries (international integration). (Johanson and Vahlne 1990, p. 20)

Johanson and Vahlne (1990) furthermore stress the possibility of the relationships to be used as bridges to other networks. Welch and Luostarinen (1993) examine the connection of the inward and outward aspects of internationalization. They claim there is a possibility that the inward process might precede and influence the development of outward activities, especially in the early stages of internationalization. The interconnections are, however, most pronounced in the various examples of countertrade or offset requirements.

Welch and Luostarinen (1993) state that the inward internationalization process may either be initiated by active international search by the buyer, including examination of different foreign sources, or in case the buyer is inactive, the sale is initiated by the foreign supplier. It is more important, however, that the buyer firm through interaction with the foreign supplier gets access to his network. "Through its network of contacts the foreign supplier may possess knowledge of interest to its foreign customers about possible customers, competitors and appropriate methods of markets entry" (Welch and Luostarinen 1993, p. 51). Hence, international purchases may be used as strategic bridges to foreign markets and networks. These relationships can help the firm, getting inside networks of foreign countries and at the same time signaling the firm as being a trustworthy partner. In some cases the relationships in domestic networks may force the procuring firm to go abroad. If the domestic customer demands that the supplier follows it abroad or to use a preferred foreign sub-supplier, it is more or less forced to do so in order to keep business at home. As Johanson and Vahlne (1990) state it: "Such bridges can be important both in the initial steps abroad and in the subsequent entry of new markets" (p. 20).

This may put the procuring firm in a dilemma. Close relationships with a domestic supplier may constitute the basis for the firm to conduct export. On the other hand, the establishing of close relationships to foreign suppliers may jeopardize the relationships already being established in the domestic network; hence, entering new foreign networks and exiting domestic networks may be a difficult task for the procuring firm.

NOTE

1. Hallen (1982) defines international purchasing as cases of imports where negotiations are carried out directly with the suppliers abroad or indirectly with its representative

in the buyer's country, and as such it is not similar to importing. International procurement refers to buyers' search for and negotiations directly with potential suppliers abroad.

REFERENCES

Carter, J. and R. Narasimhan (1990). "Purchasing in the International Marketplace." *Journal of Purchasing and Materials Management*, 26(3): 2–11.

Cavusgil, S. T. (1984). "Organisational Characteristics Associated with Export Activity." *Journal of Management Studies*, 21: 3–22.

Cunningham, Malcolm T. (1982). "An Interaction Approach to Purchasing Strategy." In H. Håkansson (ed.), *International Marketing and Purchasing of Industrial Goods*. Chichester: Wiley & Sons, pp. 345–358.

Davis, Harry, Gary Eppen, and Lars-Gunnar Mattsson (1974). "Critical Factors in Worldwide Purchasing." *Harvard Business Review* (November/December): 81–90.

Gadde, Lars-Erik and Håkan Håkansson (1993). *Professional Purchasing*. London: Routledge.

Håkansson, Håkan, Jan Johanson, and Björn Wootz (1977). "Influence Tactics in Buyer-Seller Process." *Industrial Marketing Management*, 5: 319–332.

Håkansson, Håkan and Björn Wootz (1975). "Supplier Selection in an International Environment—An Experimental Study." *Journal of Marketing Research*, 12 (February): 46–51.

Hallén, Lars (1982). "International Purchasing in a Small Country—An Exploratory Study of Five Swedish Firms." *Journal of International Business Studies* (Winter): 99–112.

Hedlund, G. and Å. Kverneland, (1985). "Are Strategies for Foreign Market Entry Changing? The Case of Swedish Firms in Japan." *International Studies of Management and Organization* (15): 41–59.

Hill, R. W. and T. J. Hillier (1977). *Organisational Buying Behavior*. London: Macmillan.

Johanson, Jan and Jan-Erik Vahlne (1990). "The Mechanism of Internationalisation." *International Marketing Review*, 7(4): 11–24.

McQuiston, Daniel H. (1989). "Novelty, Complexity, and Importance as Causal Determinants of Industrial Buyer Behavior." *Journal of Marketing*, 53 (April): 66–79.

Min, H. and W. Galle (1991). "International Purchasing Strategies of Multinational US Firms." *Journal of Purchasing and Materials Management*, 27(3): 9–18.

Möller, K. E. and Martti Laaksonen (1986). "Situational Dimensions and Decision Criteria in Industrial Buying—Theoretical and Empirical Analysis." *Advances in Business Marketing*, 1: 163–207.

Monczka, Robert and L. Giunipero (1984). "International Purchasing Characteristics and Implementation." *Journal of Purchasing and Materials Management* (Fall): 2–9.

Monczka, Robert and Robert Trent (1991). "Global Sourcing—A Development Approach." *Journal of Purchasing and Materials Management* (Spring): 2–8.

Strandskov, Jesper (1987). "Virksomheders Internationalisering" (in Danish). Copenhagen: Nyt Nordisk Forlag.

Welch, Lawrence S. and Reijo K. Loustarinen (1993). "Inward-Outward Connections in Internationalization." *Journal of International Marketing*, 1 (1): 44–56.

Part III

Importer-Exporter Interaction Issues

Chapter 8

The Impact of Culture on the Exporter– Import Agent Contract

Amal Karunaratna, Lester W. Johnson, and C. P. Rao

INTRODUCTION

An area of increasing interest in international marketing is the structure and dynamics of the international marketing channel (Anderson and Gatignon 1986). There are five main strategies available to firms wishing to enter the international market. These are: (1) export, (2) licensing, (3) joint ventures, (4) subsidiary operation, and (5) foreign direct investment. The channel structure that utilizes the services of an import agent is of particular interest due to the principal-agent nature of the relationship. Agents act as a channel intermediary on behalf of an importer or an exporter. An agent is usually located in a different country from the exporting firm. Further, an agent is distinct from a distributor, who may behave in many ways similar to an agent, with the main difference being that the distributor takes title to the goods shipped and will therefore pay the exporter prior to selling such goods to the next channel intermediary, whereas the agent does not take title to the goods. For the present discussion, we will be concerned with importing agents who act on behalf of the exporting firm and do not take title to the goods exported. The agent under these circumstances is engaged by the exporter to represent its interests in a specified market where the agent's knowledge of its environment is essential to build an international marketing channel (Dahringer and Mühlbacher 1991). An ideal agent thus offers its specialized market knowledge to the exporter to obtain an agency and acts as if the exporter itself is present in the market.

The issue of an "ideal agent" creates an interesting set of questions, which will be explored in this chapter. The international marketing literature has been focused on factors influencing market entry choice (Goodnow and Hanzi 1972; Papadopoulos and Denis 1988) and the relationship between channel members, which has been considered mainly from a transaction cost analysis perspective (Anderson and Gatignon 1986). Central to the behavior of the ideal agent is the perspective offered by agency theory, which takes a somewhat complementary view to transaction cost analysis by considering the relationship between the principal and the agent and the role of the contract (Bergen et al. 1992) by considering the type of contract most efficient (Eisenhardt 1985) under different levels of environmental uncertainty. Hence a contract, the formal vehicle of the agency relationship, that has too many conditions or does not adequately attend to the nature and circumstances of the relationship is likely to bring about mismatches leading to contractual inefficiencies. External environmental factors (political, cross-cultural, legal, and economic) beyond the control of the parties to the contract may influence the structure of the contract. Firm-specific characteristics such as experience, self-interest, corporate culture, and the types of products involved in the transaction may also cause mismatches between the outcomes desired by the parties and result in a wastage of scarce resources and contractual inefficiencies.

From a managerial point of view, a better understanding of the influences of the external environment and firm-specific characteristics and their effect on the contract will present opportunities to improve contractual efficiency. These factors impact on agency costs and carry implications for contractual efficiency. Efficiency gains in the contract would result in real cost savings to the exporter and the agent, which may create benefits to other members of the distribution chain and eventually the customer. Bergen et al. (1992), who recently surveyed the literature on agency theory, state that to date only two areas of foreign market entry mechanisms have been addressed from this perspective: licensing (Horstman and Markensen 1987) and foreign direct investment (Senbet and Taylor 1986). Therefore, an opportunity exists to contribute to the international marketing and agency theory literature by addressing the relationship between the exporter and the import agent. Of particular interest are the contractual relationships formed by firms between developed and newly industrialized countries.

We suggest in this chapter that where contracts are formed across countries between an exporter and an import agent, the cultural context may determine the formulation and structure of the contract and the efficiency of the agency contract. Where exchanges take place within an intracultural context of a culture-based network, such as those described by *Guanxi* in China (Montagu-Pollock 1991), there is potential to achieve lower agency costs. The potential to achieve this in an intercultural context may be realized only if the structural determinants of the intraculture network extend across geographic boundaries. As lower agency costs represent contracts which are more efficient, this chapter identifies several culture-based factors which may impact on contractual efficiency.

THE IMPORT AGENT AND THE CONTRACT

A contract between an exporter and an import agent embodies the tasks to be performed and the obligations of each party (Jensen and Meckling 1976). A contract between an exporter and an import agent may be implicit (verbal) or explicit (documented). The terms of an implicit contract are verbal and therefore highly flexible, and rely on the exporter having a great deal of trust that the agent will act in the exporter's best interests. Anecdotal evidence from interviews with exporting firms suggests that firms often use implicit contracts for one-off orders, and often the transaction documentation such as written orders, bills of lading, and bank drafts serve as effective contracts. For example, implicit contracts form a small percentage of total transactions in some Islamic states, where a verbal agreement is bound by religious and cultural sanction. Explicit contracts are formally negotiated documents where the terms of the relationship are clearly defined and termination and penalty conditions are specified.

Agency theory posits that the efficiency or optimality of the contract for the agent's services are maximized by minimizing agency costs. Agency costs are defined by the sum of monitoring costs (information is a commodity that can be purchased), bonding costs, and residual loss (Eisenhardt 1985). Monitoring costs are those expended by the principal to monitor the agent's actions. Bonding costs are those the principal may convince the agent to expend to guarantee that the principle's interests are not harmed, or that it will be adequately compensated if the agent's actions harm the principal (Jensen and Meckling 1976). Residual loss is an inefficiency measure brought about by a divergence between the principal's and agent's aims (lack of goal congruity between the principal and the agent) as well as the outcomes of the principal-agent relationship (Jensen and Meckling 1976). It describes the losses resulting from non-optimality (from the principal's point of view) of the agent's actions (Ellis and Johnson 1993) and results in a monetary cost to the relationship. Therefore, where the efficiency of the relationship is high, residual loss would be small. In a cross-cultural interaction, a divergence of cultural backgrounds of the parties to the contract has the potential to create residual loss, since the parties may have a large divergence of the desired outcomes from a contractual relationship.

Two types of problems create inefficiencies in the exporter–import agent contract. The first, known as moral hazard, occurs when the aims and goals of the principal (the exporter) do not coincide with those of the import agent. The second, adverse selection, occurs when it is difficult to verify the activities the agent carries out on behalf of the exporter (Jensen and Meckling 1976). Moral hazard arises when the agent's effort is not consistent with the requirements of the principal, such as in the case of an import agent who agrees to promote an exporter's goods but the agent promotes a complementary product instead. While this may not violate the contractual terms, the similarities of the tasks required to promote the product and existing cultural barriers make it difficult for management at the exporter's firm to know what the agent is doing. Adverse selection occurs when the agent withholds information from the principal, such as, for example, where an agent claims to have particular industry expertise but this cannot be verified before or after hiring (Eisenhardt 1989). These problems are brought about as a result of information asymmetries: the exporter and the import agent have different information available to them. Adverse selection and moral hazard create agency costs, and much of this is borne by the exporter unless the exporter is successful in shifting these to the agent.

Bergen and associates (1992) view the problems faced by the exporter (the principal) as pre- and post-contractual problems. The pre-contractual problems are those the exporter faces before offering an agent the contract, and post-contractual problems are those it faces after a formal contract has been entered into. Kale and McIntyre (1991) have added a third stage, identified as negotiation, initiation, implementation, and review. The latter should be a continuous process after implementation. At each of these stages, the nature of the exporter–import agent interaction depends on environmental factors such as economic conditions, competitor activity, technological changes, and the agent's behavior, which can be influenced by corporate and country culture (Bergen et al. 1992).

During the initiation stage, exporters may search for potential agents when they evaluate potential channel partners and enter into a bargaining and negotiation phase for which five negotiating steps have been described (Heiba 1990). The final of these steps results in a legal agreement (a contract) which contains each party's rights and responsibilities and will become legally binding (Heiba 1990). The contract will have a high risk of adverse selection at this stage if each of the parties withholds critical information. Next is the implementation stage, where agreement has been reached and contractual obligations are executed. During this stage, products or services (or both) are exchanged and attempts are made to influence each other's behavior. Agency opportunistic behavior is likely here, and whether or not the agent creates moral hazard problems will depend on the next stage, which reviews the channel relationship. During the review stage, each of the parties will review and re-evaluate the relationship in terms of its costs and benefits. The eventual decision to continue, change, or terminate the contract will depend on the availability of alternative solutions (i.e., other channel partners) and the cost of exit and entry into another contract. The implications for the agency relationship depend on the environmental forces (culture variables) dominant at each contractual stage.

CULTURAL INFLUENCES ON THE EXPORTER–IMPORT AGENT RELATIONSHIP

It is commonly recognized that a country's culture, political structure, and legal and economic climate constitute the major environmental forces influencing channel members (Dahringer and Mühlbacher 1991; Onkvisit and Shaw 1993). A systematic quantitative basis which may be used to analyze the impact of culture follows the well-cited work by Hofstede (1980), who defines culture as "collective mental programming: it is part of our conditioning that we share with other members of our nation, region, or group but not with members of other nations, regions or groups" (Hofstede 1983, p. 76). Starting with this definition, he identifies four cultural dimensions which focus on the differences between groups of people from 50 countries around the globe by classifying their belief systems and behavioral patterns (Hofstede 1983). These cultural dimensions are (1) individualism versus collectivism, (2) large or small power distance, (3) strong or weak uncertainty avoidance, and (4) masculinity versus femininity. Individualism describes the relationship between an individual and his or her interaction with the immediate community; those scoring high on this dimension are individualistic (focus of attitudes and values is centered on the individual), whereas low scorers concern themselves with those considered part of their in-group. Individuals from societies with high power distance tend to accept inequalities of power, whereas those scoring low on this scale tend to favor egalitarianism. Those from countries scoring high on uncertainty avoidance tend to accept uncertainty more readily and tend to be less affected by ambiguous information in decision making. Individuals from societies scoring high on masculinity tend to be competitive and achievement oriented and favor less gender equity, leaning in favor of males (Hofstede 1983).

The taxonomy developed by Hofstede has been applied to cluster markets based on the commonality of people on each of the four dimensions (McIntyre et al. 1992). Although the inherent problems in suggesting that all persons are homogeneous within a cultural cluster are acknowledged, Ralston and associates (1993) suggest that common characteristics make particular groups of nationals relatively homogeneous within and heterogeneous between clusters, and indicates the nature of the predominant influences shaping the behavior of those individuals. Ralston et al. considered this problem using four dimensions: Machiavellianism (individual's willingness to use power), dogmatism (degree to which a person is not open to new ideas), locus of control (individual's feeling of self-control, generally associated with aggression in those high on this dimension), and tolerance to ambiguity (ability to function in an uncertain environment). The last two dimensions are similar to those developed in the Hofstede framework.

These dimensions were used by Ralston and associates (1993) as the basis to compare the values of managers from mainland China (PRC), Hong Kong, and the United States. Tolerance for ambiguity scores showed that U.S. managers have the greatest level, followed by Hong Kong and Chinese managers. In the exchange interaction, Chinese managers tend to rely to a greater degree on informal means of influence than on the use of formal authority and place greater emphasis on personal relationships than on formal legal contracts. Hong Kong managers have developed a greater ability to deal with ambiguity and are more self-directed (like their Western counterparts) compared with the mainland Chinese managers. Also, Hong Kong managers were found to be more caring for their employees than their mainland counterparts. These results strongly suggest heterogeneity of cultural influences between countries and a degree of acculturation in Hong Kong, where mixed cultural influences operate. Managers able to tolerate high levels of ambiguity may favor implicit contracts and may rely on informal and flexible contracts, whereas those cultures with a high Machiavellian index may favor the use of formal contracts. Kale and McIntyre (1991) have developed a series of propositions which describe the nature of the channel relationships using Hofstede's dimensions. We have extended these propositions to consider the implications for the agency contract at each stage of the contract where the Hofstede dimensions are high or low (see Table 8.1).

Table 8.1 shows the behavioral patterns based along four cultural dimensions and the likely impact on the exporter–import agent contract. Where the exporter scores high on each of the above dimensions, the exporter is likely to prefer explicit, formal, and less flexible contractual terms than if the exporter scored low. Table 8.1 summarizes conditions facing an exporter where the exporting firm scores high or low on each of the dimensions and the implications for the agency contract at each stage of the contractual process. For example, where an exporter scores high on the dimension individualism (see the first row of Table 8.1), it is likely to incur high search costs based on objective criteria during the initiation stage. During the implementation stage there is a greater chance of conflict if dealing with a firm scoring low on this dimension with less chance of resolution. During the review stage the exporting firm is likely to claim credit for successful outcomes and blame the import agent for failures. The implications for the exporter during the initiation stage are that high agency costs may be incurred due to large expenditures on information, which seeks to determine if the exporter's goals and those of the import agent are consistent. During implementation, where conflict may occur, the agent may create moral hazard problems as the agent's goals and the exporter's goals diverge. During the review stage there may be residual loss problems as the contractual outcomes become evident to both parties, and high information costs may be incurred to verify this. In keeping with the perspective of agency theory, we have only considered the exporter's perspective rather than the cross-dimensional condition, where the exporter encounters an import agent with a different score. It is recognized that under such conditions the contractual implications may vary.

There are two considerations which follow. First, few if any cultures score high on all dimensions (McIntyre et al. 1992). Second, the interaction in a contractual relationship between parties high on some dimensions and low on others is likely to be less predictable due to the multiple combinations possible between contractual parties. While the outcomes from such interactions are difficult to predict, the above framework provides the first steps to developing a model describing an incentive structure which may be most efficient, given the cultural influences operating on the contract.

These results may allow us to suggest that a contractual relationship between a U.S. exporter and a PRC agent may be initiated informally if U.S. management

Table 8.1
Firm-Specific Cultural Characteristics Based on Hofstede's Dimensions of Cultural Groups

Cultural Dimension When Scoring HIGH at Each Phase of Contract	Conditions Faced by Exporting Firm	Agency Contractual Implications
Individualism		
Initiation	Search costs for objective criteria, strong self-interests.	High search costs drive up contractual costs.
Implementation	Greater conflict, less chance of resolution.	Moral hazard risk.
Review	Claim credit for success, blame partner for losses.	Residual loss risk.
Power Distance		
Initiation	Desire to exert greater control in negotiations.	High search costs.
Implementation	Use of coercion, powerful member attempts to dictate procedures.	Agency costs may escalate due to monitoring expenditure.
Review	Coercion leads to unsatisfactory outcome.	Unstable relationship may result in inefficient contractual outcome. Outcome-based rewards increase efficiency.
Uncertainty Avoidance		
Initiation	Requirement of "hard" information, such as past performance from potential partner.	Increasing chance of adverse selection if agent withholds information.
Implementation	Formal exchange of goods and information.	Contractual efficiency increased by outcome-based incentives.
Review	Control over events and frequent attribution of performance to channel partner.	Decision to continue or break channel depends on costs/benefit.
Masculinity		
Initiation	More assertive, focus on financial issues.	High residual loss, bonding difficult to achieve.
Implementation	High conflict, low cooperation.	High monitoring costs due to moral hazard problems.
Review	Stringent evaluation based on contractual outcome.	Efficiency increased by outcome-based reward.

Table 8.1 (continued)

Cultural Dimension When Scoring LOW at Each Phase of Contract	Conditions Faced by Exporting Firm	Agency Contractual Implications
Individualism		
Initiation	Potential channel member selected on more personal basis.	Moral hazard and adverse selection.
Implementation	Views partner as member of in-group, conflict resolution by mediation—greater tolerance.	Depends on the accuracy of "soft" information.
Review	Losses and successes considered as result of joint effort.	Incentive structure based on outcome to increase efficiency.
Power Distance		
Initiation	Driven by concerns of overall fairness.	High contractual costs due to lengthy negotiations.
Implementation	Greater communication—face-to-face and consultative decisions.	High instability of relationship if great imbalance of power.
Review	If low, power relative to partner may lead to dissatisfaction.	High contractual costs—low efficiency.
Uncertainty Avoidance		
Initiation	Willing to deal with partners having less experience.	Opportunities for moral hazard and adverse selection.
Implementation	Flexible contractual conditions.	Agency costs minimized by flexibility by both parties, otherwise high.
Review	Flexible and ad hoc process.	Low contractual costs if part of clan (intracultural).
Masculinity		
Initiation	Cooperative bargaining, less aggressive.	Opportunities for adverse selection high if information withheld.
Implementation	Focus on relationship building and keeping conflicts low.	Monitoring costs low. Good relationship with partner.
Review	Greater inclination to continue relationship, even if bottom-line expectation is poor in short term.	High contractual costs may be offset by potentially higher costs to build a new relationship.

Source: Summarized and adapted from Kale and McIntyre (1991).

is the initiating exporter. As the contract reaches implementation, it is likely to be highly formal and clearly documented. Contractual costs are likely to be high in this interaction due to the number of clauses to be negotiated, and monitoring costs may be high. Opportunities for increasing contractual efficiency are likely to be limited at the early stages but could improve as the relationship is established. The locus of control dimension results suggest that PRC managers are significantly higher on this dimension than U.S. managers (Ralston et al. 1993), indicating that while the terms of the contract may be strict, PRC managers are likely to be more responsive to requests of information, resulting in lower monitoring costs and therefore improved contract efficiency. However, intercultural forces could complicate this interaction.

CULTURAL NETWORKS

It was mentioned earlier that personal relationships play an important role in the marketing exchange process. Kale and McIntyre (1991) argue that societies low on the dimension of individualism come to view their channel partner as a member of their in-group (where a "special" relationship exists), or that a partner is chosen so that they can be treated as such. Ouchi (1979) uses an example of employees being selected who have a similar commitment to a common firm objective, which he defines as a clan. Where such a common purpose or set of shared values exist, the need to use high-cost surveillance and evaluation mechanisms are reduced, since the manager is aware that the workers are trying to achieve the "right" objective. Culture is different to clans in that where the shared values and socialization processes exist within a political unit, it is defined as culture (Ouchi 1979). Where the exporter–import agent relationship achieves the status of a clan, members of the partnership are more tolerant of each other's performance, since it can be argued that both partners are striving for each other's mutual benefit. Under such circumstances, moral hazard and adverse selection are likely to be less of a problem.

Hofstede's classification can be used to group countries along, for example, two dimensions, such as low individualism and high power distance. Countries which can be grouped together are Hong Kong, Malaysia, Korea, Taiwan, and several South American countries. In the Asian countries, the importance of personal relationships in Japan, Korea, and China (PRC) in business negotiations is gaining increasing attention. Alston (1989) describes the nature of the differences between Japan, Korea, and China and suggests the existence of a culture-based network which may operate in commercial transactions more than consumer exchanges. The nature of the relationships is described as emphasizing group loyalty (described as *Wa*) in Japan, whereas an interaction in Korea is between two parties of unequal social stature (described as *Inhwa*), and an interaction between Chinese nationals is an exchange between two individuals (described as *Guanxi*), which is different from the two previous cases. These relationships are further explained in Table 8.2.

Table 8.2
The Structure of Personal Relationships in Japan, Korea, and the People's
Republic of China

Country	Relationship	Nature of Relationship
Japan	*Wa*	• Emphasis on group loyalty and consensus.
		• Individual members profit after group profits from activities.
		• Long-term perspective.
Korea	*Inhwa*	• Harmony between unequals—links two or more persons unequal in rank, prestige, and power.
		• Linkage easily crosses corporate boundaries.
		• Corporate culture described as "clan management."
		• Family ties supersede all others.
China (PRC)	*Guanxi*	• Special relationship between two people—exchange favors.
		• Utilitarian relationship—lasts as long as relationship is profitable. Rapid changes in relationship may occur.
		• No group connotation.
		• Favors rank—exchange favors weaker member.

Source: Alston (1989).

Contracts under *Wa* could resemble an implicit contract, since they are viewed as personal agreements and are therefore fluid, changing according to the conditions. Under *Guanxi*, contracts may hold only as long as the conditions remain unchanged, and any changes are likely to supersede all prior agreements. The difference between *Guanxi* and *Wa* appears to be that under *Wa*, contracts are dependent on the firm's policies operational at the time, and these remain in force as long as the individuals who negotiated these exert sufficient influence; whereas under *Guanxi*, changes in the contract may occur as a result of changes in the environment and not due to the influence of individuals (Alston 1989). Under *Inhwa*, contracts are not merely documents stating mutual obligations and rights. They are backed by the integrity of the designers. The intentions of the parties are more important than contractual clauses. For this reason, renegotiation and redoing of contracts are expected behaviors. According to Alston, "Koreans do not consider a contract binding if conditions or interests change" (1989, p. 30). Thus, it can be seen that in all cases, contracts are likely to be highly fluid and changes could happen at any time. The differences between the three cultures are subtle and may not be visible to a party outside the culture. The implications of *Wa*, *Guanxi*, and *Inhwa* on the agency contract are twofold, namely those arising from an intracultural (within) and intercultural (between) exchange.

Where an intercultural exchange takes place between a party with low power distance and another high on individualism, a fluid contract may be needed which requires frequent renegotiation and incurs associated costs at various contractual stages. With this exchange, high agency costs may be incurred. In the intracultural context, the fluid nature of the terms is understood by both parties, and therefore costs are minimized: "no one who is part of an inhwa relationship dares upset the other" (Alston 1989, p. 30). The impact of the combination of intercultural and intracultural exchange (where, for example, an American exporter is involved in an exchange with a Chinese import agent) is less easy to predict. The Chinese agent may be able to keep its contractual costs low, resulting from low search costs to establish a distribution network in the foreign environment. How this will be translated into the agency contract with the American exporter might depend on whether or not the Chinese import agent extends its cultural network to the U.S. exporter and treats the exporter as part of its ingroup (i.e., an honorary member of the cultural network). The foregoing discussion is illustrated in Figure 8.1, which summarizes the cultural dimensions described by Hofstede and Kale and McIntyre (the resulting contractual structure and contractual efficiency which form the main variables of a model). The impact of the cultural dimensions on contractual structure and efficiency may vary depending on the negotiating stages. Throughout the exporter–import agent transaction period, cultural influences are likely to determine managerial decisions in the contractual process, and the resulting efficiency gains or losses appearing in the form of information feedback in the contractual review process might result in a modification of the structure of the contract. In this way, a set of contractual dynamics may be set up. Both the exporter and the import agent have opportunities to learn from the exchange process. Where there is positive feedback, opportunities for increased contractual efficiency may appear.

DEVELOPMENT OF PROPOSITIONS

It is evident that this model is highly idealized and assumes a status of "purity" of the intracultural network. *Guanxi* may result in an escalation of obligations between exchange partners where "repayment" might take forms which compromise extraterritoriality laws and create high transaction costs where management attempts to discharge these obligations. It is, however, appropriate to consider this model in a simple form prior to introducing more complex influences via an empirical investigation. Empirical studies where intercultural exchanges have been studied (e.g., Stewart and Keown 1989; McGuiness et al. 1991) indicate that some changes are taking place in negotiating style as PRC managers apparently become more "Westernized" in their approach. While not necessarily suggesting that negotiating style is totally culturally determined and therefore immutable, implications for the contractual process are apparent from

Figure 8.1
Culture-Based Influences on Contract Structure and Contractual Efficiency

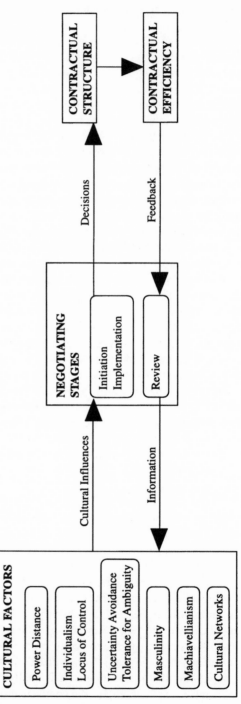

the influences of cultural networks. An examination of empirical studies allows us to develop five propositions for the agency contract. There appear to be no studies which focus on the post-negotiation relationship. Consequently we will build our propositions from the empirical evidence which examines the pre-contractual stage and extrapolate to the two later stages as a basis for future research.

Stewart and Keown (1989) surveyed a sample of 50 Hong Kong–based traders whose head offices were in the United States, Europe, and Australia. Results from a questionnaire designed to reveal the factors which contributed to a successful or unsuccessful negotiated outcome when dealing with the PRC showed that product-related factors contributed more to a successful outcome compared with personal relationships, business practices, and social customs factors; these were rated as moderately important. An "old friend" approach, which presumably based negotiations on established contacts, was rated low in importance. The most important factors contributing to an unsuccessful outcome were related to financial issues, whereas personal relationship factors such as not knowing any "old friends," communications breakdowns, and lack of patience by the non-PRC team were rated as moderately important. Other culture-based factors such as differences in business practices, negotiation styles, and social customs were rated as low. It is worth noting the upward movement of "old friends" from its contribution to success (low importance) to where its absence (moderate importance) contributes to failure, which suggests that this factor may contribute more to the contractual outcome than the respondents were aware of. These results are interpreted to suggest that as PRC negotiators gain greater experience, the emphasis on product and financial factors increases.

This conclusion is in agreement with the findings of McGuiness and associates (1991), who suggest that since the early days of China's open-door policy, where relationships were important to Chinese managers unfamiliar with foreign companies, their recent exchanges with foreign firms tend to be more Westernized as they gain greater experience. Stewart and Keown (1989) conservatively estimate that since 1978, at least 7,000 negotiations have been taken place with foreigners. McGuiness and associates show, however, that while relationships are still very important in exchanges between European, U.S., and Japanese firms, it appears to contribute no more than the value attached to past transactions and adds nothing further to the value of the product and service package.

While these findings are interesting from the pre-contractual viewpoint, what about the post-contractual and the intracultural outcome? McGuiness and associates suggest from their findings that those exchanges within the Chinese system are quite different from those outside. Extending our earlier discussion on *Guanxi*, which characterizes the exchanges based on personal relationships, it is possible that internal exchanges between a Chinese import agent and its network are based on *Guanxi*, which means that the agent has low search costs and monitoring costs based on prior knowledge of its exchange partners and high goal congruence exists between the parties, meaning that both parties desire a similar contractual outcome. For exchanges in an intercultural context between a Chinese import agent and a U.S. or Australian exporter (both low on the dimension of uncertainty avoidance but higher on power distance than those from Asian firms) outside the cultural network, there is little reason to believe that the agent would behave other than opportunistically toward the exporter. The "wild card" here is an exchange between a Chinese exporter and an expatriate Chinese national with cultural connections to the PRC. From our review of the literature, we may speculate that this cultural connection might result in a *Guanxi* relationship, and the intercountry channel structure treated as an extension of the agent's own cultural network. In this case, the contract in its implementation and review stages may be characterized by low monitoring costs and low agent opportunism. This background allows us to formulate five potentially testable propositions:

> *Proposition 1*: The rigidity or flexibility of a contract may be determined by one or both partners' tolerance for ambiguity and low Machiavellianism.

Rigid (explicit) contracts need to be efficient at the early negotiation phase, whereas flexible (implicit) contracts have the potential to increase efficiency during the implementation and review stages.

> *Proposition 2*: An import agent operating within a culture-based network operates in an intracultural network, such as *Guanxi* in China, and incurs lower agency costs within the network than outside the network.

> *Proposition 3*: An intercultural exchange, where there is a divergence along the Hofstede or other cultural dimensions, will incur agency costs which are higher than the intracultural exchange described in Proposition 2. Therefore, the greater the divergence in culture in an intercultural exchange, the greater the potential for contractual inefficiency.

The benefits of the intracultural exchange between the import agent and its network will be apparent to the exporter through lower transaction costs and rapid market penetration during the contract implementation stage.

> *Proposition 4*: An exporter operating outside a cultural network operates in an intercultural exchange and may benefit from lower agency costs if the import agent considers the exporter to be part of its in-group.

> *Proposition 5*: An exporter and an import agent who adapts to the cultural basis of the exchange will have higher goal congruency compared with one that does not; that is, there will be a great deal of harmony in what each party is willing to contribute to the relationship and its outcome.

These propositions could be tested by studying the strength of intracultural relationships and the in-country environmental variables that place limitations upon the relationship. Such a study may also consider the conditions under which an intercountry channel partner is considered a member of the in-group. A study that considers the activities at each stage of the contractual process may reveal the degree of opportunism exhibited by the agent, and this might require a longitudinal study controlling firm-specific variables. A cross-sectional study could reveal the strength of in-group behavior exhibited within a particular cultural location. The outcome from such a study would be greatly enhanced if cultural dimensions underlying behavior within a country were relatively homogeneous. While this may prove to be little more than wishful thinking, it is possible that there may be some dimensions along which cultural aspects may prove to be more homogeneous than others, such as where religion underlies the values expressed.

CONCLUSIONS

We have considered the impact of culture on the relationship between an exporter and an import agent using the framework of agency theory. Although many environmental forces impact on a contractual arrangement between an exporter and an import agent, culture impacts on the agency relationship in ways that are difficult to predict. We have presented an initial step toward developing a framework to better understand and eventually predict the contractual relationship when a cross-cultural agency relationship is negotiated and implemented. While future research in this area will need to develop empirical evidence to test the above model and propositions, there is evidence that the differences in contractual processes in an intercultural context may be due to cognitive differences between different cultures (Abramson et al. 1993). These authors found that cognitive differences between Japanese and Canadian managers, as measured by a Myers-Briggs Type Indicator, showed that Japanese management was described as having a greater concern for group harmony and emphasized the human element in problem solving, whereas Canadian managers favored a more logical, impersonal, and objective style and subordinated the human element in decision making. Their findings carry implications for contractual negotiations and communications across cultural borders. They argue that many of the problems caused by such differences lead to business failures, and these can be overcome by adequate training. These findings have implications for future research that could explore two streams while addressing the propositions outlined above. One stream may focus on the nature and structure of cultural networks; the structure and function of cultural networks outside the Asian region may provide a basis of comparison. Once such cultural networks have been described, their impact upon each stage of the contractual process could be analyzed with a view to defining the variables leading to contractual inefficiencies and those with the potential to be managerially relevant in formulating efficient contractual outcomes. The second stream of research could be aimed at describing the cognitive elements that cause impediments to efficient contractual outcomes and explore the opportunities for the use of training in overcoming these problems.

With a heightened interest in many Westernized firms of transacting with those in the newly industrialized economies, the potential for intercultural transactions and high contractual inefficiencies is high. Research aimed at reducing these inefficiencies should lead to more satisfactory contractual outcomes for firms making cross-cultural marketing exchanges.

REFERENCES

Abramson, Neil R., Henry W. Lane, Hirohisa Nagai, and Harua Takagi (1993). "A Comparison of Canadian and Japanese Cognitive Styles: Implications for Management Interaction." *Journal of International Business Studies*, 24(3): 575–587.

Alston, Jon P. (1989). "Wa, Guanxi, and Inhwa: Managerial Principals in Japan, China, and Korea." *Business Horizons*, 32(2) (March–April): 26–31.

Anderson, Erin and Hubert Gatignon (1986). "Modes of Foreign Entry: A Transaction Cost Analysis and Propositions." *Journal of International Business Studies*, 17(3): 1–26.

Bergen, M., S. Dutta, and O. C. Walker (1992). "Agency Relationships in Marketing: A Review of the Implications and Applications of Agency and Related Theories." *Journal of Marketing*, 56 (July): 1–24.

Dahringer, Lee D. and Hans Mühlbacher (1991). *International Marketing—A Global Perspective*. Reading MA: Addison-Wesley.

Eisenhardt, Kathleen M. (1985). "Control: Organizational and Economic Approaches." *Management Science*, 31(2) (February): 134–149.

——— (1989). "Agency Theory: An Assessment and Review." *Academy of Management Review*, 14(1): 57–74.

Ellis, R. Susan and Lester W. Johnson (1993). "Agency Theory as a Framework for Advertising Agency Compensation Decisions." *Journal of Advertising Research*, 33(5): 76–80.

Goodnow, J. D. and J. E. Hanzi (1972). "Environmental Determinants of Overseas Market Entry Strategies." *Journal of International Business Studies*, 3 (Spring): 35–50.

Heiba, Farouk (1990). "International Business Negotiations: A Strategic Planning Model." In Malcolm H. B. McDonald and S. Tamer Cavusgil (eds.), *The International Marketing Digest*. Oxford: Heinemann Professional Publishing, pp. 265–277.

Hofstede, G. (1980), "Motivation, Leadership, and Organization: Do American Theories Apply Abroad?" *Organisational Dynamics*, 9(1) (Summer): 442–63.

——— (1983). "The Cultural Relativity of Organizational Practices and Theories." *Journal of International Business Studies*, 14(4) (Fall): 75–90.

Horstman, I. and James Markensen (1987). "Licensing vs. Direct Investment: A Model of Internationalization by Multinational Enterprise." *Canadian Journal of Economics*, 20(3): 464–481.

Jensen, Michael, C. and William H. Meckling (1976). "Theory of the Firm: Managerial Behavior, Agency Costs and Ownership Structure." *Journal of Financial Economics*, 3: 305–360.

Kale, Sudhir H. and Roger McIntyre (1991). "Distribution Channel Relationships in Diverse Cultures." *International Marketing Review*, 8(3): 31–45.

McGuiness, Norman, Nigel Campbell, and James Liontiades (1991). "Selling Machinery to China: Chinese Perceptions of Strategies and Relationships." *Journal of International Business Studies*, 22(2): 187–207.

McIntyre, Roger P., Martin S. Meloche, and Jane M. Lang (1992). "Culture-Based Segmentation: A Potential Strategy for EC '92." *Journal of Euromarketing*, 2(1): 31–47.

Montagu-Pollock, Matthew (1991). "All the Right Connections." *Asian Business* (January): 20–24.

Onkvisit, Sak and John J. Shaw (1993). *International Marketing—Analysis and Strategy*, 2nd ed. New York: Macmillan.

Ouchi, William (1979). "A Conceptual Framework for the Design of Organizational Control Mechanisms." *Management Science*, 25(9) (September): 833–848.

Papadopoulos, N. and J. Denis (1988). "Inventory, Taxonomy and Assessment of International Market Selection." *International Marketing Review*, 5(3): 38–51.

Ralston, David A., David J. Gustafson, Fanny M. Cheung, and Robert H. Terpstra (1993). "Differences in Managerial Values: Hong Kong and PRC Managers." *Journal of International Business Studies*, 24(2): 249–275.

Senbet, Lemma and William Taylor (1986). "Direct Foreign Investment with Imperfect Information." Working Paper, University of Wisconsin–Madison.

Stewart, Sally and Charles F. Keown (1989). "Talking with the Dragon: Negotiating in the People's Republic of China." *Columbia Journal of World Business*, 24(3) (Fall): 68–72.

Chapter 9

The Role of Relationships in a Global Trading Environment: A Look at Taiwanese Importers' Perceptions of Exporters from the United States, Japan, and Western Europe

Angela R. D'Auria Stanton, C. P. Rao, and Jacob Jou

INTRODUCTION

As the trading of goods and services becomes a global phenomenon, the development, maintenance, and continuation of the buyer-seller relationship is of paramount importance (Ford 1990). Much of the international trade literature, however, has focused on the seller or exporter side of this relationship. In order for exporters to achieve continued success, it is critical that due attention be paid to the buyer or importer side as well (e.g., Ghymn 1983; Yavas et al. 1987). Although many of the internationalization models that have been created (e.g., Johanson and Weidersheim-Paul 1975; Cavusgil 1980) dictate that successful export and trade cannot take place without recognizing the importance of the importer, few studies have examined this component. Increasing competition in the global trading arena has forced exporters to be more concerned about the development and maintenance of relationships with their importer constituencies.

Modern international marketing emphasizes the importance of understanding and satisfying overseas customers' needs for success in global markets. Thus, it is imperative for international marketers to be able to discern foreign importers' expectations and strive to satisfy these expectations better than their competitors. Still, empirical research has seldom focused on importers and their concerns, despite the fact that effective export marketing management is possible only with the clear identification and analysis of the needs of the overseas customers—of whom the importers constitute a critical and necessary element. In addition, researching the exporter-importer dyadic interaction process with a focus on relationships is consistent with the relationship marketing paradigm that currently dominates the marketing discipline both domestically and internationally.

In recent years researchers have begun to pay attention to overseas importers' perspectives, their responses to export marketing practices, and to the exporter-importer relationship in general. In one of the early research efforts in this context Ghymn (1983) explored the relative importance of variables that influence the decision process of U.S. importers when they import goods from developed and developing countries. He found that such factors as timely delivery, brand name, product styling, and price were highly important to buyers of imported goods. Yavas and associates (1987) studied Saudi Arabian purchasing agents' reaction to exporter practices from the United States, Japan, England, and Taiwan. They found a significant country-of-origin effect. They noted that the Saudi importers, for example, considered the price to be an important variable with goods from Taiwan, while quality was viewed as relatively insignificant. This was completely opposite to their views of United States–based products. Quality was viewed as the most important variable for a U.S. product, while price was least important.

Kraft and Chung (1992) compared the practices of Japanese and U.S. exporters in a Korean context. They evaluated Korean importers' perceptions of such key variables as product characteristics, reputation, and negotiation style for both groups of exporters. Kraft and Chung (1992) found that the Japanese were rated more favorably on almost all of the dimensions measured.

Ghymn and Jacobs (1993) followed up Ghymn's (1983) initial study with a comparative effort that focused on influences for Japanese import managers. Although both the Japanese and U.S. samples viewed the variables of interest as important, several important differences between the groups were noted. Japanese importers valued product-specific elements such as product quality and product safety much more so than their U.S. counterparts. The U.S. importers, on the other hand, viewed such service-oriented elements as timely delivery and dependability as more significant than their Japanese counterparts. In yet another replication of this study, Ghymn and associates (1993) found that import managers in Thailand were most concerned about product quality, price, and timely delivery.

Similarly, in another recent work, Katsikeas and Al-Khalifa (1993) explored the forces that stimulated Bahraini importers to trade with U.K. exporters. They found that non-economic considerations such as effective communication and after-sales support were quite important to these importers.

The effect of a product's country of origin has led some researchers to question the role of product-origin bias in the import process. Herche (1994), for example, concluded that a country's ethnocentric tendencies had a significant impact on the development of importers' marketing strategies. This finding is in concert with earlier studies by Nagashima (1970, 1977), who found that national origin created immediate product stereotypes.

Other researchers have investigated the nature of power structure in the exporter-importer dyads involving exporters from a developing country and importers of a developed country (Leonidou 1989a, 1989b), concluding that importers generally exercise a higher degree of power over the exporters. Wortzel and associates (1988) concluded that neophyte exporters from a developing country such as the People's Republic of China are influenced by their home country business environment and culture in their dealings with U.S. importers. Other empirical research confirmed that buying firms in developed countries often are willing and even prefer to engage in long-term relationships with the supplying firms (Håkansson and Wootz 1975). In a more recent research study, Egan and Mody (1992) found that cultivating buyer-seller links is essential for export development.

In the few research studies that specifically addressed the implications of importers' perspectives for export marketing effectiveness, the major focus has been on exporters from developing countries and importers in developed countries. This stream of research has established the usefulness of identifying and analyzing importers' perspectives for developing effective export marketing strategies. However, to develop and implement effective export marketing strategies, it is imperative that an investigation encompasses examination of overseas importers' needs, expectations, and satisfactions/dissatisfactions with exporters from various countries (Rao 1977). Such detailed understanding of foreign importers' country-wise comparative evaluations of exporter business practices need to be developed in a competitive context, which then includes the alternate sources of supply to overseas importers. The identification of importers' perceptions about competing exporters from other countries will provide critical information about exporters' customer-oriented performance, which will help formulate export marketing strategies and strengthen the importer-exporter long-term relationships.

RESEARCH OBJECTIVES

In view of the increasing importance of relationships between importers and exporters, an analysis of the marketing strengths and weaknesses of exporting countries should involve product offer characteristics as well as the more subjective perceptions of exporter characteristics (Kraft and Chung 1992). The primary purpose of this research is to assess the dual roles of importer experience and affiliation with a primary trading partner on Taiwanese importers' satisfaction with the practices of U.S., Japanese, and Western European exporters.

As has been suggested by the literature, exporter characteristics are likely to be affected to some degree by their country of origin. This effect, however, can be a double-edged sword. While foreign importers are likely to stereotype the exporters' business practices based on their nationality in the absence of specific information and experience about individual exporters, this may change as a relationship develops between importer and exporter. Additionally, the length of import involvement, or importer experience, should also serve as an impact variable. As a relationship develops, importers are likely to be more satisfied with the exporters they deal with most often, regardless of nationality. Irrespective of exporter nationality, continued interaction between an importer and an exporter is likely to enable both parties to adjust and adapt to each other and their respective business practices. This import experience-based learning could take place both at a general level as well as specific levels, such as dealings with a particular country's exporters or even a specific exporter. With increased experience and interaction comes a strengthening of the importer-exporter relationship. Based on these assertions, the following research hypotheses were formulated and tested in the context of the Taiwanese importer:

H1: Importers with higher levels of export experience will place less importance on exporters' business practices, irrespective of the exporter's country of origin.

H2: Importers with higher levels of export experience will be more satisfied with the business practices of their export partners.

H3: Importers will be most satisfied with the business practices of their primary trading partner.

METHODOLOGY

Taiwan as the Country Context

The choice of Taiwan as the country of interest in this study was based on four primary reasons: (1) its long relationship of dependence on the United States; (2) its current and future importance to the United States as a major trading partner; (3) its growing international competitiveness; and (4) increasing imports into Taiwan from other countries, especially Japan and the European Community. The United States–Taiwan–Republic of China (TROC) relations have been through several evolutionary cycles over the past 50 years. From the World War II era, being heavily damaged and faced with a massive rebuilding project, to its modern-day ranking as the thirteenth largest trading nation in the world, TROC has gone through an incredible odyssey, in which the United States has played a significant developmental role.

In addition to the United States, Japan and Europe also have strong and long-term trade relationships established with TROC. As in most world markets, Japan will be an especially tough competitor. In the past, TROC authorities claimed to have given special consideration to U.S. businesses bidding on government projects. This "Buy American" policy, however, is becoming a thing of the past. Increasingly, TROC importers are becoming as sophisticated and demanding in their requirements as their counterparts in the developed countries.

Future trade between the United States and TROC will undoubtedly be characterized by free and fierce competition among the triad regions (the United States, Western Europe, and Japan).

The Sample

This study is based on a survey of Taiwanese importer agents. A sample of 500 import-export firms of both consumer and industrial products was used. The sampled companies were sent questionnaires via the national mail service. Responses were received from 201 firms, yielding a respectable response rate of 40 percent. Two of the surveys were discarded because they were judged to be incomplete and unusable for analysis.

The Questionnaire

The questionnaire used in this study was designed to measure (1) the degree of importance Taiwanese importers place on various exporter practices; (2) their satisfaction with exporters from the United States, Japan, and Western Europe on these practices; (3) how much improvement the Taiwanese importers suggest that exporters consider in their business practices; and (4) descriptive information about the importing companies. The survey instrument was framed in the context of the one major product category imported by the Taiwanese importer. The items used in the questionnaire were developed based on a staged exploratory research process. First, the import-export trade literature was examined in order to assess attributes measured in previous studies. Then, qualitative interviews were conducted with a select group of importers in Taiwan in order to assess the applicability of the developed questionnaire in the Taiwanese setting. The questionnaire was then refined and finalized based on the panel's comments. Because the original questionnaire was developed in English, a back translation (Brislin 1970) procedure was used in order to ensure translational and contextual equivalence.

RESULTS AND DISCUSSION

Importing Experience and Levels of Imports

The respondents had varying degrees of importing experience. Forty percent of the responding importers stated that they had limited experience importing, 36 percent had some importing experience, and 24 percent noted that they had considerable experience. Taiwanese importers' experience levels varied, however, based on the percentage of exports from each of the regions studied (see Table 9.1). Importers with the most experience stated that they received a far greater percentage of their imports from the United States than they did from

Table 9.1
Taiwanese Importer Experience and Percentage of Imports from the United States, Western Europe, and Japan

	United States— Percentage Imports	Western Europe— Percentage Imports	Japan— Percentage Imports
Limited Importing Experience	25.8%	24.1%	47.5%*
Some Importing Experience	25.9%	29.0%	32.7%
Considerable Importing Experience	42.0%*	19.8%	29.4%

*Significant difference between experience levels at p < .001.

Table 9.2
Percentage of Imports by Country

	Primary Partner— United States	Primary Partner— Western Europe	Primary Partner— Japan
Exports from United States	72%*	9%	11%
Exports from Western Europe	13%	75%*	9%
Exports from Japan	10%	10%	75%*

*Significant difference between experience levels at p = .000.

Western Europe or Japan (p ≤ .006). On the other hand, purchasing agents with the least experience noted that they received the highest percentage of their imports from Japan (p ≤ .006). This does not seem particularly surprising when one considers that the United States has been a major player in the Taiwanese trading arena for the past 50 years, while the Japanese are much newer entrants in this market.

The importance of relationships between Taiwanese importers and their exporters was also evident (see Table 9.2). Importers purchased a significantly higher proportion of products from the country they dealt with most often (p < .000). In fact, over 70 percent of the purchases transacted by Taiwanese importers were made with their one primary exporting partner.

The Importance of and Satisfaction with Exporter Business Practices

In addition to providing current trading figures, the importers were asked to evaluate the importance of specific exporter business practices (see Table 9.3, column 1). The business practices most important to the Taiwanese importers studied were communications (X = 4.71, using a 1 to 5 scale), dependability of long-term supply (X = 4.68), price adjustments (X = 4.54), timely delivery (X = 4.46), quality levels (4.45), and willingness to cooperate with unforeseen difficulties (X = 4.41). The importance measures were also evaluated based on an importer's experience. Although importers who stated that they had considerable experience rated the importance of exporter business practices higher than those with less experience, none of the differences were statistically significant in a one-way analysis of variance. Thus, hypothesis H1, which postulated that more experienced importers will attach less importance to exporter business practices, was not supported.

The respondents were also asked to assess their satisfaction with U.S., Western European, and Japanese exporters on these business practices. Dissatisfaction with the business practices of U.S., Western European, and Japanese exporters was evident. Regardless of an importers' experience level, their satisfaction scores fell below their importance ratings (see Table 9.3). Hypothesis H2 stated that importers with more experience will be more satisfied with the business practices of exporters than those with less experience. Although Taiwanese importers with limited experience appeared to be the most dissatisfied of all, the relationship between satisfaction and experience was not linear in all cases. In fact, there tended to be little distinction among importers with some experience and those with considerable experience. Thus, hypothesis H2 was only partially supported. Dissatisfaction was particularly evident (for all three exporting regions) among importers with limited experience for ordering procedures. Additionally, those with the least experience were also the most dissatisfied with the U.S. and Western European exporters on communications and the dependability of long-term supply. These less experienced importers were also more dissatisfied with both Western Europe and Japan in their understanding of the Taiwanese way of doing business and willingness to cooperate with unforeseen difficulties. Finally, dissatisfaction with exporter practices was much more prevalent between importers with limited experience and their Western European counterparts.

Hypothesis H3, which stated that importers would be most satisfied with the business practices of their primary trading partner, was not supported. The level of involvement with a particular exporting region seemed to have little impact on an importer's satisfaction level (see Table 9.4). While importers were generally more satisfied with the exporting region they dealt with most often, very few of the differences were statistically significant. It must also be noted that Taiwanese purchasing agents who stated that they received the majority of their

Table 9.3
Satisfaction with Exporter Practices Based on an Importer's Experience

Practice	Imp.	Satisfaction with U.S. Exporters			Satisfaction with Western European Exporters			Satisfaction with Japanese Exporters		
		Ltd.	Some	Cons.	Ltd.	Some	Cons.	Ltd.	Some	Cons.
Communications	4.71	3.41*	3.89	3.45*	3.37*	3.96	3.82	3.89	3.92	4.03
Ordering procedures	4.02	3.45*	3.91	3.60	3.40*	3.91	3.71	3.61*	3.90	3.91
Method of payment	4.01	3.51	3.82	3.79	3.36*	3.93	3.64	3.60	3.61	4.00
Price adjustments	4.54	3.02	3.23	3.03	2.85	3.02	3.36	2.87	3.10	3.21
Product modifications	3.68	3.23	3.26	3.38	3.32	3.32	3.54	3.56	3.57	3.73
Quality levels	4.45	3.44	3.68	3.68	3.41*	3.83	3.96	3.76	3.79	4.03
Styling of the product	3.73	3.24	3.40	3.36	3.06*	3.53	3.50	3.58	3.57	3.78
Timely delivery	4.46	3.15	3.45	3.28	3.13*	3.57	3.32	3.66	3.83	3.82
Right type of sales literature	3.51	3.09	3.41	3.30	3.20	3.41	3.43	3.39	3.62	3.39
Parts list/service manuals	3.83	3.42	3.73	3.60	3.41	3.72	3.68	3.55	3.63	3.45
Training sales personnel	4.06	3.33	3.43	3.60	3.24	3.51	3.57	3.41	3.45	3.58
Understands Taiwanese way of doing business	4.16	3.00	3.25	3.37	2.87*	3.39	3.50	3.67	3.80	4.09
Willingness to cooperate with unforeseen difficulties	4.41	3.38	3.73	3.68	3.47*	3.87	3.97	3.66*	3.96	4.09
Long-term supply dependability	4.68	3.55*	3.98	3.85	3.58*	3.98	4.04	3.90	3.90	4.09

Imp. = Imports; Ltd. = Limited; Cons. = Considerable; * = p < .05.

Table 9.4
Satisfaction with Exporter Practices Based on Country of Main Trading Partner

Practice	Satisfaction with U.S. Exporters Primary Trading Partner				Satisfaction with Western European Exporters Primary Trading Partner				Satisfaction with Japanese Exporters Primary Trading Partner			
	U.S.	W.E.	Japan	Overall	U.S.	W.E.	Japan	Overall	U.S.	W.E.	Japan	Overall
Communications	3.68	3.58	3.38	3.55	3.61	3.74	3.62	3.66	3.82	3.71	4.02	3.93
Ordering procedures	3.64	3.75	3.52	3.62	3.32	3.77	3.74	3.64	3.82	3.67	3.76	3.76
Method of payment	3.81	3.67	3.57	3.69	3.61	3.67	3.66	3.65	3.79	3.30*	3.79	3.72
Price adjustments	3.10	3.17	3.00	3.08	3.25	2.93	3.00	3.04	3.00	3.05	3.04	3.03
Product modifications	3.28	3.33	3.17	3.25	3.39	3.43	3.29	3.37	3.79	3.32*	3.55	3.57
Quality levels	3.68	3.50	3.41	3.55	3.75	3.64	3.53	3.63	3.93	3.57	3.83	3.82
Styling of the product	3.37	3.21	3.23	3.30	3.54	3.25	3.25	3.33	3.85	3.32*	3.58	3.61
Timely delivery	3.34	3.33	3.20	3.29	3.54	3.29	3.32	3.36	3.85	3.76	3.64	3.71
Right type of sales literature	3.24	3.22	3.22	3.23	3.39	3.37	3.27	3.34	3.45	3.50	3.47	3.47
Parts list/service manuals	3.61	3.63	3.45	3.56	3.82	3.61	3.45	3.61	3.61	3.52	3.57	3.57
Training sales personnel	3.51	3.46	3.34	3.44	3.54	3.56	3.19*	3.42	3.45	3.15	3.49	3.43
Understands Taiwanese way of doing business	3.28	3.21	3.02	3.17	3.25	3.21	3.22	3.22	4.12*	3.52	3.67	3.77
Willingness to cooperate with unforeseen difficulties	3.72	3.58	3.31	3.55	3.82	3.74	3.68	3.74	3.88	3.65	3.85	3.82
Long-term supply dependability	3.92	3.75	3.53	3.75	4.07	3.88	3.56	3.82	3.88	3.71	4.01	3.93

* = $p < .05$.

imports from Japan rated greater satisfaction with the United States on product modifications, product styling, and understanding the Taiwanese way of doing business.

DISCUSSION

Importers with the least experience with a particular country's exporters generally reported lower satisfaction ratings with exporter business practices regardless of country. This seems to suggest that experience may have a positive effect on satisfaction with exporters. Thus, it may be possible that satisfaction among importers with limited experience will improve as they gain continued competencies in international trade. It must also be noted, however, that satisfaction gains seem to be more apparent at the earlier stages of the experience curve. Since there were few differences between importers with some experience and considerable experience, it may be possible that the expectations of importers increase over time and, subsequently, gains in satisfaction levels may be much greater to achieve. It is also imperative to understand the role experience plays in terms of future relationships with regional exporters. When participants were asked to project the prospects for strengthening business relations between their company and their suppliers, differences were evident based on the importer's level of experience. Importers who stated that they had considerable experience stated that they anticipated their prospects for improved relationships with their exporting constituencies as much brighter than those with lesser experience. This was especially true for relationships with exporters from the United States (p = .0001) and Western Europe (p = .0007).

Interestingly, however, the relationship between increased satisfaction levels and an importer's primary trading partner did not hold. This may be a result of the changing Taiwanese international trade environment or may simply indicate that although an importer may have a primary trading partner, the notion of a relationship between buyer and seller has not been forged. Thus, U.S., Western European, and Japanese exporters cannot rely on their past successes and must continually strive to not only provide their Taiwanese importers with a product, but with the requisite services and considerations as well.

CONCLUSIONS

Results of this exploratory study provide significant strategic implications for marketing managers. An importer's level of expertise plays an important, but often overlooked, role in international trade. Additionally, exporters should focus on building and maintaining relationships with their importer constituencies. Future studies should test the strength of this relationship further through measurement of the length of the relationship, as well as longitudinal measures over time. Additionally, the notion of assessing not only importer satisfaction with business practices but also the importance placed on these elements may help exporters better position themselves with respect to their competition. Exporters' competitive advantage, however, not only comes from the practices deemed important by the importers but must also take into account the experiential qualities of the importer and the relationship that has been developed between importer and exporter. It follows that exporters must allocate their scarce marketing resources in order to enhance their relationships with their importer constituencies.

Undoubtedly, the relative importance placed on exporter business practices may vary by country. Future research focusing on other countries, both within and outside the Pacific Rim region, should offer a basis of comparing this decisional criterion. As indicated, the import purchasing area has received relatively little attention in the import-export literature and has yet to be fully explored. Further studies in this area will certainly serve to improve marketers' understanding of this element of international marketing.

REFERENCES

Anonymous (1989). "Market Taiwan: Recent Changes Create New Opportunities." *Business America*, June 19.

———— (1991). "The ABC's of Doing Business in Taiwan." *Business America*, July 29.

BFT (1991a). *1991 Foreign Trade Development of the Republic of China*. Board of Foreign Trade, Ministry of Economic Affairs, TROC.

———— (1991b). *The Republic of China on Taiwan in the 1990s: An Increasingly Important Trading Partner in the Pacific Region*. Board of Foreign Trade, Ministry of Economic Affairs, TROC, June.

Brislin, Richard W. (1970). "Back-Translation for Cross-Cultural Research." *Journal of Cross-Cultural Psychology*, 1(3): 185–216.

Cavusgil, S. T. (1980). "On the Internationalization Process of Firms." *European Research*, 8: 273–281.

CEPD (1991a). *Detailed Action Plan for Strengthening Economic and Trade Ties with the United States*. Council for Economic Planning and Development, TROC.

———— (1991b). *The Six Year National Development Plan for Taiwan, Republic of China (1991–1996): Macroeconomic Development Targets*. Council for Economic Planning and Development, TROC.

Cheng, Chu-Yuan (1986). "United States–Taiwan Economic Relations: Trade and Investment." *Columbia Journal of World Business*, 21(1): 87–96.

Egan, Mary Lou and Ashok Mody (1992). "Buyer-Seller Links in Export Development." *World Development*, 20(3): 321–334.

Ford, David (1990). *Understanding Business Markets: Interaction, Relationships, Network*. London: Academic Press.

Ghymn, Kyung-il (1983). "The Relative Importance of Import Decision Variables." *Journal of the Academy of Marketing Science*, 11(3): 304–312.

Ghymn, Kyung-il and Laurence W. Jacobs (1993). "Import Purchasing Decision Behaviour: An Empirical Study of Japanese Import Managers." *International Marketing Review*, 10(4): 4–14.

Ghymn, Kyung-il, B. Srinil, and P. Johnson (1993). "Thailand Import Managers' Purchasing Behaviour." *Journal of Asian Business*, 9(1): 1–12.

Håkansson, H. and B. Wootz (1975). "Supplier Selection in an International Environment—An Experimental Study." *Journal of Marketing Research*, 12(1): 46–51.

Herche, Joel (1994). "Ethnocentric Tendencies, Marketing Strategy and Import Purchase Behavior." *International Marketing Review*, 11(3): 4–16.

International Trade Administration (1991). *Notes from the President's Export Council Mission to Taiwan*. Washington, DC: United States Department of Commerce.

Johanson, Jonny and F. Weidersheim-Paul (1975). "The Internationalization of the Firm: Four Swedish Cases." *Journal of Management Studies*, 3 (October): 3–25.

Katsikeas, Constantine S. and Ali Al-Khalifa (1993). "The Issue of Import Motivation in Manufacturer-Overseas Distributor Relationships: Implications for Exporters." *Journal of Marketing Management*, 9 (January): 65–77.

Kraft, Frederic B. and Kae H. Chung (1992). "Korean Importer Perceptions of U.S. and Japanese Industrial Goods Exporters." *International Marketing Review*, 9(2): 59–73.

Leonidou, Leonidas C. (1989a). "Behavioral Aspects of the Exporter-Importer Relationship: The Case of Cypriot Exporters and British Importers." *European Journal of Marketing*, 23(7): 17–23.

——— (1989b). "The Exporter-Importer Dyad—An Investigation." *Journal of Managerial Psychology*, 4(2): 17–23.

Nagashima, A. (1970). "A Comparison of Japanese and U.S. Attitudes toward Foreign Products." *Journal of Marketing*, 34(1): 68–74.

——— (1977). "A Comparative 'Made in' Product Image Survey among Japanese Businessmen." *Journal of Marketing*, 41(3): 95–100.

Rao, C. P. (1977). "Spanish Importers' Evaluation of the U.S. Exporters." *Journal of the Academy of Marketing Science* (Special Issue): 103–106.

Rosson, Philip J. and Stanley R. Reid (1987). *Managing Export and Expansion: Concepts and Practice*. New York: Praeger.

Seringhaus, Rolf F. H. and Philip J. Rosson (1991). *Export Development and Promotion: The Role of Public Organizations*. London: Kluwer Academic Publishers.

Weinberger, Caspar W. (1991). "Taiwan's Rosy Future." *Forbes*, October 28.

Wortzel, Heidi Vernon, Lawrence H. Wortzel, and Shengliang Deng (1988). "Do Neophyte Exporters Understand Importers?" *Columbia Journal of World Business*, 23(4): 49–56.

Yavas, U., S. T. Cavusgil, and S. Tunclap (1987). "Assessment of Selected Foreign Suppliers by Saudi Importers: Implications for Exporters." *Journal of Business Research*, 15(3): 237–246.

Part IV

Market Communications Issues

Chapter 10

Culture and Communication: Implications for Sales Force Training Involving Intercultural Interactions

Kumar C. Rallapalli and C. P. Rao

Selling as a function is becoming more global and transcultural (Walle 1986). Dramatic economic, political, and social changes around the world in recent years have made businesses expand their operations beyond the national boundaries. Events such as opening the markets of Eastern Europe, the reunification of Germany, changing trade relations with Canada and Mexico, continued competition with Japan, and the rise of other manufacturing powers in the Far East have made global marketing and international interaction everyday activities for thousands of American businesses (Bovee et al. 1995). The tremendous growth in global marketing has resulted in new challenges for the multinational corporation that has operations in more than one country. More specifically, assessing the social elements in the international marketing context that involves dealing with a diverse customer base requires a highly skilled and trained sales force.

Several researchers have recognized the importance of culture in the international marketing context (e.g., Graham 1988; Clark 1990). There has been, however, relatively little research conducted in the area of international sales training (e.g., Kale and Barnes 1992). In order to provide some insights into sales training, the authors present an integration of cross-cultural communication research and sales research. This is an attempt to address the differences in communication styles that would affect the sales performance. Based on the discussion of the predominant communication styles across different cultures, the authors also present several guidelines for global sales force training and development.

ISSUES IN GLOBAL SALES FORCE TRAINING AND DEVELOPMENT

Lederer and Burdick (1958) in their book, *The Ugly American*, characterized American businessmen as profoundly lacking the understanding of the host culture's customs. This lack of understanding resulted in several failed attempts to interact with their trading partners. Fortunately, in the last two decades much research has been conducted in cross-cultural psychology and anthropology to advance our understanding of different cultures (e.g., Hall 1966, 1976, 1983; Hofstede 1980, 1983; Okabe 1983).

Perhaps no other function in marketing is more affected than personal selling with the increased globalization of businesses (Hill and Still 1990). This is largely due to the nature of the task itself. Personal selling involves one-on-one interaction with the prospect that should result in a profitable transaction. The emphasis is on the ability of the salesperson to convince the buyer that the product will help solve the buyer's problems. Much research has been conducted on analyzing and improving selling effectiveness (e.g., Weitz et al. 1986). One of the key determinants in improving selling effectiveness was found to be sales training. Hill and Birdseye (1989) noted that when it comes to selling across cultures, most of the businesses have difficulty finding well-qualified and well-trained sales people.

There is a need to train salespersons before they venture into the real world of business. This training should not only impart the necessary information pertaining to the industry and the competition but also help the trainee understand the effects of cultural differences on everyday business transactions as can be seen from the example below:

All nationalities possess unique characteristics. The failure of managers to comprehend the cultural differences adequately has led to many international business blunders. In one case, in Saudi Arabia, one U.S. executive turned down a Saudi businessman's offer to join him for a cup of coffee. The American was in a hurry to close the deal, and naturally, the Saudi was hurt at the rejection and the negotiation process was much less successful than it would have been. (Ricks 1983, p. 9)

In today's business world, many organizations are comprised of individuals from different cultural, ethnic, and religious backgrounds. Intercultural context refers to a situation where two individuals from different cultural backgrounds interact. Most of the time individuals interact with people from different cultures, for different lengths of time, and with mixed effectiveness. With the increased desire of businesses to develop a global orientation, intercultural contacts are more and more becoming a common scenario. An example of an intercultural context would be a U.S. manufacturer negotiating with a Japanese vendor or German supplier. Significant amounts of time, effort, and money are invested in these interactions. Therefore, any insights, information, and knowledge pertaining to the cultural differences would make these intercultural sales transactions more effective.

As businesses expand beyond the borders of their countries, they are demanding the salespersons to succeed in intercultural settings (e.g., Weitz et al. 1992). When dealing with different cultures, however, interpretation and behavioral prediction will become difficult. In order to successfully sell the products or services, salespersons should develop an understanding of cognition and behaviors of the customers' culture. This understanding can be achieved through effective sales training and development. Kale and Barnes (1992) presented a broad framework for understanding cross-national buyer-seller relationships. The framework included national character, organizational culture, and individual personality of the salesperson as the major dimensions affecting the sales process. Kale and Barnes (1992) concluded that the framework provides some guidelines for sales training and development in an intercultural situation. However, the framework developed by Kale and Barnes (1992) does not provide any specific propositions in guiding multinational corporation in developing sales training policies.

The purpose of this chapter is to analyze the impact of culture on sales communication styles in an intercultural setting in order to provide some guidelines for global sales force training and development. First, the influence of culture in an intercultural situation will be discussed with the help of a theoretical model (see Figure 10.1). Second, the influence of cultural dimensions on communication styles will be discussed by deriving several research propositions to guide sales training and development.

A Model for Improving Sales Training in an Intercultural Context

A considerable amount of research involving cross-cultural interactions exists pertaining to variables such as communications, personality, self-concepts (Hall 1966), perceptions (Bond 1979), and affective processes. All these play an important role in an effective selling situation. The model borrows extensively from model of behavior and cultural variability (Triandis 1977, 1980, 1984), the model of communication and cultural variability (Gudykunst et al. 1988) and the model of impression management (Gardner and Martinko 1988). The major premise of the model is that cultural dimensions influence the characteristics of salesperson and customer, which in turn affect the sales communication style. Sales communication style then leads to congruence/incongruence. Congruence refers to the matching of sales communication style to the expectations of the customer. When the sales communication style is not consistent with customer expectations, it results in an incongruence. Congruence and incongruence of behavior expectations lead to success and failure, respectively. The success or failure of the sales interaction is shown to be related to the salesperson and the customer in the form of feedback for future interactions.

Figure 10.1
A Model for Improving Sales Training in an Intercultural Context

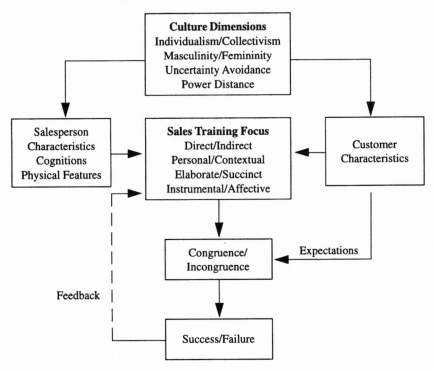

In the next section of the chapter, we examine the different cultural dimensions and how they influence the sales communication styles.

Dimensions of Cultural Variability

Poyatos (1983) defined culture as a series of habits shared by members of a group living in a geographic area, learned but biologically conditioned, such as the means of communications, social relations at different levels, the various activities of daily life, the products of that group and how they are utilized, the peculiar manifestations of both individual products of that group and how they are utilized, the peculiar manifestations of both individual and national personalities, and their ideals concerning their own existence and their fellow people. This is the most comprehensive definition of culture to date.

Although several researchers have identified variety of cultural dimensions (e.g., Hall 1976), we will use the factor-analytically derived dimensions of Hofstede (1980). Hofstede's dimensions have been used to explain behavior at the interpersonal level, like equity and equality norms across cultures (Bond et al. 1982), perceptions of interaction episodes (Forgas and Bond 1985), perceptions of communication associated with relationship terms (Gudykunst and Nishida 1986), and cultural differences in affective communication (Gudykunst and Ting-Toomey 1988)—all interpersonal phenomena. Hofstede's four dimensions were found to be relatively robust in predicting cultural differences (McGrath et al. 1992). Hofstede (1980) identified four dimensions of culture. They are individualism-collectivism, power distance, uncertainty avoidance, and masculinity-femininity.

Individualism-Collectivism

This dimension has been identified as a major component of cultural variability (Parsons and Shils 1951). In individualistic cultures, "people look after themselves and their immediate family only," whereas in collectivistic cultures, "people belong to groups or collectives which are supposed to look after them in exchange for loyalty" (Hofstede 1980, p. 390). Individualistic cultures score high on McClelland's (1961) achievement motive, whereas collectivistic cultures score high on the affiliation motive. The United States is an example of individualistic culture, while Japan is a collectivistic culture.

Power Distance

Power distance is defined as "the characteristic of culture, that defines the extent to which the less powerful person in a society accepts inequality in power and considers it as normal" (Hofstede 1980, p. 390). High power distance cultures accept greater inequality as opposed to low power distance cultures. Arab countries are good examples of high power distance cultures, and Austria is a low power distance culture. In high power distance cultures, parents value obedience in their children more than those in low power distance cultures. Power distance has important implications for sales communication styles. In high power distance cultures subordinates try to manage their self-presentations by pleasing their superiors (e.g., giving gifts); conversely, in low power distance cultures, where the relative inequality between superior and subordinate is less, subordinates tend to manage their images in the eyes of superiors through their performance.

Uncertainty Avoidance

Uncertainty avoidance refers to a "characteristic of culture that defines the extent to which people within a culture are made nervous by situations that they consider to be unstructured, unclear, or unpredictable, and the extent to which they try to avoid such situations by adopting strict codes of behavior and a belief in absolute truths" (Hofstede 1980, p. 390). Japan and Singapore are examples of strong and weak uncertainty avoidance cultures, respectively. According to Hofstede, cultures of high uncertainty avoidance display emotions more than low uncertainty avoidance cultures. In addition, low uncertainty avoidance cultures exhibit lower stress levels, weaker super egos, greater acceptance of dissent, and more risk-taking than high uncertainty avoidance cultures. Based on this dimension we can say that the sales presentations of individuals from high uncertainty avoidance cultures tend to be less successful in a novel situation than those of individuals from low uncertainty avoidance cultures.

Masculinity-Femininity

According to Hofstede (1980), high masculinity refers to "the high value placed on things, power and assertiveness while systems in which people, quality of life and nurturance prevail are low on masculinity or high on femininity" (Hofstede 1980, p. 390). Norway and Japan are examples of feminine and masculine cultures, respectively. Masculine cultures emphasize differentiated sex roles, performance, ambition, and independence, whereas feminine cultures place importance on overlapping social roles for the sexes, quality of life, service, and interdependence. Therefore, a person from a masculine culture may not be successful in his or her sales communication style when dealing with a woman from a feminine culture, since women are not treated equally in many masculine cultures and are not expected to perform a variety of tasks. This dimension is more important in an organizational context considering an increase in the numbers and jobs of working women.

Customer Characteristics

The customer characteristics play a key role in the success/failure of the sales interaction. Sales communication styles are constantly guided by beliefs about what the customers expect. Familiarity of customer affects the sales communication behavior. When the customer is familiar, the sales communication behavior will be more congruent with the expectations of the customer, resulting in a successful sales transaction. However, in most of the intercultural situations, customer expectations are not known. This paper will highlight general similarities and differences in the communication styles among cultures that would reduce the unfamiliarity considerably in an intercultural context.

Salesperson Characteristics

Salesperson characteristics can be broadly divided into cognitions and physical characteristics. The social cognitive processes influence the behaviors. The term *social cognition* refers to how people think about people. Salespersons' physical characteristics such as age, gender, race, and attractiveness influence the success or failure of sales interaction. Witkin and associates (1962) found that individuals from high power distance cultures manage their impressions based on physical characteristics, while individuals from low power distance cultures manage based on their individual achievements, ideas, and contributions. Other salesperson characteristics that vary with cultures are personality, self-monitoring, and communication apprehension. Gudykunst and associates (1987) concluded that individualism is positively related to self-monitoring. This study restricts itself to influence of culture on sales communication styles.

Sales Communication Styles

Sheth (1976) defines sales communication style as "representing the format, ritual or mannerism which the buyer and the seller adopt in their interaction." Weitz, Castleberry, and Tanner (1992) suggest that when planning a sales call one should consider the cultural difference to suit their presentations to customers' expectations. For example, when selling to an Arab customer the salesperson should plan to get to know the customer by meeting him several times before actually trying to sell a product. Although the importance of cultural differences has been recognized by sales management textbooks (e.g., Weitz et al. 1992), none of them provide any explicit guidelines for sales training to adapt their sales communications to suit the customers' cultures (e.g., individualistic versus collectivistic cultures). Research pertaining to communication styles in sales interactions in intercultural situations is limited. However, few studies have examined the effects of communication style on the success of sales interaction (e.g., Williams and Spiro 1985). These studies have primarily used the communication paradigm developed by Sheth (1976), according to whom communication styles can be categorized as task oriented, interaction oriented, or self-oriented. However, we use the communication styles identified in the cross-cultural psychology since these styles are more applicable in different cultures. Several research propositions will be derived that would provide some guidelines for improving sales training in an intercultural context. These major communications styles that make a sales presentation effective in an intercultural context are the direct versus indirect, elaborate versus succinct, personal versus contextual, and instrumental versus affective styles.

Direct versus Indirect Style

Research in cross-cultural psychology reveals that individuals from individualistic and low context cultures prefer a direct mode of interaction in day-to-day life, whereas a similar behavior would be considered inappropriate in a collectivistic culture (Ting-Toomey 1988). When one considers the growing importance of negotiation in a selling exchange, the need to understand the direct versus indirect style of communication styles becomes highly important. According to Ting-Toomey (1988), individuals from an individualistic culture would consider negotiation process as an overt communication process based on immediate cost-benefit analysis, whereas individuals from a collectivistic cultures would consider a similar process as an accumulative, long-term process based on long-term cost-benefit comparisons. Therefore, in order to successfully manage the verbal sales presentations, sales training must consider the predominant mode of interaction. These findings about the mode of interaction regarding individualistic and collectivistic cultures imply that:

Proposition 1: For a sales interaction to be successful, the sales training should focus on a more direct mode of communication style when interacting with customers from individualistic cultures.

Proposition 2: For a sales interaction to be successful, the training should focus on an indirect style of communication when dealing with customers from collectivistic cultures.

Elaborate versus Succinct Style

This style refers to quantity of talk that is considered necessary in different cultures. According to Grice (1975), "an elaborate style refers to the use of rich, expressive language in everyday conversation, while a succinct style includes the use of understatements, pauses and silences." Arab cultures tend to use an elaborate style of verbal communication. Prothro (1970) analyzed the differences between Arab and American communication styles and found that mere statements of Arabs are considered extreme by Americans. Johnson and Johnson (1975) found that Japanese lie on the other end of the continuum with regard to using a succinct style. Japanese tend to use indirection, circumlocution, and silence in everyday language. Based on these findings, individuals from moderate uncertainty avoidance tend to use an elaborate style; individuals from high uncertainty use a succinct style of verbal communication. Therefore, we propose that:

Proposition 3: For a sales interaction to be successful, the sales training should focus on a succinct mode of communication style when interacting with customers that belong to cultures with high uncertainty avoidance.

Personal versus Contextual Style

Gudykunst and associates (1988, p. 109) defined the personal versus contextual style as follows:

Verbal personal style is individual-centered language, while verbal contextual style is role-centered language. Verbal personal style refers to the use of certain linguistic derides to enhance the sense of "I" identity, and verbal contextual style refers to the use of certain linguistic signals to emphasize the sense of "role" identity. In the verbal personal style, meanings are expressed for the purpose of emphasizing "personhood," while in the verbal contextual style, meanings are expressed for purpose of emphasizing prescribed role relationships.

Several researchers examined the personal and contextual dimensions among different cultures. Mishra (1982) found that Indian English-speakers provide many minor contextual parts of a story before presenting the main thesis, whereas speakers of British English provide the topic first and then present the relevant information. Young (1982) found that Chinese use an extensively contextual style. Both Japanese and Koreans were found to use context-oriented language. These findings suggest that cultures high on power distance and collectivistic cultures tend to use a contextual style of verbal communication. Based on these findings we propose that:

> *Proposition 4*: For a sales interaction to be successful, the sales training should focus on a personal style of communication when dealing with customers from individualistic and low power distance cultures.

> *Proposition 5*: For a sales interaction to be successful, the sales training should focus on a contextual communication style when interacting with customers who are primarily from collectivistic and high power distance cultures.

Instrumental versus Affective Style

Gudykunst and associates (1988, p. 112) noted that "instrumental verbal style is sender-oriented language usage and the affective verbal style is receiver-oriented language usage. The instrumental style is goal-oriented in verbal exchange and the affective style is process-oriented in verbal exchange." Adelman and Lushing (1981) found that Arabs use a dramatic, affective style of verbal communication in everyday discourse. For Americans, the digital level of verbal communication is the prime concern for effective face-to-face communication. Other studies found the Japanese and Korean languages emphasize an affective, intuitive style (Okabe 1983; Park 1979). Conversely, members of individualistic cultures tend to engage in a instrumental style of verbal communication. Denmark, the Netherlands, Switzerland, and the United States are some of the cultures that use instrumental styles of verbal communication, while most Arab, Latin American, and Asian cultures use an affective style of verbal interaction. Thus, we propose that:

> *Proposition 6*: For a sales interaction to be successful, the sales training should focus on an instrumental style of communication when dealing with customers from individualistic cultures.

> *Proposition 7*: For a sales interaction to be successful, the sales training should focus an affective style of communication when dealing with customers from collectivistic cultures.

Congruence/Incongruence

Congruence/incongruence refers to the match/mismatch of sales presentation styles and customer expectations. If the sales training is consistent with the expectations of the customer, it will result in congruence of behavior (sales presentation)-expectations (customers expectations of salesperson's behavior). If the sales training does not take into consideration the culture differences and attempts to make a sales presentation that is not consistent with customers' expectations, it will result in an incongruent behavior-expectation. Based on this reasoning we propose that:

> *Proposition 8*: A sales presentation will be congruent with customer expectations if the sales training focuses on a communication style (e.g. direct vs indirect) that is consistent with the customers' culture.
>
> *Proposition 9*: A sales presentation will be incongruent with customer expectations if the sales training focuses on a communication style that is not consistent with the customers' culture.

Success/Failure

The consequences of sales training are categorized into success and failure. Success/failure refers to whether the sales person was able to achieve his or her sales call objectives or not. The success of sales presentation depends on how appropriate the sales training is. In other words, the sales call is likely to be successful if the sales presentation is congruent with customer expectations. When there is congruence, the sales presentation is likely to be effective. On the other hand, if the sales presentation and customer expectations are incongruent, the sales presentation will meet negative attributions, resulting in an ineffective sales call. Therefore we propose that:

> *Proposition 10*: When sales training and customer expectations are congruent, the sales presentation is more likely to be effective in achieving the sales call objectives.
>
> *Proposition 11*: When the sales training and customer expectations are incongruent, the sales presentation is more likely to be ineffective in achieving the sales call objectives.

CONCLUSION

Knowledge pertaining to intercultural communication is of critical importance to multinational corporations that have to deal with people from diverse cultural backgrounds. The major implication of this study is its ability to present a model that gives an overview of the impact of culture on sales communication in an intercultural situation. This has some important implications for global sales force training and development. These propositions presented in this study can be utilized in developing a training program that would enable the salespeople to role play the predominant communication styles in dealing with the customer's culture. There is an increasing trend toward business expanding their operations across the borders, requiring marketers to interact with customers with different cultural backgrounds. This model would allow a sales manager to use training that would take into account the differences in communication styles of different cultures that can potentially affect the sales presentation strategy. One has to also take into consideration certain inherent limitations with Hofstede's dimensions. The objective of this chapter is to recognize the impact of culture on global sales force training involving an intercultural context. Literature in cross-cultural psychology suggests that there are several other variables that would potentially affect the sales interaction in an intercultural context such as personality, self-concept, self-monitoring, information processing, and conflict resolution processes. Future research should examine these influences in order to provide a more comprehensive framework to guide sales training and development.

REFERENCES

Adelman, M. and M. Lushing (1981). "Intercultural Communication Problems as Perceived by Saudi Arabian and American Managers." *International Journal of Intercultural Relations*, 5: 349–364.

Bond, M. (1979). "Dimensions of Personality Used in Perceiving Peers: Cross-Cultural Comparisons of Hong Kong, Japanese, American, and Filipino University Students." *Journal of Cross-Cultural Psychology*, 13: 186–200.

Bond, M., K. Leung, and K. Wan (1982). "How Does Cultural Collectivism Operate? The Impact of Task and Maintenance Contributions on Reward Allocation." *Journal of Cross-Cultural Psychology* 16: 186–200.

Bovee, L. Courtland, Michael J. Houston, and John V. Thill (1995). *Marketing*, 2nd ed. New York: McGraw-Hill.

Clark, Terry (1990). "International Marketing and National Character: A Review and Proposal for an Integrative Theory." *Journal of Marketing*, 54(4): 73–79.

Forgas, J. and M. Bond (1985). "Cultural Influences on the Perception of Interaction Episodes." *Personality and Social Psychological Bulletin*, 11: 75–88.

Hill, John S. and Meg Birdseye (1989). "Selling and Sales Management in Action: Salesperson Selection in Multinational Corporations: An Empirical Study." *Journal of Personal Selling and Sales Management*, 9 (Summer): 39–47.

Hill, John S. and Richard R. Still (1990). "Organizing the Overseas Sales Force: How Multinationals Do It." *Journal of Personal Selling and Sales Management*, 10 (Spring): 57–66.

Gardner, W. and J. M. Martinko (1988). "Impression Management in Organizations." *Journal of Management*, 14(2): 321–338.

Graham, John L. (1988). "Deference Given the Buyer." In Farok J. Contractor and Peter Lorange (eds.), *Comparative Strategies in International Business*. Lexington, MA: Lexington Books.

Grice, H. (1975). "Logic and Conversation." In P. Cole and J. Morgan (eds.), *Impression Management in the Organizations*. Hillsdale, NJ: Erlbaum.

Gudykunst, W. and T. Nishida (1986). "Attributional Confidence in Low- and High-Context Cultures." *Human Communication Research*, 12: 525–549.

Gudykunst, W., T. Nishida, and E. Chua (1987). "Perceptions of Social Penetration in Japanese–North American Dads." *International Journal of Intercultural Relations*, 11: 171–190.

Gudykunst, W. and S. Ting-Toomey (1988). "Affective Communication Across Cultures." *American Behavioral Scientist*, 31: 384–400.

Gudykunst, W., S. Ting-Toomey, and E. Chua (1988). *Culture and Interpersonal Communication*. Beverly Hills, CA: Sage.

Gudykunst, W., S. Yang, and T. Nishida (1987). "Cultural Differences in Self-Consciousness and Self-Monitoring." *Communication Research*, 14: 7–36.

Hall, E. T. (1966). *The Hidden Dimension*. New York: Doubleday.

————— (1976). *Beyond Culture*. New York: Doubleday.

————— (1983). *The Dance of Life*. New York: Doubleday.

Hofstede, G. (1980). *Culture's Consequences: International Differences in Work-related Values*. Beverly Hills, CA: Sage.

————— (1983). "Dimensions of National Cultures in Fifty Countries and Three Regions." In J. Deregowski, S. Dzuirawiec, and R. Annis (eds.), *Explications in Cross-Cultural Psychology*. Lisse, The Netherlands: Swets and Zeitlinger.

Johnson, C. and F. Johnson (1975). "Interaction Rules and Ethnicity." *Social Forces*, 54: 452–466.

Kale, Sudhir H. and John W. Barnes (1992). "Understanding the Domain of Cross National Buyer-Seller Interactions." *Journal of International Business Studies* (First Quarter): 101–131.

Lederer, William and Eugene Burdick (1958). *The Ugly American*. New York: Norton.

McClelland, D. C. (1961). *The Achieving Society*. New York: Van Nostrand Reinhold.

McGrath, Rita Gunther, Ian C. MacMillan, and Sari Scheinberg (1992). "Elitists, Risk-Takers, and Rugged Individualists? An Exploratory Analysis of Cultural Differences Between Entrepreneurs and Non-Entrepreneurs." *Journal of Business Venturing*, 7(2): 115–135.

Mishra, A. (1982). "Discovering Connections." In J. Gumperz (ed.), *Language and Social Identity*. Cambridge: Cambridge University Press.

Okabe, R. (1983). "Cultural Assumptions of East and West: Japan and the United States." In W. Gudykunst (ed.), *Intercultural Communication Theory*. Beverly Hills, CA: Sage.

Park, M. (1979). *Communications Styles in Two Different Cultures: Korean and American*. Seoul, Korea: Han Shin Publishing Company.

Parsons, T. and E. Shils (1951). *Toward a General Theory of Action*. Cambridge, MA: Harvard University Press.

Poyatos, F. (1983). *New Perspectives in Nonverbal Communication*. Oxford: Pergamon Press.

Prothro, E. (1970). "Arab-American Differences in the Judgment of Written Messages." In A. Lutfiyya and C. Churchill (eds.), *Readings in Arab Middle-Eastern Societies and Cultures*. The Hague: Mouton.

Ricks, David (1983). *Big Business Blunders: Mistakes in Multinational Marketing*. Homewood, IL: Richard D. Irwin.

Sheth, Jagdish M. (1976). "Buyer-Seller Interaction: A Conceptual Framework." *Proceedings of the Association for Consumer Research*. Cincinnati, OH: Association of Consumer Research, pp. 382–386.

Ting-Toomey, S. (1988). "A Face Negotiation Theory." In Y. Kim and W. Gudykunst (eds.), *Theory in Intercultural Communication*. Newbury Park, CA: Sage.

Triandis, H. (1977). *Interpersonal Behavior*. Monterey, CA: Brooks/Cole.

—— (1980). *Values Attitudes and Interpersonal Behavior*. In M. Page (ed.), *Nebraska Symposium on Motivation, 1979*, vol. 27. Lincoln: University of Nebraska Press.

—— (1984). "A Theoretical Framework for the More Efficient Construction of Culture Assimilators." *International Journal of Intercultural Relations*, 8: 301–330.

Walle, H. Alf (1986). "Conceptualizing Personal Selling for International Business: A Continuum of Exchange Perspective." *Journal of Personal Selling and Sales Management*, 6 (November): 9–17.

Weitz, Barton A., S. B. Castleberry, and J. F. Tanner (1992). *Selling, Building Partnerships*. Homewood, IL: Irwin.

Weitz, Barton, Harish Sujan, and Mita Sujan (1986). "Knowledge, Motivation and Adaptive Behavior: A Framework for Improving Selling Effectiveness." *Journal of Marketing*, 50 (October): 174–191.

Williams, Kaylene C. and Rosann L. Spiro (1985). "Communication Style in the Salesperson-Customer Dyad." *Journal of Marketing Research*, 22 (November): 434–442.

Witkin, H., A. Dyk, H. Faterson, D. Goodenough, and S. Karp (1962). *Psychological Differentiation*. New York: John Wiley.

Young, L. (1982). "Inscrutability Revisited." In J. Gumperz (ed.), *Language and Social Identity*. Cambridge: Cambridge University Press.

Chapter 11

International Copy Testing: Recent Developments in the Measurement of Advertising Effectiveness

Flemming Hansen

BACKGROUND

Advertising testing has become an increasingly international business. Major advertisers, such as Coca-Cola, Colgate-Palmolive, and Procter and Gamble, develop their own standardized system, which they apply uniformly in different countries. The experiences they gain accumulate and define norms, based upon which subsequent test results are evaluated.

Standardized international pretests are also offered by several commercial research institutes. The Buy Test, Incorporated, is available in many countries around the world; with a main office in London, they have test scores for several thousand different tests from all over the world. The American McCullum-Spielman test is marketed internationally through the German GFK company, under the name of Advantage. In the posttesting, or tracking, area, the Millward-Brown system, originating in London, is becoming more and more widely used all over the world. Also, the major research chains, such as Gallup, INRA, IRIS, and Research International, offer more or less standardized advertising pretesting. All of these tests rely heavily upon different measures of "persuasion," that is, the ability of the tested advertisement to convince the consumer of the advantages of the product advertised and to create purchasing intentions. Papers have been published proving some validity of such effect measures in terms of correlation with subsequent sales results. However, in later years, theoretical research, particularly with what has been labelled "attitudes towards the ad" (A-ad) and ad-liking measures has thrown new light upon the way in which advertising works. Similarly, Advertising Research Foundation's large-scale copy-testing study—findings that became available around 1991—has thrown some doubt on the validity of the rather simple persuasion measures applied in most standard research systems. Consequently a new generation of tests is emerging. In the following we shall look briefly upon the development of international advertising pre-tests and particularly upon the more recent development in modelling advertising effects.

It is a well-known observation, made in many presentations regarding advertising, that advertising works—sometimes. Underlying this, of course, is the fact that remarkably little in reality is known about how, when, and why it works.

It is also a well-established fact that the measurement of advertising effect is a complicated business. Basically one would like to quantify the effect by relating advertising spending to sales or revenue results. Most frequently, however, there is a time distance between the two, the length of which is not always known. Additionally, in the intervening time, a number of other factors such as price, distribution, point of purchase activities, and competitors' activities may have their influence.

To avoid these problems, advertising effects are normally measured with the use of some intervening variable, reflecting the immediate impact of the advertising upon the consumer. The concept is borrowed from social psychology and is often referred to as the SOR model, where the S represents the stimulus (advertising); the R represents response (sales), and the O represents some intervening variables upon which the exposure taking place at one point in time has its influence and where again at some other point in time the same intervening variable influences the response—that is, the sale. In principle such intervening variables cannot be observed themselves, but questioning and other measurement techniques can be used to obtain some information about them. Attitudes of different kinds are typical representatives of such variables. In reality you cannot be sure of what an attitude is and where it is, but by asking various questions one may form hypotheses as to the structure and role of the attitude.

Both in pretesting and in posttesting of advertising, the search for useful intervening variables is vital. Of course where direct sales data are available and can be related to advertising, the need for such intervening variables disappears. These cases are rare, however, but they do exist, for instance, in connection with classified advertising, coupon advertising, direct marketing, and probably also some retail advertising.

In the following we shall look upon the historical development of advertising testing and its use. Next we shall look in more detail at the variables used and some theoretical underlying considerations. Finally we shall look at some more recent developments inspired by problems repeatedly observed in connection with traditional variables and techniques.

In this chapter no direct distinction is made between print and television advertising, although of course the influence that the increasingly dominant role of television has had upon advertising testing will be seen. As will become evident, however, print versus television is just one of several important factors the advertiser will have to consider before deciding upon what to measure, in order to understand the way in which his or her advertising works.

HISTORICAL DEVELOPMENT

In this chapter we shall primarily be concerned with pretesting, that is, tests carried out on copy before it has been inserted or broadcast. More aggregated measures or "tracking" of effects as the campaign progresses are not included. However, it is not uncommon that pretesting is carried out on the air, that is, related to single exposures, either experimentally inserted or simply by tying the test in with the very first broadcast of the spot or insertion of the advertisement. It makes good sense to include a discussion of such tests with tests of pretesting in general.

Quantitative advertising testing has passed through three stages.

1. The age of the recognition versus recall debate (1930–1970)
2. The persuasion age (1960–2000)
3. The age of model base research (1900–   )

In parallel with this, a changing use of varying qualitative techniques has taken place. This subject is not a major topic of this presentation, but a few remarks should be made, since some interaction between the two lines of research development has taken place.

Starting in the 1950s with traditional motivation research, the standard depth and focus group interview techniques have developed, and they have dominated the scene until recently. In later years, semiotic approaches have become popular also. Originating in France, it was not initially related to advertising but has been used increasingly, both in France and later in other countries, to gain insights into the nature of the messages and their meaning to consumers.

The Dichter (1964) motivation research tradition was a strictly American initiative of the early 1950s. In reaction to its somewhat invalidated findings, great emphasis was put upon developing quantitative advertising evaluation techniques. It is also worth noting that when more quantitative techniques (the Schwerin test) became available in Europe, first in London, in the early 1960s, they were met with severe criticism because of their lack of sensitivity to the creative process and its elements. Consequently, in many places in Europe and certainly in the United Kingdom, focus group interviews and in-depth interviews remained dominant in the area of advertising testing. This different importance of the approaches in New York and London may also reflect differences in the relative strengths of the advertising manager, with the company and the account manager with the major agencies. Whereas in New York the first approach has had a very strong position, the dominant account manager in the agency became a typical London phenomenon. It is obvious that the agency researcher prefers qualitative work to support the creative process (and to avoid quantitative effect discussions), whereas the advertising manager of the company will put more emphasis on budgetary considerations and quantitative testing, related to possible sales results.

The need for qualitative information in relation to the more quantitative tests has also become more and more obvious, so that today a number of measurements are built into nearly all test forms, giving the possibility of evaluating which elements in the tested advertisement have a positive or negative effect and in which connection. Such semi-qualitative ingredients in otherwise more quantitative tests are often described as diagnostics. In the history of quantitative approaches to advertising testing, the first phase originates with the Gallup/ Robinson recognition methodology developed in the late 1920s. It may take the form where the respondent goes through the publication indicating what has been read, seen, or noted, and it may include questions about what elements have been observed with more or less attention. It may also take the form of a poster containing various more-or-less competing material. It can be used to follow up on what has happened to material that has actually appeared in a publication, or it can be used to evaluate selected material in an experimental setting. In any event, the basic measurement is the recognition of what has been seen.

The use of recognition data for advertising testing has been decreasing until very recently. Only in connection with copy testing in the form of page traffic studies of print media has it been used frequently. However, in academic research it has survived, and in later years an understanding of the structurally different psychological processes underlying the recognition and the recall processes has generated renewed interest in the measure. It is suggested that whereas recall relies upon activating basically coded information structures of processed attitudinal and informational items, (some would say information stored in the left side of the brain), the recognition process relies to a much larger extent on the regeneration of holistic impressions stored very differently in the brain.

A major problem that has been suggested with the method is that people tend to overclaim what they have recognized. (The reverse may also occur, particularly with "unpleasant" material.) The effect can be observed by asking people to inform on what they have observed and including material in a test material that they cannot possibly ever have seen. There will still be some respondents claiming recognition. For a review of these problems see Du Bow (1994).

In a response to this criticism the so-called proven recall technique was developed by the Starch organization in the late 1930s (Lipstein 1984/1985). In its original version the method was to ask respondents what they remembered having seen in a particular publication, be it yesterday's newspaper or last week's magazine. The technique may involve different levels of aid, ranging from just asking, "What advertisements did you see in xx newspaper yesterday," over "what coffee advertisements did you see," to "did you see a Maxwell House Coffee ad yesterday." Particularly with the aided recall versions it has been stressed that the respondent should report back at least some positively correct information regarding the content of the advertisement claimed to have been seen. Only then would he or she be counted as "having seen."

With the advent of television and with television advertising becoming increasingly important, this technique lent itself to adoption in terms of the "day after recall" measure. This version of the recall measure was originally developed with Procter and Gamble, but eventually the rights to administer the test were licensed to Burke and around this grew the largest advertising testing organization of the 1960s and 1970s. The idea here is to identify a sufficiently large number of people who have watched the television program on which the commercial to be tested has been broadcast within the previous 24 hours. Part of the usefulness of this measure was that it could easily be combined with audience measures obtained in diaries or through meters. You not only knew from audience research how many viewers had been on the program, you also, from "day-after recall," could estimate how many of those had actually seen and recalled the commercial. The methodology has been heavily criticized, however. Not least, advertising people have claimed that recall is not necessarily related to sales.

Later research has proved that this is certainly correct (du Plessis 1994). It was also claimed that one could easily create high recall scores by producing spots relying upon dramatic, attractive, and not necessarily product-related effects.

In its early days the use of recall measures in relation to advertising effects primarily took the form of advertising recall. However, with growing concern for brand recall in a competitive world where there is not room for 100 percent recall for many brands in a market, change in brand recall following advertising exposure has also become a frequently used measure. In this connection the structure of brand recall in specific markets is of interest. Laurent and associates (1989) have provided interesting results on this. Basically they find that in a majority of markets only a few brands account for very high unaided brand recall scores. The typical relationship is illustrated in Figure 11.1. This is ascribed to a limited mental capacity for storing brand name in any given product area. Since, for many fast-moving consumer trends, brand recognition is a predominant factor in influencing what brands will occur in the aroused set of the consumer at the time of the purchase, the struggle for brand recall is important and the inclusion of its measurement in advertising testing obvious. However, at least for major brands, it is unlikely that advertising exposure in a test situation will create much change in brand recall. For minor brands, however, the measurement may be more sensitive and therefore useful.

This whole debate led to a quest for other valid measures of advertising effects. What was asked for were simple measures that related to the sales effect that was likely to be generated by the advertisements when they were inserted. A number of advertising evaluation procedures came into use. "Advertising lik-

Figure 11.1
Theoretical Relationship between Aided and Unaided Awareness of Brands

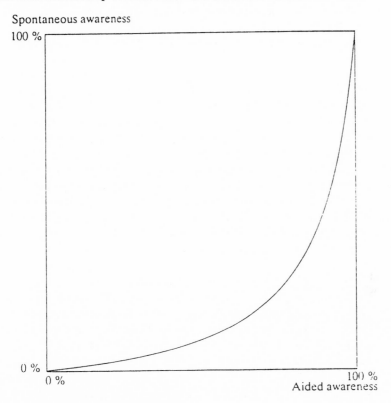

Spontaneous awareness

Source: Laurent, Kapferer, and Roussel (1989).

ing" was the critical term (Thorson 1991). Here the respondents judged the advertisement on a number of dimensions, such as

- Is it convincing?
- Does it have relevant information?
- Do you like it?
- Is it interesting?
- Does it change your opinion of the product?

In one way or another all these measures ask the respondent to evaluate aspects of the advertisement. Such scales have become labelled attitudes toward the ad, or "A-ad." They became widely used in academic communication research (for instance, Park and Wyer 1993; Mitchell 1986), but they were met with strong criticism from many practitioners. It was claimed that it was of no importance whether the respondent liked the ad or not. What was important was that it generated a sale. They assumed that ad liking had no direct relationship with subsequent purchases, an assumption that later was proved wrong (Walker and Dubitsky 1994).

In some instances, particularly with highly information-loaded campaigns, one may simply measure learning or the extent to which the message is understood. With advertising informing about new legal regulations, about changing train schedules, new store locations, and the like, probably the most relevant measure of effect is one that reveals the extent to which the consumers who have been exposed to the message have learned from it what was intended. Here, obvious measures are multiple-choice or true/false questions (Hansen and Bache 1972).

Other researchers claimed that what were needed were measurements that directly related to sales. Some kind of measures of attitudes, intentions, preferences, or changes in the same towards the brand was what was needed. Under one label these have later been named attitudes toward a brand, or A-brand. Basically two kinds of measures came into use. Predominant has been the measurement of change in attitude, preference, purchase intention, or the like between before and after exposure. Various kinds of scaled preferences have also been used.

Such preference measures have in several instances been shown to relate to subsequent sales results. However, a major problem with them is that they require very large samples to provide statistically significant results. Changes in purchase intentions for fast-moving consumer goods and similar products—if they occur at all immediately after the exposure—are small and few. Therefore, the measurements tend to be insensitive. When attempts are made to overcome this weakness by strengthening the exposure, either by giving more exposure or more opportunity to emphasize the message, it is still difficult to observe significant changes in attitudes and preference. With an audience with a large proportion of loyal consumers, it is not likely that behavior intention will change much following exposure to a single commercial. Also, the artificial exposure situation may create unpredictable effects.

Other test systems have tried to develop persuasion measures that, rather than relying on attitude shifts, directly attempt to quantify the persuasive effect of the advertisement. One such example is the buy-test system where a scale is developed in such a way that a high score relates to subsequent purchasing behavior. Other similar attempts rely upon self-ratings of expected change in behavior following the exposure. Regardless of what measure is used, doubt has also been thrown upon these persuasion measures. On the whole it seems that if a relationship can be established, it varies greatly from product area to product area and from situation to situation. This leads to a need for accumulated experiences for evaluating findings from studies of this kind (a need that can be said to exist also in connection with recognition, recall, and A-ad measures). Since the effect measured may vary between product areas, between countries, and between different types of consumers, it is important to have accumulated

Table 11.1
Model and Measurements in the Information Processing Model (Effect Hierarchy Model)

The Model	The Measurements
Exposure	Viewing and readership
Awareness	Recognition, ad and brand recall, mechanical measurements
Understanding	Multiple choice; true–false
Interest (in ad)	Ad-liking and other evaluations of ad (A-ad)
Persuasion	Attitude shifts, self-rated changes in preferences and intentions
Behavior	Market share, requests, sales

experience, providing norms for relevant categories based upon which particular test score can be judged as "good" or "bad."

The different measures discussed so far reflect a traditional view of advertising, which has been labelled the information processing model. The early versions of these circulated in the 1930s under the name of "AIDA," standing for Attention, Interest, Desire, Action. In theories of innovations concerned with the acceptance of new products, a flow from attention, interest, evaluation, trial to purchase is suggested. Among cognitive psychologists, in its most popular form it is stated as a three-step process, where the receiver of the communication is supposed to pass through the following stages:

• Cognition—a cognitive phase
• Evaluation—an evaluation phase
• Conative—a meaning phase

The information being received is processed in a computer-like way and creates evaluations, attitudes, and preferences leading to purchase.

We can summarize this discussion of the classical information-processing model of how consumers treat information as is shown in Table 11.1: The steps—exposure, awareness, interest, understanding, persuasion, behavior—are shown on the left-hand side of the diagram, and on the right-hand side typical examples of measures that are used in the different steps of the information processing are given.

MODEL-BASED TESTING

Over the years, however, there have been doubts as to whether this one-string information-processing approach is always an appropriate description of the way in which people receive information. It is not the purpose here to review this extensive literature. (For an orientation, see Hansen 1985; Petty and Cacioppo 1986). However, a few indications of the different lines of thinking that apply are useful for an understanding of the way in which advertising testing is moving at present.

When looking upon the role information played in the kind of information-processing situations I was concerned with (Hansen 1972), I suggested the concept of "forced exposure," that is, situations where the information is not actively sought out by the receiver, but rather is perceived because it is more less forced upon him. In particular it may be found in connection with television advertising. The exposure is there is no or almost no motivation on behalf of the receiver to process it.

Another early observation is made by Zajonic (1968) in his "Mere exposure theory." Just to illustrate the line of thinking and the nature of the findings emerging, Figure 11.2 is shown.

Zajonc exposed a number of students to Chinese characters; some of them (without the knowledge of the respondents) were shown two, five, or ten times, others only one. On the following day he asked the same students to indicate what they thought the words meant in terms of positive/negative meaning. The results in the figure are obvious. The more students had been exposed to a particular character, the more positive the meaning they ascribed to it. Over the years many similar experiments have been conducted, with four-syllable words in Turkish, with pictures of persons and landscapes, and so on, all with the same results.

An interesting Danish observation that may relate to this is presented in Figure 11.3. Here the evaluation of 42 different Danish companies is shown. Both the evaluation done by the entire population and that done for the minor group that claims to know the particular companies are shown. The consistency of the more positive evaluation among those with more information is remarkable. Obviously, with completely unknown constructs such as Chinese characters, there are no prior associations that can be made and can interfere with the mere-exposure effect. In reality, however, such inferences do occur. If one observes number 42 in the Danish data, it can be seen that here the company is less liked among those who know it the best. It can be added that it was a very badly functioning chemical company, well known to have environmental problems. Somehow these observations suggest a simple mere-exposure effect, which of course may interfere with many other things, but if it does not, it may create effects, not assuming very much cognitive activity.

Another interesting line of research, which originates in perceptual psychology but which has been brought to the attention of consumer behavior researchers by the German researcher Kroeber-Riel (1984), concerns itself with picture perception. Here it is studied how little time people need to see pictures in order to be able to recognize them. Generally it has been found that one or two seconds is enough, suggesting that very little exposure is needed in order

Figure 11.2
Average Rated Affective Connotation of Chinese-Like Characters Exposed with
Low and High Frequencies

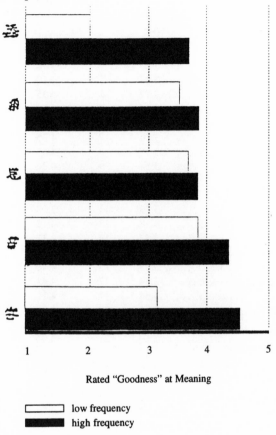

Rated "Goodness" at Meaning

☐ low frequency
■ high frequency

Source: Zajonic (1968).

to generate recognition. In order to illustrate the findings, a typical experiment from this line of research is described.

If, for example, 100 respondents are shown a sequence of 100 slides, each exposed two seconds, be it of landscapes, faces, paintings, or other meaningful material (abstract painting takes more) and then the following day the same 100 persons are exposed to 200 slides including those shown the first day, and after each slide each respondent is asked to indicate whether he or she can remember having seen them before, one will find that almost 100 percent recognize the slides from the preceding day correctly. There are variations, depending upon the type of material, such as meaningfulness, degree of differentiation, and so on. However, it is remarkable that even after a period of one week or more, the

Figure 11.3
Evaluation of 42 Danish Companies among All and among Those Knowing the Companies Well

Company No.	All		Knows Well		
1	4.12	1	4.60	1	(0)
2	3.85	2	4.40	4	(−2)
3	3.85	2	4.40	4	(−2)
4	3.77	4	4.35	9	(−2)
5	3.75	5	4.22	11	(−6)
6	3.75	6	4.14	15	(−7)
7	3.74	7	4.35	6	(+1)
8	3.55	8	4.05	20	(−12)
9	3.54	9	4.36	6	(+3)
10	3.53	10	4.25	10	(0)
11	3.53	11	4.07	17	(−6)
12	3.59	11	3.98	24	(−13)
13	3.58	13	4.12	14	(−1)
14	3.57	14	4.17	12	(+2)
15	3.55	15	4.03	22	(−7)
16	3.55	15	4.46	2	(+13)
17	3.54	17	4.41	3	(+14)
18	3.54	17	4.11	16	(+1)
19	3.53	19	3.39	30	(−11)
20	3.52	20	3.91	29	(−9)
21	3.50	21	3.94	26	(−5)
22	3.49	22	4.36	6	(+16)
23	3.46	23	4.03	22	(+1)
24	3.44	24	3.56	39	(−15)
25	3.40	25	3.83	33	(−8)
26	3.37	26	3.77	35	(−9)
27	3.35	27	3.88	31	(−4)
28	3.35	27	3.97	25	(+2)
29	3.33	29	3.92	27	(+2)
30	3.30	30	3.55	42	(−12)
31	3.28	31	3.85	32	(−1)
32	3.28	31	3.79	34	(−3)
33	3.25	33	3.75	36	(−3)
34	3.25	33	3.74	38	(−5)
35	3.25	35	3.92	27	(+8)
36	3.24	36	4.06	18	(+18)
37	3.22	37	3.51	41	(−4)
38	3.21	38	3.75	36	(+2)
39	3.20	39	3.46	43	(−4)
40	3.18	40	4.05	20	(+20)
41	3.18	40	4.12	14	(+26)
42	3.17	42	4.05	18	(+24)

percentage correctly recognized is still high. It is also found that if the pictures in the first exposure are shown with no interval in between and if the exposure time is short, then recognition drops rapidly. The shortest possible exposure combined with approximately half a second following the exposure provides the best recognition. Seemingly the information stored enabling the person to recognize the picture later takes about half a second. Still another line of research introduced in this connection has been the study of brain lateralization. The theory holds that while verbal, numerical, and symbolic information seems to be stored in the left side of the brain, pictorial, holistic, and similar impressions are stored in the right side of the brain, suggesting that there may be two very different ways in which to store information. The theory is complicated and its practicability questionable (Hansen 1984), but it does suggest that information may be treated in very different ways in different situations.

Other research suggests that emotional impressions and responses may follow exposure that cannot easily be related to the information-processing hierarchy upon which advertising research traditionally has been based. In the early 1980s a number of researchers introduced the idea that emotions could be generated without cognition and that they may even be stored, not in the brain, but in muscles in different locations of the body. Again, a simple classical experiment may illustrate this (Bornstein 1989). One takes two groups of students and places them in two rooms and provides them with a Walkman on which are recorded music, speech, and combinations, and then asks them to listen to what is on the Walkman. The only difference between the two groups is that in the first, it is explained to the students that since Walkmen are often used when moving around, cycling, or walking, to make the evaluation more fair, they should shake their heads while listening. To the other group the same explanation is given, only it is suggested that they should nod while listening. After the experiment, when they are asked to express their evaluation of the quality of what they have just listened to, amazing results emerge. After having listened for a short period of time, the group that had nodded evaluated the Walkman significantly better than those who had been shaking their heads. A somewhat related illustration comes from an extension of the aforementioned Zajonic Chinese character experiment. If, following the completion of the original experiment, people are asked whether they have been aware that they have seen some Chinese characters more than others, it appears that some actually have become aware of this. When this group is then compared with the group that has not been aware of seeing the characters more than once, it is found that the latter group has the stronger mere-exposure effects. Here, seemingly, cognition interferes with the exposure effect.

Finally, a line of research that has also become more and more important since the mid-1980s concerns itself with various aspects of feelings and emotions in relation to advertising perception (Bornstein 1989). Findings show how having seen different kinds of movies prior to watching an advertisement has an effect upon various recall and A-ad type measures. In other experiments

Figure 11.4
Advertising Response Model: Conceptual Model Based on the Elaboration Likelihood Model

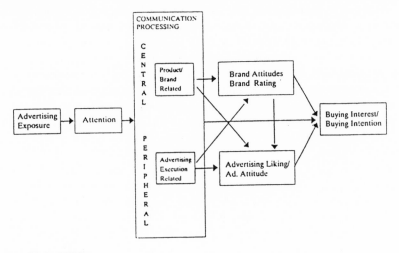

Source: Metha (1994).

respondents are brought into different moods before being exposed to the same printed material. Again, clear effects occur. The development of special scales for the measurement of mood and feelings has also made it possible to find marked differences in the moods generated by different types of commercials upon different types of respondents.

Altogether these findings suggest that people may have very different ways of perceiving information in different situations: They may store information in an emotional as well as in a pictorially recognizable way, in addition to the information-processing information storage. One factor that has been studied intensively and been shown to influence how people treat information is involvement (Petty et al. 1983). Involvement reflects the extent to which the person is motivated in relation to the product in question, the message in question, or the specific situation in question (Zaichkowsky 1985).

Several models have been proposed suggesting different ways of information processing. Probably the most extensive and the most influential is the "Elaboration Likelihood Model" (ELM) proposed by Petty and Cacioppo (1986). The essence of the model is illustrated in Figure 11.4.

In this model the central route processing is very similar to the traditional information-processing model's picture of the way in which consumers treat information. The peripheral processing, however, is different. Here information is received but stored more or less unprocessed, and traces have to be found in terms of recall or recognition of the advertisement, rather than in terms of brand recall or changes in attitude toward the brand. Eventually, if the stored advertising information is aroused in a subsequent purchasing situation and is linked to the brand advertised, this may, at this time, influence the purchasing behavior. The extent to which central versus peripheral routing is applied depends upon a number of factors, among which involvement probably is the most critical one.

Petty and Cacioppo say:

We have outlined two basic routes to persuasion. One route is based on the thoughtful (though sometimes biased) consideration of arguments central to the issue, whereas the other is based on affective associations or simple inferences tied to peripheral cues in the persuasion context. When variables in the persuasion situation render the elaboration likelihood high, the first kind of persuasion occurs (central route). When variables in the persuasion situation render the elaboration likelihood low, the second kind of persuasion occurs (peripheral route). Importantly, there are different consequences of the two routes to persuasion. Attitude changes via the central route appear to be more persistent, resistant, and predictive of behaviour than changes via the peripheral route.

The effect of some of the factors pointed out by Petty and Cacioppo are shown in Figures 11.5 and 11.6. In their theoretical studies, they have proven distraction, repetition, involvement, number of evaluators, need for cognition, message form, source attractiveness, source expertise, number of sources, and body position to be of importance. More specifically, in advertising testing, factors one would look for would be:

• Product area involvement
• Loyal versus non-loyal target group
• New versus established product
• Type of campaign: story, informational, or emotional

Associated with the peripheral route we also find emotional responses. An attempt to quantify these is reported by Haley and associates (1994).

Departing in such a model it is not sufficient with one overall effect measure; rather, one has to work with a repertoire of measures have to be be applied, depending upon the specific situation. Such measures could naturally be found among:

1. Recognition (total and part)
2. Mechanical attention measures
3. Learning effects (true/false, multiple choice)
4. Recall, R-ad, and R-brand
5. Message recall and particularly brand linking contained in it
6. A-ad and A-brand measures
7. Emotional response measures

Figure 11.5
Variables That May Enhance or Reduce Elaboration in a Relatively Objective Manner

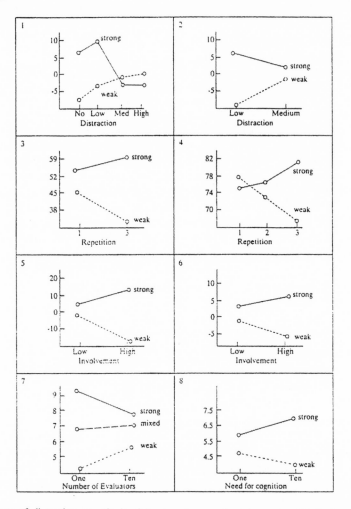

(1) Effects of distraction on attitudes following strong and weak counter-attitudinal messages. (2) Effects of distraction on attitudes following strong and weak pro-attitudinal messages. (3) Effects of message repetition on initial attitudes following strong and weak messages. (4) Effects of message repetition on delayed attitudes following strong and weak messages. (5) Effects of personal relevance on attitudes following pro- (strong) and counter-attitudinal (weak) messages (data from Petty and Cacioppo 1979, Experiment 1). (6) Effects of personal relevance on attitudes following strong and weak counter-attitudinal messages (data from Petty and Cacioppo 1979, Experiment 2). (7) Effects of personal responsibility on attitudes following strong, weak, and mixed messages (data from Petty, Harkins, and Williams 1980, Experiment 2). (8) Effects of need for cognition on attitudes following strong and weak messages (data from Petty, Cacioppo, and Schumann 1983, Experiment 2).

Source: Petty and Cacioppo (1986), Figure 3.

Figure 11.6
Additional Variables That May Affect Information Processing in a Relatively Objective Manner

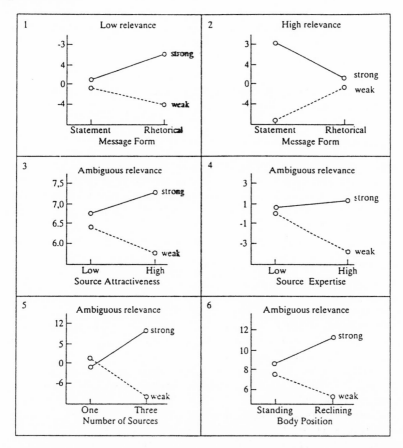

(1) Effects of rhetorical questions on attitudes following strong and weak messages of low relevance. (2) Effects of rhetorical questions on attitudes following strong and weak messages of high relevance. (3) Effects of social attractiveness on attitudes following strong and weak messages of uncertain relevance. (4) Effects of expertise on attitudes of field-dependent subjects following strong and weak messages of uncertain relevance. (5) Effects of multiple sources on attitudes following strong and weak messages of uncertain relevance. (6) Effects of recipient posture on attitudes following strong and weak messages of uncertain relevance.
Source: Petty and Cacioppo (1986).

Which one to choose in this specific situation will depend upon the factors just discussed.

With advertising pretesting tailormade, as suggested here, the quest for norm data also changes. A need arises for looking into different kinds of experiences in different kinds of test situations and comparing findings with those. For individual advertisers norms will, to a larger extent than before, be something they will establish themselves.

A development in this direction toward what one could label "semi-standardized tests" makes the use of norm data considerably more complicated and leaves more to the skilled interpretation of the test results. Also the choice of test design relies heavily upon the researcher's ability to judge the campaign along those important dimensions previously discussed. In an international context, this is likely, at least for major advertisers, to pull them in the direction of developing their own individual experience and norms for variables that are useful in their particular market situation.

REFERENCES

Bornstein, Robert F. (1989). "Exposure and Affect: Overview and Meta-Analysis of Research, 1968–1987." *Psychological Bulletin*, 106(2): 265–289.

Dichter, Ernest (1964). *Handbook of Consumer Motivations*. New York: McGraw-Hill.

Du Bow, Joel S. (1994). "Recall Revisited: Recall Redux." *Journal of Advertising Research* (May/June).

du Plessis, Rik (1994). "Recognition versus Recall." *Journal of Advertising Research* (May/June).

Haley, R. J. and A. L. Baldinger (1991). "The ARF Copy Research Validity Project." *Journal of Advertising Research*, 31(2).

Haley, R. J., James Stafforoni, and Arthur Fox (1994). "The Missing Message of Copy Testing." *Journal of Advertising Research* (May/June).

Hansen, Flemming (1972). *Consumer Choice Behavior*. New York: The Free Press.

——— (1984). "Towards an Alternative Theory of the Advertising Communication Process." *International Journal of Research in Marketing*, 1(1).

——— (1985). *Studies of Communication Effects: Methodological and Theoretical Papers on Left/Right Lateralization*. Copenhagen: Civiløkonomernes Forlag.

Hansen, Flemming and Erik Bache (1972). "A Pretesting Procedure That Works." European Society for Marketing Research (ESOMAR) Conference Proceedings.

Kroeber-Riel, W. (1984). *Konsument Verhalten*. Munchen: Vahlen.

Laurent, G., J. N. Kapferer, and F. Roussel (1989). "Thresholds in Brand Awareness." In *Developments in Advertising and Communications*, European Society for Marketing Research (ESOMAR) Annual Conference Proceedings.

Lipstein, Benjamin (1984/1985). "An Historical Retrospective of Copy Research." *Journal of Advertising Research*, 24(6).

Metha, Abdilasha (1994). "How Advertising Response Modelling (ARM) Can Increase Ad Effectiveness." *Journal of Advertising Research* (May/June).

Mitchell, Andrew A. (1986). "The Effect of Verbal and Visual Components of Advertisements on Brand Attitudes and Attitude toward the Advertisement." *Journal of Consumer Research*, 13(1).

Park, Jong-Woh and Robert S. Wyer, Jr. (1993). "The Effect of Pictorial Distance and the Viewer's Sociability on Ad Liking." *Journal of Consumer Psychology*, 2(4).

Petty, R. E. and J. T. Cacioppo (1979). "Issue-Involvement Can Increase or Decrease Persuasion by Enhancing Message-Relevant Cognitive Responses." *Journal of Personality and Social Psychology*, 37: 1915–1926.

——— (1986). *Communication and Persuasion: Central and Peripheral Routes to Attitude Change.* New York: Springer-Verlag.

Petty, R. E., S. G. Harkins, and K. D. Williams (1980). "The Effects of Group Diffusion of Cognitive Effort on Attitudes: An Information Processing View." *Journal of Personality and Social Psychology*, 38: 81–92.

Petty, Richard E. and John T. Cacioppo (1986). "The Elaboration Likelihood Model of Persuasion." *Advances in Experimental Social Psychology*, 19: 123–205.

Petty, Richard E., John T. Cacioppo, and David Schumann (1983). "Central and Peripheral Routes to Advertising Effectiveness: The Moderating Role of Involvement." *Journal of Consumer Research*, 10.

Thorson, Ester (1991). "Likeability: 10 Years of Academic Research." In *Proceedings from the Eighth Annual Advertising Research Foundation Copy Research Workshop*, New York.

Walker, David and Tony M. Dubitsky (1994). "Why Liking Matters." *Journal of Advertising Research* (May/June).

Zaichkowsky, Judith Lynne (1985). "Measuring the Involvement Construct." *Journal of Consumer Research*, 12 (December).

Zajonic, R. B. (1986). "Attitudinal Effects of Mere Exposure." *Journal of Personality and Social Psychology*, 9(2) (Part 2) (June) (Monograph Supplement).

Chapter 12

Are There Global Dimensions of Beliefs toward Advertising in General? A Multicultural Investigation

Srinivas Durvasula and Steven Lysonski

INTRODUCTION

The world is undergoing a dramatic transformation as the pace of globalization intensifies. Many firms have entered international markets, hoping to increase sales and gain market share. To achieve this goal, advertising has become a major vehicle to position products and communicate their benefits and attributes. Yet, our understanding of consumers' beliefs toward advertising in various countries is incomplete. We simply do not know enough about the reactions of consumers toward the advertising they see, nor their general perceptions of advertising. A plethora of articles have been written in the United States concerning how Americans feel about advertising (cf. Larkin 1977; Sandage and Leckenby 1980; Dubinsky and Hensel 1984; Muehling 1987; Andrews 1989; Andrews et al. 1991; Shavitt et al., 1998). Yet, our knowledge about the sentiments toward advertising, whether they are positive or negative, in other countries continues to be scant (Wills and Ryans 1982; Semenik et al., 1986; Tuncalp 1990). Only a few of these studies have focused on specific countries outside the United States (Tuncalp 1990; Zhang and Gelb 1996).

Measuring advertising perceptions are of concern to academics and practitioners. It is believed that these perceptions (e.g., cognitions, beliefs, and attitudes) affect consumers' attitudes toward advertising in general (Muehling 1987). Attitudes toward advertising precede the attitudes consumers have toward specific ads, which subsequently are linked to consumers' brand perceptions and purchase behavior (MacKenzie and Lutz 1989; Biehal et al., 1992). For practitioners, understanding consumers' advertising perceptions helps them design and implement more effective advertising campaigns. If consumers are negative toward aspects of advertising, it may be necessary to use more factual appeals rather than slick, persuasive ones. On the basis of comparing England to the

United States, O'Donohue (1995) found both complexity and ambivalence in the attitudes consumers hold toward advertising. She recommends more research to probe this complexity. Recently, a study by Shavitt and associates, (1998) on attitudes toward advertising in the United States found that Americans view advertisements as informative and useful in their decision making as well as enjoyable. Yet, a study in Saudi Arabia by Safran and associates (1996) found that some Saudis view television advertising as a serious cultural threat, while others see it as benign. Hence, there appears to be considerable variance in perceptions toward advertising.

As barriers to trade steadily decline, as witnessed by the progress of the World Trade Organization, the world is becoming more interdependent commercially. Cross-cultural investigations of advertising perceptions add immensely to our appreciation of cultural and attitudinal differences. If cross-cultural studies find similarity in ad perceptions, Levitt (1983) may be correct; standardization of advertising and development of global ad campaigns are feasible. However, if beliefs about advertising are different cross-culturally, effective advertising may require country-specific and customized efforts due to these differences on advertising perceptions (cf. Fullerton and Nevett 1986). Witkowski and Kellner (1998) found that attitudes toward television advertising in Germany and the United States were largely convergent, but cultural differences exist. A study by Grier and Brumbaugh (1999) identified asymmetries in cultural groups that impact the meaning consumers attach to ads. Another study by Rustogi and associates (1996) also found that cultural values do have an influence on attitudes toward advertising appeals.

The goal of this study is to provide a greater understanding of the beliefs consumers have toward advertising by looking at five different countries, located on four different continents. The main goal was to assess if the social and economic dimensions of these beliefs identified in the United States apply to other countries. Each country differs on per capita advertising expenditures, media mix, and the extent of advertising exposure. Data were analyzed using covariance structure analysis to determine whether the social and economic dimensions can indeed be construed as global. Multivariate tests of mean comparisons were performed to identify similarities and differences in belief perceptions.

The chapter is structured as follows. First, previous research on advertising thoughts, beliefs, and attitudes is briefly reviewed. Second, the study methodology and sample selection are discussed. Next, the results of the study are provided and discussed. The last part of the chapter examines implications and conclusions.

BACKGROUND RESEARCH ON ADVERTISING PERCEPTIONS

The majority of previous studies on advertising perceptions have investigated attitudes toward advertising. Andrews (1989) argues that this research has focused more on beliefs toward advertising vis-à-vis attitudes toward advertising. The term "perceptions of advertising" refers to cognitive responses (i.e., thoughts, beliefs, and attitudes toward advertising). As discussed by Durvasula and associates (1993), these perceptions of advertising are viewed as an integral part of models that examine advertising's effect on purchase behavior. In particular, consumers' attitude-toward-the-advertisement (A_{ad}) is considered as an important determinant of their brand attitudes and purchase intentions. One of the important determinants of attitudes-toward-the-advertisement is the attitude-toward-advertising-in-general (attitude-general) construct (MacKenzie and Lutz 1989). This construct, in turn, is determined by beliefs toward advertising in general.

In the academic literature, advertising has been viewed both positively and negatively. The supporters of advertising maintain that advertising provides information about product attributes, which is necessary for decision making. Potter (1954) contends that advertising is a facilitating mechanism in helping a society develop material prosperity. Others view advertising as essential in giving consumer sufficient and accurate information so that they are educated and informed (Sandage 1972; Sandage and Leckenby 1980). Despite the praise that has been given to the role advertising plays in assisting consumers and benefiting society (Hite and Bellizzi 1986; Holbrook 1987), other research has been critical of advertising's methods to persuade. As advertising has evolved in U.S. society, it has become more concerned with persuasion, according to Carey (1960).

Several researchers maintain that advertising is used to manipulate people (Bauer and Greyser 1968; Greyser and Reece 1971; Larkin 1977; Feldman 1980; Reid and Soley 1982; Pollay 1986) or to deceive them (Anderson et al. 1978; Barksdale et al. 1982; Durand and Lambert 1985; Muehling 1987). Others charge that advertising is offensive and disrespectful (Larkin 1977; Anderson et al. 1978; Reid and Soley 1982; Hite and Fraser 1988). Pollay (1986) and Kirkpatrick (1986) have particularly been strident in their attacks on advertising by suggesting that it creates needs and wants, insults intelligence, and exploits the vulnerabilities of consumers. Advertising is seen as a powerful force that can shape and mold a society so that products are viewed as the means to happiness and fulfillment.

To understand the complexity of advertising perceptions, several studies have focused on the dimensionality of beliefs about advertising in general. These studies identified two primary dimensions, consisting of economic aspects and social factors (Bauer and Greyser 1968; Andrews 1989). Several studies used these two dimensions in their exploration of consumer advertising perceptions (Greyser and Reece 1971; Haller 1974; Larkin 1977; Sandage and Leckenby 1980; Reid and Soley 1982; Muehling 1987; Ho and Chen 1989).

Most of these studies used respondents from the United States; hence, we do not know the extent to which these beliefs prevail in other countries. There is some evidence suggesting that other industrialized countries may share the same attitudes toward advertising. For example, Thorelli and associates (1975) found consumers in Germany and the United States had favorable beliefs toward the economic benefits of advertising, but both groups voiced negativity toward the social aspects of advertising. Similarly, Barksdale and associates (1982) found that respondents in an analysis of six developed countries expressed negative views about advertising.

Studies on developing countries also seem to show a similar pattern. For Kenya, Waruingi (1980) found that consumers acknowledged the economic and information benefits of advertising but also were critical of the some of the economic effects, such as higher prices. These consumers were also critical of the social aspects and regarded government regulation of advertising as necessary. Analyses of South Korean consumers by Ye (1986) and Thai consumers by Thorelli and Sentell (1982) found positive beliefs about advertising coexisting with negative ones, such as the belief that advertising manipulates people to buy and distorts information. For China, Ho and Chen (1989) and Semenik and associates (1986) found comparable results in that Chinese respondents were favorable to the economic aspects of advertising while being negative to some of the practices used in advertisements. Even a study in Saudi Arabia by Tuncalp (1990) found similar favorable and unfavorable attitudes toward advertising.

RESEARCH METHOD

About the Samples

This study is based on data collected from five countries, representing different regions of the world. Among them, India and Singapore are both located in Southeast Asia. Two other countries, Greece and Denmark, are part of Western Europe. New Zealand represents the South Pacific region. New Zealand has a small population of 3.7 million and can be considered developed. The country has gone through a dramatic deregulation period beginning in the mid-1980s. Advertising expenditures have increased substantially during this period. Denmark is also a small country, with about 5.3 million people. Advertising is subject to some government controls in this country. Greece, with a population of 10.5 million, has experienced significant change as the European Community injected funds into this country to encourage its development. Advertising expenditures have increased significantly over the last few years.

India occupies the major portion of the Indian subcontinent, has a population of about 1 billion people, and is classified as a developing country. Singapore is a small city-state with a population of about 3 million and is viewed as a newly industrialized country. These two countries share some similarities in social values in that people of both countries have a positive view of family, exhibit respect for elders, and do not display forthright criticism of others. There is also a sizable population of those with Indian origin in Singapore (about 6 percent). However, this country in many ways is culturally different from India, with people of Chinese origin forming a dominant majority (i.e., about 80 per-

Table 12.1
Selected Socioeconomic and Advertising Characteristics

Population and Social Indicators	New Zealand	Denmark	Greece	India	Singapore
Population (million)	3.7	5.3	10.5	976	3.5
Literacy	99	99	97	53	91
Life expectancy at birth					
males	75	73	76	62	75
females	80	78	81	63	80
Infant mortality (per 1,000 live births)	7	7	8	5	7
Economic Indicators					
GDP per capita (U.S.$)	18,765	30,223	11,420	396	25,908
Advertising Expenditures					
Advertising as a percent of GNP	1.18	.52	.70	.25	.80
Advertising expenditures per capita (U.S.$)	192	170	81	.80	223
Print expenditures per capita (U.S.$)	99	130	36	na	111
TV expenditures per capita (U.S.$)	67	32	39	na	91
Radio expenditures per capita (U.S.$)	23	3	4	na	13

Sources: European Marketing Data 1999; International Marketing Data 1999; World Bank's World Development Indicator 1999.

cent). Given its strong tourism base and an open economy, Singapore has modern international retailing and other marketing institutions, making this country a truly global or international city, while India represents primarily a traditional, domestic marketing environment with considerable isolation from international markets. The change orientation in these two countries is equally different with Singapore, as a high-growth economy, being more dynamic than India, where changes take place at a much slower pace.

Table 12.1 features socioeconomic and advertising characteristics of the countries in the study (*European Marketing Data 1999; International Marketing Data 1999; World Bank's World Development Indicator 1999*). There is a significant difference among the countries in terms of advertising expenditures. For example, the ad expenditure in India is $0.80 per capita and represents .25 percent of the gross national product (GNP). At the other extreme is Singapore, which spends $223 per capita (.80 of GNP) and New Zealand, which spends $192 per capita, representing 1.18 of the GNP. The differences are even more revealing when examining the per capita print and television ad expenditures. Print expenditures are only $36 per capita in Greece, compared to substantially higher levels in the other countries.

Across the five countries, the samples consisted of young adults, all having educational background in business administration. Since much of the research about advertising beliefs used young adults, for comparative purposes we also employed similar samples. The average age was close to 21 and the samples were divided evenly by sex. A total of 179 subjects in New Zealand, 86 subjects in Denmark, 89 subjects each in Greece and India, and 299 subjects in Singapore participated in the study.

When studying cross-national consumer perceptions, it is crucial to use comparable samples. It has been suggested that sample comparability can be achieved by matching the samples on certain characteristics of interest (Douglas and Craig 1983; Irvine and Carroll 1980; Sekaran 1983). In this study, even though the five samples are not representative of their countries' populations, they are relatively more homogeneous in a matched-sample sense with respect to age, sex, English language usage, and educational background. Hence, these samples can be considered as comparable and therefore appropriate for making cross-national comparisons.

About the Measures and Questionnaire Administration

Beliefs toward advertising in general were measured with seven seven-point Likert type (i.e., agree/disagree) statements (cf. Bauer and Greyser 1968). They include four statements measuring the economic aspects (i.e., "advertising is essential"; "in general, advertising results in lower prices"; "advertising helps raise our standard of living"; "advertising results in better products for the public") and three statements measuring the social aspects of advertising (i.e., "most advertising insults the intelligence of the average consumer"; "advertising often persuades people to buy things they shouldn't buy"; "in general, advertisements present a true picture of the product being measured").

The subjects in India and Singapore were fluent in communicating in English. Hence, together with the subjects in New Zealand, these subjects received the questionnaire in English. In Greece and Denmark, the questionnaire was administered in Greek and Danish, respectively, after translating the English version of the questionnaire into those local languages. To ensure equivalency between the foreign language versions, standard questionnaire translation procedures were followed. Bilingual experts assisted in these procedures.

RESULTS

The global dimensionality of the advertising belief measures was assessed first using covariance structure analysis of the data. To establish support for the economic and social dimensions of advertising beliefs, it is necessary to show that the scales measuring those two dimensions exhibit measurement invariance, internal consistency, and discriminant validity. For this purpose, several multiple-group analyses were performed and their results examined.

Configural (or Factor Structure) Invariance

As assumed in several research studies (cf. Aaker and Myers 1982; Andrews 1989; Bauer and Greyser 1968), the hypothesized model is one where the economic and social aspects dimensions are assumed to be separate, yet correlated. The minimum requirement for this two-dimensional scale to be invariant cross-nationally is to show that it provides a good fit across the countries. That is, items of the scale must exhibit significant non-zero loadings on salient factors and zero loadings on non-salient factors (Horn and McArdle 1992). For example, a four-item scale measured beliefs toward economic aspects of advertising. These four items must have significant and non-zero loadings on the economic aspects dimension. Similarly, the three items measuring beliefs toward the social aspects of advertising must exhibit non-zero loadings on that factor but zero loadings on the economic aspects factor. If the fit of this model, based on confirmatory factor analysis results, is acceptable, then the beliefs toward advertising in general measure have the same factor structure cross-nationally, and it has configural invariance.

As shown in Table 12.2, when the factor structure is assumed to be similar cross-nationally (i.e., configural invariance), the hypothesized model has a χ^2 value of 133.80 (65 df.). Since χ^2 is affected by sample size, some researchers suggest that other fit indices also be examined (Marsh 1994). For this purpose, four other fit indices, the goodness-of-fit index (GFI), comparative fit index (CFI), root-mean-square error of approximation (RMSEA), and the χ^2/df ratio are obtained, as they have been widely used to evaluate measurement scales in cross-national research (cf. Durvasula et al. 1993; Steenkamp and Baumgartner 1998). For adequate fit, high GFI values, CFI values in the high .80 range and above, χ^2/df ratio of 3 or less, and RMSEA of .10 or less are desired (Browne and Cudeck 1993; Hu and Bentler 1995; Netemeyer et al. 1991). Both GFI and CFI are .80 or above for the hypothesized model under the assumption of configural invariance. These fit indices, along with a low RMSEA of .80 and a χ^2/df ratio of 2.06, are all in the acceptable range.

Table 12.3 provides factor loadings for the hypothesized model under the assumption of configural invariance. Out of a total of 35 loading estimates across the five countries, 91.5 percent (i.e., 32) are statistically significant. Further, a high percent of the loadings (77%) is sizable in magnitude (above .3). These

Table 12.2
Multiple-Group Analysis of the Hypothesized Model of Advertising Beliefs

	Configural Invariance	Metric Invariance	Factor Covariance Invariance	Error Variance Invariance
χ^2	133.80	168.38	169.68	173.45
df	65	93	97	125
GFI	.96	.95	.95	.95
CFI	.80	.79	.79	.86
RMSEA	.08	.07	.07	.05
χ^2/df	2.06	1.81	1.75	1.39

Note: The configural invariance model assumes similar factor structure across the five samples, but the loadings, factor covariances, and error terms are freely estimated. The metric invariance model constrains the factor loadings to be invariant across the samples. The factor covariance invariance model constrains both factor loadings and factor covarience to be invariant. The error variance invariance model is the most restrictive, constraining the loadings, factor covariance, and error variances to be invariant across the countries.

various fit indices and factor loading estimates provide support for the configural invariance assumption, implying that the hypothesized two-factor correlated model fits the data well across the five countries.

Tests for discriminant validity are performed next on the hypothesized model. For this purpose, the ϕ estimates (i.e., correlation between the social aspects dimension and economic aspects dimension) are reported in Table 12.3. These ϕ estimates range from .37 in India to .82 in Denmark. All of these correlations are statistically significant and none of them in unity. However, when confidence intervals are computed around these correlations, only the confidence interval around the correlation of .37 in the Indian sample does not contain a value of 1. This means cross-cultural support for the discriminant validity of the two dimensions of advertising beliefs does not exist (cf. Fornell and Larcker 1981).

Based on various analyses performed so far, it can be concluded that the hypothesized model fits the data well cross-nationally, with a high percent of significant and non-zero factor loadings on salient factors and zero loadings on non-salient factors. Discriminant validity tests, however, provide mixed results. Not all confidence intervals around economic aspects and social aspects correlation are below unity. Hence, configural invariance or cross-national similarity of factor structure for advertising beliefs is not fully supported.

Metric Invariance

Whereas configural invariance indicates that the factor structure is similar across the countries, it does not imply that consumers in those countries respond

Table 12.3
Factor Loadings

	New Zealand (N = 179)	Denmark (N = 86)	Greece (N = 89)	India (N = 89)	Singapore (N = 299)
Social Dimension					
Insults intelligence	.36	.49	.51	.67	.15
Often persuades	.07 ns	.45	.33	.55	.08 ns
Presents true picture	.46	.34	.39	.10 ns	.58
Economic Dimension					
Advertising is essential	.40	.37	.51	.25	.24
Results in lower prices	.51	.38	.18 ns	.43	.24
Raises standard of living	.63	.66	.68	.50	.56
Results in better products	.62	.48	.37	.61	.69
Correlation between the social and economic dimensions	.63	.82	.75	.37	.68

Note: All of the factor loadings are significant at $\alpha = .05$ level unless stated otherwise as ns (not significant).

to the items in the same way. A stronger test for measurement invariance is to show that the scale has metric invariance. If an individual scale item exhibits metric invariance, then it has similar scale intervals across countries. As a consequence, difference scores on the item can be meaningfully compared across the countries. If the entire scale, consisting of various items, is metrically invariant, then cross-national difference scores on the scale indicate corresponding cross-national difference on the underlying construct (cf. Rock et al. 1978; Steenkamp and Baumgartner 1998). Metric invariance can be established by showing that factor loadings of the scale items are invariant (or similar) cross-nationally.

Table 12.2 shows the fit indices of the hypothesized model when constraining the factor loadings to be invariant (or similar) across the four samples. The χ^2 fit statistic for this metric invariance model is 168.38 (93 df.). The χ^2 difference in fit between this model and the configural invariance model is 34.58 (28 df., $p < .05$). This test shows better support for the configurance model. However, given the sensitivity of χ^2 to sample size, other fit indices should also be examined. Among the alternative fit indices, the GFI, RMSEA, and χ^2/df ratio are all in the acceptable range and provide support for the metric invariance model as well. The CFI value, while less than .80, is not very much different from the CFI value of the configural invariance model. Hence, it is assumed that the more restrictive metric invariance model fits the data equally well; the factor loadings can be considered as invariant cross-nationally.

Factor Covariance Invariance

The factor covariance invariance model is more parsimonious than the metric invariance model, because it assumes that the covariance between beliefs toward economic aspects factor and beliefs toward social aspects factor is invariant across the countries. The χ^2 fit of this model is 169.68 (97 df.). The fit of this model is not significantly different from the metric invariance model (χ^2 difference = 1.30, 4 df., p > .05), implying that even factor covariance is the same across the five countries.

Error Variance Invariance

For a measurement scale to be equally reliable across the countries, it must be shown that factor loadings, factor covariances, and error variances are all invariant or similar across the countries. The error variance invariance model is based on this assumption. The χ^2 fit of the error variance invariance model, where factor loadings, factor covariance, and error variances are assumed to be the same across the countries, is 173.45 (125 df.). This fit is not significantly different from the fit of the factor covariance invariance model (χ^2 difference = 3.77, 28 df., p > .05). High GFI and CFI values (.95 and .86, respectively), coupled with low RMSEA and χ^2/df ratio values (.05 and 1.39, respectively), also provide support for the error variance invariance model.

In sum, results of various multiple group analysis suggest the hypothesized two-factor correlated model of beliefs toward advertising in general has marginal support for configural invariance, metric invariance, factor covariance invariance, and error variance invariance. Establishment of metric invariance is the minimum condition necessary for making practical mean comparisons on the scale cross-nationally.

Internal Consistency

To assess internal consistency of the two advertising belief dimensions, composite reliability estimates were computed from the confirmatory factor analysis output. These estimates are considered to be analogous to coefficient alpha (Fornell and Larcker 1981). A reliability estimate of .7 is regarded as the minimum necessary value for acceptable scale reliability. Across the five samples, these reliability estimates are all below the acceptable level for both the economic aspects factor and the social aspects factor.

Given the low reliability values and the lack of discriminant validity for the two advertising belief dimensions, there is only a marginal support for the hypothesized two-factor correlated model. Consequently, support for global di-

Table 12.4

Mean Comparisons of Advertising Belief Items: MANOVA Results

	New Zealand a	Denmark b	Greece c	India d	Singapore e	F	p-value
Social Dimension							
Insults intelligence	4.58 bde	3.82 ac	4.84 bde	4.01 ac	3.53 ac	19.23	.00
Often persuades	5.19 de	5.02 cd	5.97 abde	3.81 abc	4.72 ac	17.16	.00
Presents true picture	3.06 cd	3.29 d	3.66 ad	4.56 abce	3.14 d	16.23	.00
Economic Dimension							
Advertising is essential	5.29 de	5.37 de	5.35 de	6.30 abc	5.87 abc	13.76	.00
Results in lower prices	3.29 ce	2.78	2.39 ad	3.19 ce	2.38 ad	11.26	.00
Raises standard of living	4.17 b	3.07 acde	4.74 bd	3.87 bc	4.26 b	14.60	.00
Results in better products	4.14 c	3.67 cde	5.27 abde	4.51 bc	4.27 bc	13.66	.00

Note: Mean values are presented on a 7-point scale where 1 = strongly disagree and 7 = strongly agree. The mean score for "Raises standard of living" is 3.07 for Denmark (country b). This mean is significantly different ($p < .05$) from the means of New Zealand (a), Greece (c), India (d), and Singapore (e).

mensionality of advertising beliefs does not exist. Therefore, the seven statements measuring beliefs toward advertising in general are treated separately when examining mean differences across the countries.

Cross-National Differences in Beliefs toward Advertising in General

Since the economic and social aspects factors have not exhibited acceptable measurement properties, sum scores for the two factors are not computed. Instead, items representing the two factors are treated separately and the differences in responses to those items are examined cross-nationally. Table 12.4 shows the mean differences across the five samples. Since the seven belief statements are theoretically correlated, a multivariate analysis of variance is performed first to find out whether the vector of means representing the seven belief statements is significantly different across the five countries. As shown in Table 12.4, a low Wilk's Λ (.589) and a high F-value (14.924) imply that the mean vector is indeed significantly different across the five countries ($p < .00$).

Next, results of several univariate analyses of variance show that all seven belief statements exhibit significant mean differences across the samples ($p < .00$). Further, Table 12.4 also shows the results of Bonferroni multiple comparison tests that determine, for each belief statement, which countries have sig-

Figure 12.1
Percent Agreed with Social Dimension Statements

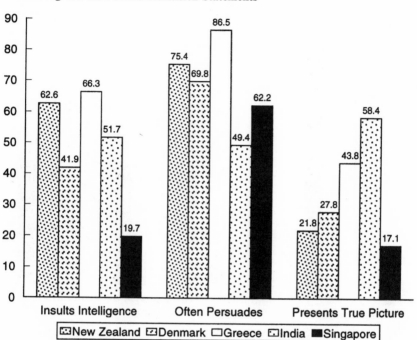

nificantly different mean values. These tests are considered to be very conservative, and they adjust p-values for the inflated type I error when making several pair-wise mean comparisons.

The mean responses presented in Table 12.4 can be interpreted on a seven-point scale where, for any belief statement, a value of "1" indicates strong disagreement with that statement, a value of "7" indicates strong agreement, and a value of "4" indicates neutral response. Based on this, it is clear that across the five samples, people on average agree that advertising is essential while disagreeing that advertising results in lower prices. For the other belief statements, the mean responses show some variation across the countries, with the values being neither consistently high nor consistently low. Moreover, some of these pair-wise differences are also statistically significant. Table 12.4 clearly shows statistically significant differences among the countries.

To get a better perspective of these differences, the responses labeled "somewhat agree," "agree," and "strongly agree" with values 5, 6, and 7, respectively, are recoded as "agree." The percent of subjects providing positive response to any belief statement by agreeing to that statement is then computed. Across the five samples, the agreement percentages are plotted on a bar chart. Figure 12.1 shows the agreement percentages for beliefs toward the social aspects, and

Figure 12.2
Percent Agreed with Economic Dimension Statements

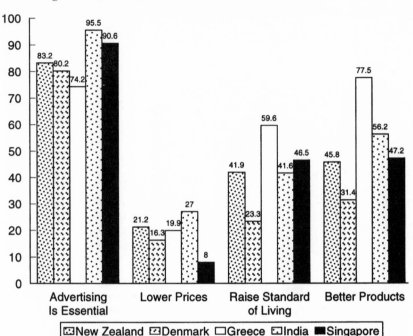

Figure 12.2 shows those percentages for beliefs toward the economic aspects of advertising. These two figures can be viewed together with Table 12.4 for a better interpretation of the results.

Figure 12.1 reveals that while a high percentage of subjects in New Zealand, Greece, and India feel that advertising insults intelligence, there is a lower percentage of agreement by those in Denmark and Singapore. One of the objectives of advertising is to persuade people to buy the advertiser's product. In general, subjects across the countries agreed in response to this statement, especially those in Greece. While the Indian subjects feel that advertising presents a true picture of the advertised products, the majority in the other countries do not agree with that statement. In sum, across the countries, subjects in general do not have positive opinions about the social aspects of advertising. These results parallel findings reported in other studies as discussed in the "Background Research" section.

Examining Figure 12.2 on the economic dimensions, we find that subjects across the five samples agree that advertising is essential and disagree that it leads to lower prices. The Greek subjects have a relatively more favorable opinion about the economic aspects of advertising; they agree with three of the four statements, whereas the Danish subjects have the exact opposite opinion. In general, even in the other countries, the majority of subjects do not consider the economic impact of advertising to be so favorable, despite having mean scores above 4. The great variation among countries also indicates the diversity in beliefs about advertising.

DISCUSSION

The results provide a useful perspective on the beliefs toward advertising in a cross-cultural context. Understanding consumers' advertising beliefs is considered important because these perceptions eventually influence brand attitudes and purchase intentions via their impact on attitude-toward-the-advertisement. For advertising practitioners a better awareness of what consumers believe about advertising will help them design better advertising campaigns. Nationally, if advertising beliefs vary among different consumer groups, then a separate ad campaign may be warranted for each market segment. Cross-nationally, an assessment of the similarities and differences in consumer ad beliefs would place researchers in a better position to decide whether to run standardized or customized ad campaigns across various countries. Given the usefulness of this stream of research, our study examined whether consumers in five different countries (that have both commonalities and differences in culture, social values, economic orientations, and ad expenditures) share beliefs about advertising. As such, our work extends previous cross-national studies in this area.

A sample of 742 young adults in five countries that represent Asia, the South Pacific, and Europe responded to the inventory by Bauer and Greyser (1968) concerning beliefs toward advertising in general. Following the accepted procedures in cross-national research (cf. Durvasula et al. 1993; Steenkamp and Baumgartner 1998), data were analyzed at the multiple group level using covariance structure analysis. Results indicate that the hypothesized model that assumes the presence of two correlated dimensions of advertising beliefs, economic aspects and social aspects, fit the data well and also exhibited invariance of factor loadings, factor covariance, and error variances across the five countries. However, the two advertising belief dimensions do not possess discriminant validity and acceptable reliability estimates. Hence, for the sample of young adults, this study does not support the view that the economic aspects and social aspects of advertising exist as separate dimensions globally. Some of the studies in the past did not report reliability of the dimensions, thus making any comparisons difficult. However, those studies, in contrast to the present study, suggest the existence of two separate advertising belief dimensions (cf. Andrews 1989; Darley and Johnson 1994).

Among the five countries, the results of mean comparisons demonstrate noteworthy differences and similarities. Overall and across the five countries, young adults feel that advertising is essential. They also agree that advertising often persuades people to buy the advertiser's product. This result is not surprising, given that persuasion is one of the goals of advertising. Subjects in general disagree that advertising results in lower prices, suggesting that they view advertising as an expense that is added to the price of a product. In four of the countries, respondents also believe that advertising results in better products. However, subjects in New Zealand, Greece, and India believe that advertising insults consumers' intelligence. It is likely that advertisements in these countries may feature simplistic and naïve arguments in their selling propositions.

When examining responses to the economic aspects of advertising, there are two noteworthy findings. First, subjects in Denmark disagree with three of the four statements ("lower prices," "raises standard of living," and "results in better products"). In contrast, subjects in Greece express agreement with three of the four statements ("advertising is essential," "raises standard of living," and "results in better products"). These results indicate that there is not a common perception of advertising among EC countries. Further research is needed to explore this notion, especially if Pan-European advertising is to be used.

The results also indicate that a high percent of Singaporeans do not think that advertising insults consumer intelligence, but they also do not feel that advertising presents a true picture of the advertised products. This is in sharp contrast to Indians, who have opposite views. Further research is needed to explore this finding. It is possible that ads in Singapore feature clever, persuasive appeals that are not factual but are entertaining and not insulting to one's intelligence. In India, ads may be trivial (and therefore not mentally challenging) but factual. Nonetheless, young adults in general feel that advertising insults a consumer's intelligence. This finding is consistent with conclusions reached by previous research in this area (cf. Pollay 1986).

An interesting question is whether our study supports those who advocate standardization in advertising and use of common campaigns across countries. This issue is particularly relevant to the two pairs of countries, India and Singapore and Greece and Denmark, as the economic cooperation between them is increasing. With Singaporean companies marketing products in India, and Indian firms encouraged to do the same in Singapore, is it possible for these companies to use the same ad campaigns in the two countries? While some results of this study (e.g., similar beliefs and generally favorable advertising attitudes between India and Singapore) provide support for standardization in advertising, other results show differences, suggesting that attempts to develop standardized cross-national ad campaigns must take place cautiously. Similarly, given the interdependence between Greece and Denmark resulting from European Community membership, it is wise to consider localized campaigns in view of the disparity in advertising beliefs in those two countries.

The rapid industrialization, change orientation, and Western economic practices may have contributed to the type of ad beliefs of Singaporeans. In contrast, subjects in a 1973 study (Mehta 1973) conducted in Western India had almost similar advertising perceptions as found for the Indian subjects in this study, implying that two decades of economic development efforts do not seem to have brought any significant changes in advertising perceptions of Indians, particularly in advertising beliefs.

The results have other implications regarding recruiting young adults for advertising positions. To the extent that these young adults are cynical or negative about the advertising industry, this may carry over to their career decisions. Andrews and associates (1991) explore this issue in greater depth and suggest methods to deal with these cynical attitudes, such as consciousness raising about the benefits of advertising.

Future research needs to answer other important questions. Is the lack of support for the two-factor model of economic dimensions and social factors of advertising beliefs universal or limited to young adults? Do these two dimensions for advertising beliefs exist for samples with other demographic and socioeconomic profiles? Or are there other models with other dimensions that are superior in describing beliefs? Do other European countries hold similar advertising beliefs as noted for Greece and Denmark? How do these beliefs affect consumers' attitudes toward ads they see? Are consumers likely to "turn off" to ads they see due to their overall negative beliefs about ads? How can ads be developed so that consumers are not likely to be cynical? These are only a few of the issues that this research has exposed. In sum, by systematically comparing advertising beliefs from five very different nations, this study contributes to a better understanding of cross-national consumer advertising perceptions.

REFERENCES

Aaker, D. A. and J. G. Myers (1982). *Advertising Management*, 2nd ed. Englewood Cliffs, NJ: Prentice-Hall.

Anderson, R., J. Engledow, and H. Becker (1978). "How *Consumer Reports* Subscribers See Advertising." *Journal of Advertising Research*, 18 (December): 29–34.

Andrews, Craig (1989). "The Dimensionality of Beliefs toward Advertising in General." *Journal of Advertising*, 18(1): 26–35.

Andrews, Craig, Srinivas Durvasula, and Richard Netemeyer (1994). "Testing the Cross-National Applicability of U.S. and Russian Advertising Beliefs and Attitude Measures." *Journal of Advertising*, 21(1): 71–82.

Andrews, Craig, Steven Lysonski, and Srinivas Durvasula (1991). "Understanding Cross-Cultural Student Perceptions of Advertising in General: Implications for Advertising Educators and Practitioners." *Journal of Advertising*, 20(2): 15–28.

Barksdale, H., W. Perreault, J. Arndt, J. Bamhill, W. French, M. Halliday, and J. Zif (1982). "A Cross-National Survey of Consumer Attitudes towards Marketing Practices: Consumerism and Government Regulations." *Columbia Journal of World Business*, 17 (Summer): 71–86.

Bauer, R. and S. Greyser (1968). *Advertising in America: The Consumer View*. Boston: Harvard University, Graduate School of Business Administration, Division of Research.

Biehal, Gabriel, Debra Stephens, and Eleonora Curlo (1992). "Attitude toward the Ad and Brand Choice." *Journal of Advertising*, 21(3): 19–36.

Browne, M. W. and R. Cudeck (1993). "Alternative Ways of Assessing Model Fit." In K. A. Bollen and J. S. Long (eds.), *Testing Structural Equation Models*. Newbury Park, CA: Sage Publications, pp. 136–162.

Carey, J. (1960). "Advertising: An Institutional Approach." In C. H. Sandage and V. Fryburger (eds.), *The Role of Advertising: A Book of Readings*. Homewood, IL: Richard D. Irwin.

Darley, W. and D. Johnson (1994). "An Exploratory Investigation of the Dimensions of Beliefs toward Advertising in General: A Comparative Analysis of Four Developing Countries." *Journal of International Consumer Marketing*, 7(1): 5–21.

Douglas, S. and C. S. Craig (1983). *International Marketing Research*. Englewood Cliffs, NJ: Prentice-Hall.

Dubinsky, A. and P. Hensel (1984). "Marketing Student Attitudes toward Advertising: Implications for Marketing Education." *Journal of Marketing Education*, 6 (Summer): 22–26.

Durand, R. and Z. Lambert (1985). "Alienation and Criticisms of Advertising." *Journal of Advertising*, 14(3): 9–16.

Durvasula, Srinivas, Craig Andrews, Steven Lysonski, and Richard Netemeyer (1993). "Assessing the Cross-National Applicability of Consumer Behavior Models: A Model of Attitude toward Advertising in General." *Journal of Consumer Research*, 19(4): 626–636.

European Marketing Data 1999. London: Euromonitor.

Feldman, L. (1980). *Consumer Protection: Problems and Prospects*. New York: West Publishing Company.

Fornell, Claes and D. Larcker (1981). "Evaluating Structural Equation Models with Unobservable Variables and Measurement Error." *Journal of Marketing Research*, 18 (February): 39–50.

Fullerton, R. A. and T. R. Nevett (1986). "Advertising and Society: A Comparative Analysis of the Roots of Distrust in Germany and Great Britain." *International Journal of Advertising*, 5(3): 225–241.

Green, R. T., W. H. Cunningham, and I. C. Cunningham (1975). "The Effectiveness of Standardized Global Advertising." *Journal of Advertising* (Summer): 25–30.

Greyser, S. and B. Reece (1971). "Businessmen Look Hard at Advertising." *Harvard Business Review*, 49 (May/June): 18–26, 157–166.

Grier, Sonya and Anne Brumbaugh (1999). "Noticing Cultural Differences: Ad Meanings Created by Target and Non-Target Markets." *Journal of Advertising*, 28(1): 79–93.

Haller, T. (1974). "What Students Think of Advertising." *Journal of Advertising Research*, 14 (February): 33–38.

Hite, R. and J. Bellizzi (1986). "Consumers' Attitudes toward Accountants, Lawyers, and Physicians with Respect to Advertising Professional Services." *Journal of Advertising Research*, 26 (June/July): 45–54.

Hite, R. and C. Fraser (1988). "Meta-Analysis of Attitudes toward Advertising by Professionals." *Journal of Marketing*, 52 (July): 95–103.

Ho, S. and C. Chen (1989). "Advertising in China—Problems and Prospects." *International Journal of Advertising*, 8: 79–87.

Holbrook, M. (1987). "Mirror, Minor, on the Wall, What's Unfair in the Reflection on Advertising?" *Journal of Marketing*, 51 (July): 95–103.

Horn, John L. and J. Jack McArdle (1992). "A Practical and Theoretical Guide to Measurement Invariance in Aging Research." *Experimental Aging Research*, 18 (Fall–Winter): 117–144.

Hu, Li-tze and P. M. Bentler (1995). "Evaluating Model Fit." In R. Hoyle (ed.), *Structural Equation Modeling Concepts, Issues, and Applications*. Thousand Oaks, CA: Sage Publications, pp. 76–99.

International Marketing Data 1999. London: Euromonitor.

Irvine, S. H. and W. K. Carroll (1980). "Testing and Assessment across Cultures: Issues in Methodology and Theory." In Harry C. Triandis and John W. Berry, eds., *The Handbook of Cross-Cultural Psychology*, Vol. 2. Boston. Allyn & Bacon, pp. 127–180.

Kirkpatrick, J. (1986). "A Philosophic Defense of Advertising." *Journal of Advertising*, 15(2): 42–48, 64.

Larkin, E. (1977). "A Factor Analysis of College Student Attitudes toward Advertising." *Journal of Advertising*, 6(2): 42–46.

Levitt, T. (1983). "The Globalization of Markets." *Harvard Business Review*, 61 (May–June): 92–102.

Lysonski, Steven and Richard Pollay (1990). "Advertising Sexism Is Forgiven, But Not Forgotten: Historical and Cross-Cultural Differences in Criticism and Purchase Boycott Intentions." *International Journal of Advertising*, 9(4): 319–331.

MacKenzie, S. B. and Richard Lutz (1989). "An Empirical Examination of the Structural Antecedents of Attitude-Toward-the-Ad in an Advertising Pretesting Context." *Journal of Marketing* 53(2): 48–65.

Marsh, H. W. (1994). "Confirmatory Factor Analysis Models of Factorial Invariance: A Multifaceted Approach." *Journal of Structural Equation Modeling*, 1(1): 5–34.

Mehta, S. C. (1973). "The Consumers' View of Marketing in India." *Indian Management*, 12(9) (September): 37–42.

Muehling, D. D. (1987). "An Investigation of Factors Underlying Attitudes toward Advertising in General." *Journal of Advertising*, 16(1): 32–40.

Netemeyer, R., S., Durvasula, and D. R. Lichtenstein (1991). "A Cross-National Assessment of the Reliability and Validity of the CETSCALE." *Journal of Marketing Research*, 28 (August): 320–327.

O'Donohue, Stephanie (1995). "Attitudes to Advertising: A Review of British and American Research." *International Journal of Advertising*, 14(3): 245–262.

Pollay, R. (1986). "The Distorted Mirror: Reflections on the Unintended Consequences of Advertising." *Journal of Marketing*, 50 (April): 18–36.

Potter, D. (1954). *People of Plenty*. Chicago: University of Chicago Press.

Reid, L. and L. Soley (1982). "Generalized and Personalized Attitudes toward Advertising's Social and Economic Effects." *Journal of Advertising*, 11(3): 3–7.

Rock, Donald, A., Charles E. Werts, and Ronald L. Flaugher (1978). "The Use of Analysis of Covariance Structures for Comparing the Psychometric Properties of Multiple Variables across Populations." *Multivariate Behavioral Research*, 13 (October): 403–418.

Rustogi, Hemant, Paul Hensel, and Willem Burgers (1996). "The Link between Personal Values and Advertising Appeals: Cross-Cultural Barriers to Standardized Global Advertising." *Journal of Euromarketing*, 5(4): 57–79.

Safran, Al-Makaty, Norman van Tubergen, Scott Whitlow, and Douglas Boyd (1996). "Attitudes toward Advertising in Islam." *Journal of Advertising Research*, 36(3): 16–29.

Sandage, C. (1972). "Some Institutional Aspects of Advertising." *Journal of Advertising*, 1(1): 9.

Sandage, C. H. and J. D. Leckenby (1980). "Student Attitudes toward Advertising: Institutions vs. Instruments." *Journal of Advertising*, 9(2): 29.

Sekaran, Uma (1983). "Methodological and Theoretical Issues and Advancements in Cross-Cultural Research." *Journal of International Business Studies*, 14 (Fall): 61–73.

Semenik, R., N. Zhou, and W. Moore (1986). "Chinese Managers' Attitudes toward Advertising in China." *Journal of Advertising*, 15(4): 56–62.

Shavitt, Sharon, Pamela Lowrey, and James Haefner (1998). "Public Attitudes toward Advertising: More Favorable Than You Might Think." *Journal of Advertising Research*, 38(4): 7–22.

Steenkamp Jan-Benedict, E. M. and Hans Baumgartner (1998). "Assessing Measurement Invariance in Cross-National Consumer Research." *Journal of Consumer Research*, 25 (June): 78–90.

Thorelli, H., H. Becker, and J. Engledow (1975). *The Information Seekers: An International Study of Consumer Information and Advertising Image*. Cambridge, MA: Ballinger Publishing Co.

Thorelli, H. and G. Sentell (1982). *Consumer Emancipation and Economic Development: The Case of Thailand*. Greenwich, CT: JAI Press.

Tuncalp, S. (1990). "Attitudes towards Advertising among Executives in Saudi Arabia." *International Journal of Advertising*, 9(3): 219–231.

Waruingi, C. (1980). *The Consumer and the Marketing System in a Developing Country: Kenya*. Unpublished Doctoral dissertation, Indiana University.

Wills, J. and J. Ryans (1982). "Attitudes toward Advertising: A Multinational Study." *Journal of International Business Studies*, 13 (Winter): 121–129.

Witkowski, Terrence and Joachim Kellner (1998). "Convergent, Contrasting, and Country-Specific Attitudes toward Television Advertising in Germany and the United States." *Journal of Business Research*, 42(2): 167–174.

World Bank's World Development Indicator 1999. London: Euromonitor.

Ye, J. (1986). *The Experience, Attitude and Behavior of Consumers as Actors in the Marketplace: The Case of South Korean Consumers*. Unpublished Doctoral dissertation, Indiana University.

Zhang, Yong and Betsey Gelb (1996). "Matching Advertising Appeals to Culture: The Influence Products' Use Conditions." *Journal of Advertising*, 25(3): 29–46.

Zhariullah, Durriya and Zahid Zhariullah (1999). "Relationships between Acculturation, Attitude toward the Advertisement, and Purchase Intension of Asian-Indian Immigrants." *International Journal of Commerce and Management*, 9(3–4): 46–65.

Part V

Sectoral Management Issues

Chapter 13

Globalization and Its Effects on Strategies for Small and Medium-Sized Businesses

R. K. Asundi

GLOBALIZATION

The 1990s are characterized by dramatic global developments that change the nature of international business as well as domestic business. These dramatic developments include the political and economic changes in Eastern Europe and Russia, which in turn have led to opening the doors of a wide variety of business activities. Multinational enterprises are moving into these areas to take advantage of new opportunities. Japan is becoming an economic power in the Asia Pacific region. Europe is moving toward economic integration, leading to a united European Community (EC). A recent major development is the extension of the free trade agreement from the United States and Canada to Mexico, resulting in what is known as NAFTA, the North American Free Trade Agreement. In the new century, regrouped major economic markets that would include North America, Europe, and Asia Pacific may emerge. Other markets outside these regions will also develop new alliances and emerge as major economic markets.

Revolution in information technology and advances in transportation are leading to a globally integrated business system. In such a system, knowledge, skilled people, goods, and services become extremely mobile. Producers of goods and services often compete both domestically and internationally. Thus small businesses and service sectors, which were considered traditionally by economists as "non-trade" sectors, have to become involved in international business and competition. The large multinational corporations (MNCs) rely on small businesses for goods and services and thus affect their success based on performance at the levels of international standards. While large multinational enterprises (MNEs) dominate world trade, small and medium-sized enterprises (SMEs) now account for a growing amount of world trade also.

The increasing world trade, which as of 1992 as reported in the *Directory of Trade Statistics* (1993) of the international Monetary Fund stood at $3,687 billions of exports and $3,846 billions of imports involving goods and services, can be used as a good indicator of globalization of markets. The major trading units contributing to this world trade are the European Community (exports $1,458 billion; imports $1,524 billion), Asia, including Japan (exports $916 billion; imports $850 billion), and North America (exports $623 billion; imports $744 billion). In addition to international trade involving exporting and importing, international business activities include foreign direct investment, licensing, and joint ventures.

Trade activities help one to understand MNE practices and strategies. They also help one to understand the impact of international business on the economy. Research indicates that exporting and international business activity are critical to the success of a country's economy by opening additional markets. If employment is growing at a faster rate than the export sector, then a country must either emphasize exports and create more jobs or find employment for people in faster-growing domestic industries (Mandel and Bernstein 1990). Imports on the other hand affect those seeking jobs in industries relating to this sector, who will find work scarcer and wages lower. Jobs lost by the importing sector of an economy need to be filled by the exporting sector.

A second international business activity as a result of globalization is the growing foreign direct investment (FDI, or equity funds invested in other nations). These investments range from industrialized nations to less developed countries (LDCs) and newly industrialized countries (Hong Kong, Korea, and Singapore). Most of the world FDI is in the United States, EC, and Japan. The European Community (EC) or Common Market was founded in 1957. Its initial members were Belgium, Germany, Italy, France, Luxembourg, and the Netherlands. Since then Denmark, Ireland, the United Kingdom, Greece, Portugal, and Spain have joined. Foreign holdings in the United States by 1990 amounted to about $1.5 trillion, while the U.S. holdings abroad totaled about $1.2 trillion. In 1992 alone the FDI in the United States was $420 billion and FDI by the United States was $487 billion (U.S. Department of Commerce, *Survey of Current Business*, July 1993). As nations become more affluent they have pursued foreign direct investments in geographic areas that have economic growth potential.

THE GLOBAL DEVELOPMENT CHALLENGE

To become strong in markets conditioned by recent global developments, nations must excel in three areas. They must:

1. maintain economic competitiveness;
2. influence trade regulations and advance reciprocity in trade; and
3. encourage business enterprises to develop a global orientation.

Economic competitiveness requires quality products and ability to develop unique capabilities in certain areas (such as Italy's leather goods and ceramic tiles, Germany's printing press industry, U.S. mainframe computers, and the like. In the service areas, specialty retailing in Britain, design services in Italy, and fast-food services of the United States).

Economic competitiveness is in a continual state of flux whose determinants are generally believed to be labor costs, interest rates, exchange rates, and economies of scale. However, this view fails to take into consideration the true sources of international competitive advantage (Porter 1990).

The best way for companies to achieve competitive advantage is with innovation. To maintain this competitive advantage, firms have to make their past innovations obsolete by developing new products to replace old ones. Ability to innovate rests in four broad attributes: factor conditions, demand conditions, related and supporting industries, and the environment in which firms compete. These attributes individually determine national competitive advantage (Porter 1990).

The premise of international trade theory is that a nation will export those goods that make most use of the factor conditions with which it is relatively well endowed. The factor conditions are land, labor, and capital. Export of labor-intensive goods by a country with an uneducated workforce and sophisticated finished goods by a country that has a highly educated labor force are examples of the impact of distinctive factor conditions that other countries may find hard to match. Nations at times have developed factor conditions they need through innovative approaches (by Italy, technologically advanced minimills that use less energy and modest capital and locate close to sources of scrap and end-use customers, with efficiency at small scale).

To be innovative a company needs to have access to people with necessary skills (factor conditions), domestic competition that creates pressure to innovate (rivalry), customers who want a better or less expensive product (demand conditions), and suppliers who can supply low-cost materials (supporting industry). Further, a firm needs to find ways to solve the problem through innovation rather than look for an easy way around a disadvantage (firm strategy).

A strong local demand for its goods and services strengthens a nation's competitive advantage. Local demand helps the seller to understand buyer wants and also helps to monitor need for changes in the product, based on customers' signals of desires. Related and supporting industries that are internationally competitive act as low-cost suppliers and adjust to changing conditions that help producers maintain their competitive position and thus add to the national competitive advantage.

The structure of the firms and a rivalry that is distinctive to an industry and is congruent with its nation's culture and characteristics provide yet another dimension of national advantage. Small and medium-sized firms managed like extended families (Italy's lighting, furniture, footwear industries), hierarchical organizations emphasizing technical and engineering content and a disciplined management structure (Germany's optics, machinery industries), and organizations with unusual cooperation across functional lines (as in Japan) are all instances of national advantages based on firms' strategy, structure, and rivalry. Competitive global success thus comes from vigorous competition at home that pressures companies to improve and innovate and puts them in a position to compete globally.

THE EFFECT OF GLOBALIZATION ON SMALL AND MEDIUM-SIZED ENTERPRISES

Among other criteria the Small Business Administration of the United States of America (SBA) utilizes the number of employees in a firm as a measure of the size of the firm. Accordingly, a firm with less than 500 employees is considered a small business. Other countries and some authors define a firm with 100 employees as a small business. Throughout this chapter enterprises with less than 500 employees will be termed small and medium-sized enterprises (SMEs).

Only limited studies have been undertaken to assess the effect of globalization and growth of international trade on small businesses. There are a few publications dealing with problems of small exporting firms (Miesenbrock 1988; Kathawala et al. 1989). Studies of the effects of opening up national borders on small businesses indicate that SMEs are not well equipped to face increases in international trade (Filion 1990; OECD 1991).

Global markets, increased international trade, and export-import opportunities have advanced as a result of the series of General Agreement on Tariffs and Trade (GATT) among several nations of the world, Free Trade Agreements (FTA) among blocs of countries, and common markets. The SMEs, however, continue to face restrictions in their international trade. Because of their size they face a variety of barriers, such as distance, limited markets, and cultural differences. The opening of markets is found to affect different regions in different ways. Regions that are unable to adapt to open markets and face increasing competition close out when tariff barriers are eliminated. Regions with new resources (for example, Lombardia in Italy) may develop new trade flows and create new channels of transportation and attract new technologies. SMEs in such regions could expand their exports and work as subcontractors for medium-sized and large firms to assist in their export expansion.

An investigation to examine the impact of globalization on SMEs in three small regions of Quebec has been recently reported by Julien, Joyal, and De-shaies (1994). They assess the behavior of firms with respect to the 1988 FTA between the United States and Canada. How do small firms (in this study they utilized firms with less than 250 employees) face up to an increase in potential competition, and how do they take advantage of reduced customs duties? Their survey results initially showed that only a small number of firms knew about the FTA and had taken steps to take advantage of the reduced taxes or to counter potential competition. Further analysis revealed that actions were taken by SMEs within the wider framework of economic globalization. Some firms had taken steps to reinforce their competitive position in terms of general international trade and not specifically in response to FTA. Thus their focus was to adapt to world competition by designing strategies to develop a specific market.

A plot of the "exposure factor" versus the "dynamism" of the responding firms generates a mapping that leads to groupings of the firms as follows: 94 firms that are dynamic but not threatened and 38 firms operating in closed markets, giving a total of 132 firms not vulnerable to the agreement (see Figure 13.1). The central part of the graph includes 57 firms that can be classified as vulnerable. They are either highly dynamic and highly affected or moderately dynamic and moderately aware. The third group contains 53 very vulnerable firms that are highly affected and yet very passive. The clothing sector is found to be the most vulnerable but having taken few or no steps to improve their competitiveness. On the other hand, machinery, commercial printing, and wood sectors reacted well to the market opening. The smallest firms (1–10 employees) operated in niche markets with specialized products and were found not vulnerable. The medium-sized firms (50–250 employees) were found to be vulnerable or highly vulnerable. Exporting firms were only moderately vulnerable.

An interesting finding of the study is that when the capacity of SMEs to react to removal of international barriers consisting of trade between two countries is considered, the measure is found to be insufficient compared to a measure that widens the notion of competitiveness in terms of national and international markets. This is reflected in the number of firms reacting to opening of markets, 28.9 percent of the firms in the former case (trade between two countries) versus 78.1 percent in the latter case (international markets). The findings confirm that increasing numbers of SMEs realize the new challenges created by market globalization. The FTA with the United States becomes just one element in the new international structure that includes Common Market countries, Japan, and the newly industrialized countries as well.

SMEs develop different ways to face the challenge of market globalization (Acs and Andretsch 1990):

1. Use of new production technologies (computerization, CAD system, etc.)
2. Creating differentiation through innovation at the national and international market levels.

Research tends to show that international competitiveness depends as much on product differentiation as on the use of new production technologies. SMEs

Figure 13.1
Classification of Firms According to Their Level of Exposure and Dynamism

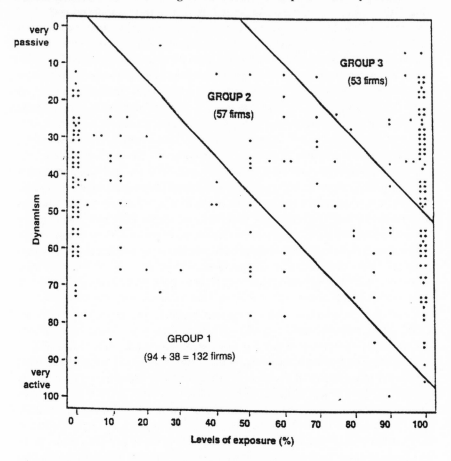

Key: Each dot represents a firm on the open market.
Firms with specialized production or operating in local markets (38 in all) were transferred to Group
  1 and therefore have not been shown in their initial placings.

refusing to adapt to new international environment while operating in open markets will find it hard to survive. Knowledge and some basic understanding of external environment in the context of the national as well as global developments and changes, together with an evaluation of the firm's resources, is necessary for the small firm's survival. Small businesses lack the resources to acquire such information and to conduct an analysis of its implication, to develop appropriate policies, and to undertake innovative programs to address this shortcoming.

SMALL AND MEDIUM-SIZED ENTERPRISES IN AN ECONOMY

SMEs constitute a substantial part of many economies of the world, including those of advanced and developed countries. For example, in the United States in 1992 there were over 5.711 million businesses with employees. Only about 14,000 of these employ more than 500 workers and are considered large businesses. The remaining 5.697 million are small businesses. Small businesses account for nearly half of all U.S. employment. In 1990 small business employment share from all industries was 53.67 percent. Further, the trend of payroll employment away from manufacturing and toward the service sectors is accompanied by a shift from large business–dominated industries to small business–dominated and intermediate-sized industries. A small business–dominated industry is an industry in which 60 percent or more of employment is in firms with fewer than 500 employees, and vice versa for large business–dominated industries. Intermediate industries are those in which the large or small business share falls between 40 and 60 percent of industry employment.

This same trend is observed within manufacturing. Manufacturing is an important sector involving growth of SMEs and affected by globalization in the United States. Manufacturing accounts for 20.0 percent to 22.5 percent of the U.S. gross national product in inflation-adjusted terms. It generates 4.5 times as many secondary jobs as the retail sector and almost three times as many secondary jobs as the personal and business service sectors (Baker and Lee 1992).

Since the mid-1970s there has been a steady increase in the number of small and medium-sized industrial firms (typically defined as lower than 500 employees, U.S. SBA 1992). In the United States the number of manufacturing establishments grew from 319,000 in 1980 to about 374,000 in 1990. Among these more than 98 percent are SMEs and employ 40 percent of the total manufacturing work force. The increase in the number of manufacturing establishments has been dominated by smaller facilities. As shown in Figure 13.2 the number of firms with one to four employees increased 38.8 percent and those with five to nine employees increased 23.2 percent during 1980–1990. In contrast the number of establishments with more than 250 employees decreased.

Thus, while small business created jobs, large businesses were losing jobs. Apart from job creation, small businesses are responsible for a high proportion of innovations in products and services. New small firms produce 24 times more innovations per research dollar than do the large *Fortune* 500 firms (Kents and Bracker 1988).

Notwithstanding this economic contribution and performance by the small business sector, thousands of small companies fail every year. For the fiscal year 1992 a total of 96,913 business failed, an 18.1 percent increase over 1991; there were 71,139 bankruptcies, a 1.7 percent increase over 1991. Business bankruptcies are also a subset of the population of business terminations reported by the Employment and Training Administration. A business bankruptcy is the legal

Figure 13.2
Percentage Change in Number of Facilities, 1980–1990

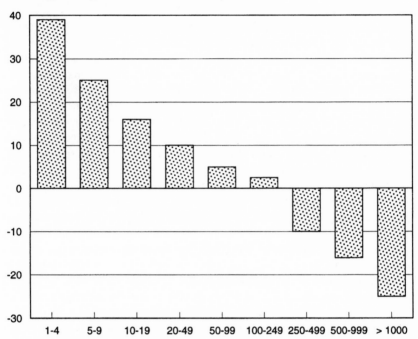

recognition that a company is solvent and not able to satisfy creditors or discharge liabilities. Information about business failures is from the SBA Office of Advocacy, adapted from the Dun & Bradstreet corporation record of business closing (1991–1992); information about bankruptcies is from data of administration of the U.S. Courts.

The failure rate as determined in a study by Dun and Bradstreet shows that 53 percent of all failures and bankruptcies reported in 1980 occurred in less than five years from a firm's founding and 83 percent of new businesses failed in less than ten years (Romanelli 1989). Small businesses and in particular new small businesses are very risky and susceptible to failure.

A survey of 703 small business owners (*USA Today*, March 13, 1987, p. 13) in 1987 found that the main reasons new firms fail are as follows (respondents could choose more than one answer):

Lack of capital	48%
No business knowledge	23%
Poor management	19%
Inadequate planning	15%
Inexperience	15%

Although shortage of capital is the greatest problem facing small business owners, we can see that inadequate management resulting from limited knowledge, poor planning, and inexperience constitute the other great problem. Globalization and opening of markets would make management, information, and decision-making issues more critical for the survival of the small enterprise.

INNOVATIVE PROGRAMS TO ASSIST SMALL BUSINESSES TO FACE THE CHALLENGES OF GLOBAL DEVELOPMENTS AND OPEN MARKETS

Cooperative Program: A U.S. Case Study

This case study describes a three-way cooperative program to assist SMEs in long-term survival and growth. The program is called the Small Business Institute Program (SBI) and provides managerial and functional area counseling to small business firms. The SBI program, established in 1972, provides this counseling service throughout the United States, through 520 colleges and universities in 50 states and several territories, and assists 8,000 businesses a year (Johnson 1990). Teams of qualified university students (around 20,000 students each year) provide the counseling to small businesses as part of their educational program. Since 1972 over 152,000 small businesses have received assistance from the SBI program.

The SBI cooperative program has been presented in the form of a model to understand the relationship among the three entities involved in the program by Asundi (1995). The model representing the SBI cooperative program is shown in Figure 13.3 and can be understood as follows.

The cooperative program model is represented by a triangle in which the three cooperating entities—the educational institution, the small business community, and the government—are placed at the three apex points. Bilateral, mutually beneficial relations between any two of the three entities are represented by two-way arrows. The nature of the interaction between the educational institution and the government leads to the university receiving financial support and informational material from the government agency (the Small Business Administration) and in turn providing reports of business cases, their analyses, and their problems, opportunities, and solutions. The same report is given to the owner or manager of the business enterprise, in addition to an oral presentation by the students on their findings. The interaction between the business units and the university students leads to an opportunity for the students to analyze a real business operation, identify business problems, and develop proper solutions. The business unit in turn receives an analysis of its operations from an outsider's perspective by dedicated students with business education at no cost. A continuing successful business then contributes to government revenue and reduces unemployment. Thus we can see the reciprocity of benefits and contributions between each pair of the three entities, Business, University, and Government,

Figure 13.3
Cooperative Program Model

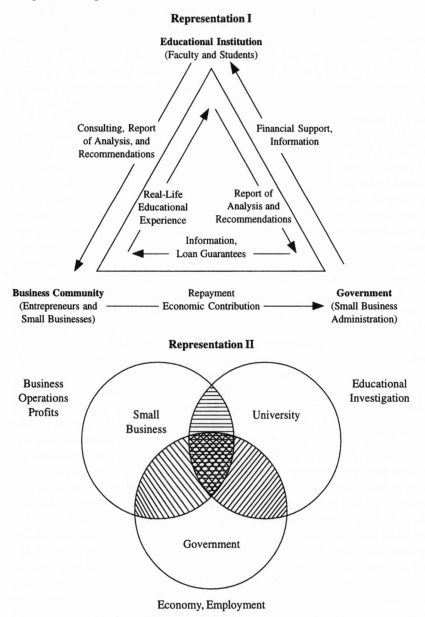

Representation I

Educational Institution
(Faculty and Students)

Consulting, Report
of Analysis, and
Recommendations

Financial Support,
Information

Real-Life
Educational
Experience

Report of
Analysis and
Recommendations

Information,
Loan Guarantees

Business Community
(Entrepreneurs and
Small Businesses)

Repayment
Economic Contribution

Government
(Small Business
Administration)

Representation II

Business
Operations
Profits

Educational
Investigation

Small
Business

University

Government

Economy, Employment

White part: Primary role unique to each entity. Single line: Bilateral interactions. Triple line: Linkage
of the three entities (SBIDA).

in the Small Business Institute program. The overall benefits and contributions in the SBI program are presented in Table 13.1.

Studies of the evaluation of the SBI program by the participating enterprises and by former students and the effect of the SBI intervention on the perception of business problems has been made by Weinstein et al. (1992), Fontenot et al. (1991), and Jackson et al. (1992). Weinstein, Nicholls, and Seaton identify other literature on student business consulting on the issue of evaluation of SBIs and the academic benefits of student consulting projects published from 1977 to 1988. These studies, based on regional and national samples, deal with the evaluation of client perception, faculty perception, and student perception of student business consulting. The findings of Weinstein et al. and the findings of the literature in general show that the SBI program provides valuable service to entrepreneurs and small business.

They note that the majority of clients were receptive to new ideas presented by the students and found the report practical and valuable. Clients viewed the students' levels of professionalism to be average (14.6%) to above average (75.4%) and their business knowledge to be average (39.7%) to above average (50.0%). The authors also note that business knowledge and practicality of recommendations are the key predictors of client satisfaction, as revealed by a stepwise regression model. Since small businesses do not normally utilize costly consultant services, SBI assistance appears to be of particular value. Their study adds credence to the idea that SBI programs are a viable model for assisting small business and improving the prospects of fledgling firms.

A survey of 504 SBI student alumni of schools across the United States by Fontenot et al. (1991) to assess the students' perceptions of the skills gained by participating in an SBI case analysis shows the following results. To determine the effectiveness of the SBI course, the authors compare it to the business policy course. Survey results indicate that the students found the business policy course to be more effective in developing analytical skills and to be more useful in their careers than the SBI course. The SBI course, however, was perceived to be more effective in developing interpersonal skills and operational skills than the policy course.

Another important area in which SBI counseling by students plays a significant role is in the change in perception of existing problems by the business owner after SBI intervention (Jackson et al. 1992). As noted by Sanfield (1981) more than a decade ago, the proximity and frequency of the real-world problems faced tends to force the small business owner away from analytical frameworks into more intuitive and practical ways of dealing with things. The students can offer an alternative approach to a problem (based on an outsider's view), which in combination with the owner's way of thinking results in a stronger total approach than either method by itself. Since perceived problems may not be actual problems, proper problem identification may very well hold the secret to reduced business failure.

An economic impact study of the SBI program for the 1990–1993 period is

Table 13.1
Overall Benefits and Contributions in the SBI Program

Contributions	Benefits
University	
Time and effort of students and faculty	Students:
Current knowledge base	Experiential learning from a real business situation
Analysis of business problems, opportunities, and recommendations in the form of oral and written report	Opportunity to interact with manager/owner
Counseling by students under faculty guidance	Appreciation of business difficulties and hard work
Resources of university	Applying classroom learning to real-world situations
	Faculty:
	Interactions with business community
	Guiding students in a variety of business situations
	Opportunity for investigation
	University community relations
Business	
Access to business operation and information base	Analysis and counseling on opportunities, problems, and solutions (an external perspective) by senior business students
Time and business knowledge of manager/owner	Indirect faculty input
	Written report of recommendations and solutions at no cost
	Potential business success and growth
Government	
Grant support for universities	Information about small business problems across a sample of business
Information and guidelines for management and counseling	Reduced failures of small business resulting in loan repayments
Management and financial assistance to small business	Employment, economic development, and tax revenues

Table 13.2
Data of Economic Impact Study, 1994 SBIDA (SBI Clients, 1991–1992: 7,100)

Net new jobs created	10,697
Average hourly wage	$9.77
Corresponding employee wages	$203 million
Additional revenue increase (1992) 1991 revenues × marginal growth rate = additional revenues ($9.13m × 0.8% = $79m)	$79 million
Additional sales taxes	$13 million
Employee taxes (Medicare, Social Security, and federal income tax)	$55 million
Cost of generating each new job	$280
Employee wage increase (national average wage increase 3.7%)	6.8%
Employment growth rate (1992 average growth rate for the U.S. small business = 0.42%)	12.8%
Increase in growth revenue	38%
Additional tax revenues per dollar spent by federal government in supporting SBI Program (total increment tax revenues) (sales tax + employment tax + federal income tax) ÷ cost of consulting by all SBI programs) 60,069,226 ÷ 2,990,000 = 20.1	$20.1

reported by Fontenot (1994). The study is based on client data collected in a mail survey with the help of SBI programs throughout the United States and its territories. The survey involved clients who received consulting between 1990 and 1993. An estimated 2,375 surveys were sent to clients, from which 499 usable responses were received.

In this study the change in sales, employment, and wages between the year in which consulting was received and the year after consulting was received were calculated for SBI clients. Rates of sales and employment growth are then compared with average growth rates for the United States on each measure. The difference between the growth rate for clients and the growth rate of all business in the nation are used to compute the marginal changes in sales and employment growth of SBI clients. To determine the growth as a result of SBI consulting, the marginal growth rates are multiplied by the average sales and employment of the respondents for the year before consulting. Marginal changes are computed for 1991–1992. Table 13.2 shows a summary of the economic impact data as a result of SBI counseling activities.

In the economic impact study the SBI clients rated the SBI consultants and the consulting experience as very high. Nearly 50 percent of respondents rated the consultants as excellent, and 66 percent rated their working relationship with SBI student consultants as also excellent.

ENTREPRENEURSHIP TRAINING AND EDUCATION—A BRAZILIAN CASE

Since 1990 Brazil has experienced large changes that include four economic plans, three different currencies, and two presidents. The country faced inflation rates of around 1,517 percent a year from November 1993 to November 1994. Consequently large corporations began to downsize and demand professionals with an entrepreneurial bent to be creative, innovative, visionary, and risk taking (Shils and Zucker 1979).

Such entrepreneurs within an organization are called intrapreneurs (internal entrepreneurs). The entrepreneur's risk is at the career level, while the intrapreneur's risk may involve major financial risk (Timmons 1990). The downsizing of the multinationals and the turmoil in the state-owned companies led some Brazilians to start their own businesses. In 1994 in the state of Minas Gerais, more than 44,000 new small and medium-sized businesses were created.

This shift from large multinational and state-owned corporations to the development of small and medium-sized enterprises has accentuated the disparity between the education of the student body in the universities (particularly in the areas of business and engineering) and the demands of the marketplace. Business colleges in the universities emphasized management principles, decision making, quantitative methods, marketing, and financial theory, and practices in the context of large corporations. The cases utilized also invariably related to large corporations. To address this issue, SEBRAE, a nationwide small business development agency created in 1972, undertook a large reorganization in 1990 to become a nonprofit private institution.

SEBRAE develops an entrepreneurship education model that is distinct from the traditional approach to management education offered in business colleges in Brazil. The entrepreneurship education program involves three phases and related activities. The three phases are (1) information and sensitization, (2) training, and (3) evaluation of results and future directions. Associated with the first two phases are the activities of seminars and lectures on entrepreneurship; identification of partners for the program; international, regional, and local workshops to disseminate training methods; and courses at universities.

SEBRAE Minas utilized the works of Filion (1992) and Timmons (1990) to develop the entrepreneurship education program. A model presented by Timmons distinguishes the characteristics of managers and administrators from those of an entrepreneur (Figure 13.4). Current Brazilian education emphasizes the needs of the manager in a large corporation rather than those of the entrepreneur. Filion's approach to education emphasizes:

Figure 13.4
A Typology of Entrepreneurial/Managerial Skills

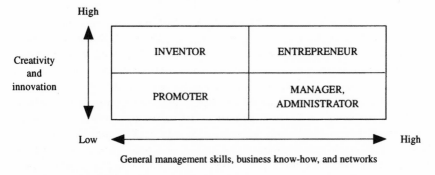

Source: Timmons (1990).

1. The importance of learning methods over content.
2. Entrepreneurial development based on who you are and what you do rather than what to do and how to do it.
3. Resourcefulness to create one's own jobs.

According to Timmons, entrepreneurial attitudes and behaviors can be acquired; people have an astounding capacity to change and learn if they are motivated and committed to do so. Entrepreneurship can thus be advanced through a proper educational process. Accordingly SEBRAE designed an entrepreneurship education program that includes vision, creativity, small business management, and other important aspects of entrepreneurship.

To provide vision the program orients students to new ideas of production and service, good use of available resources and new management approaches, and finding new ideas in existing business and trade shows.

To encourage creativity the program utilizes games, nonconventional thinking, and team creativity. Professors and students are encouraged to adopt Roger von Oech's (1983) approach on creative thinking to avoid "mental blockers" such as assuming the existence of a right answer, a given thinking is not logical, to err is wrong, and the like.

To effectively manage small enterprises the program adapts advanced management techniques to the realities of the small enterprise. Small enterprises involve simple structures, informal control, limited resources, and limited market influence (Gibb 1983).

Other aspects of the program include the development of leadership, persistence, self-confidence, and networking. To enhance the program, local case studies, student exposure to successful entrepreneurs, and the establishment of small business centers in universities are encouraged.

The universities and colleges provide the space, faculty, and students, while

SEBRAE helps with equipment and literature on new venture creation, business opportunities, conferences, and workshops at the regional and national levels.

As of 1994 SEBRAE Minas Management Information System has provided seminars and lectures to 2,274 organizations, implemented 30 courses, developed twelve videos and two books, and created one entrepreneur nucleus. Starting with universities with similar views about entrepreneurship training and education, SEBRAE is continually increasing the number of participating institutions to provide assistance and information to the 736 municipalities of Minas Gerais. It cooperates with local commerce and industrial chambers, as well as universities. Minas Gerais has more than 30 SEBRAE counters linked with boards of trade, banks, business associations, and trade shows. A SEBRAE counter is an open door for a wide range of information and data on management, technology development, and markets relating to small and medium-sized enterprises. A variety of other services are also developed and offered by SEBRAE, from project preparation to financing sources.

SEBRAE Minas business philosophy and its products have made it a successful Brazilian entity to help and support small and medium-sized businesses to strengthen the developing economy and social well-being of Brazil.

IMPLICATIONS OF ADOPTING THE SBI OR ENTREPRENEURSHIP PROGRAMS FOR THE INDIAN SETTING

Since the early 1990s there has been an increasing interest on the part of multinational enterprises from different parts of the world to focus on India. The combination of global developments and the greater operating freedom offered to foreign investments in India has led to this interest and focus. Total FDI in India in 1990 was less than $100 million, but by 1992 it had increased to $1.2 billion and continues to rise. U.S. multinationals represent the largest and fastest-growing investors. Implications of this growth and its impact on SME survival become important issues.

SMEs in India as in other countries will need information, management, modernization, and adaptation to new technologies. An assessment of the feasibility of some form of assistance and education through a well-coordinated program such as the SBI or other similar cooperative program such as the Small Business Development Centers and the Service Care of Retired Executives could be made. Such a program can be developed to cover the entire country, in view of the numerous colleges and universities throughout the different states of India. Whether a government agency should be involved, as in the case of the SBI (or the SBDC) in the United States, or whether a private enterprise should promote it, as in the case of Brazil, is an issue that is worth investigation for subsequent adoption to strengthen the small and medium-sized enterprise sector and its contribution to the economy of India.

REFERENCES

Acs, Z. and D. B. Andretsch (1990). *Innovation and Small Firms*. Cambridge, MA: MIT Press.

Asundi, R. K. (1995). "Possible Model of a Cooperative Program for Business and Entrepreneurship in Latin America." In *Memorias, Il Mesa Redonda en la Formación y Desarrollo de Pequeñas Empresas*. IX Congreso Latinoamericano sobre Espíritu Empresarial, Mayaguez, Puerto Rico, pp. 22–34.

Baker, D. and T. Lee (1992). *Employment Multipliers in the U.S. Economy*. Washington, DC: Economic Policy Institute.

Filion, L. J. (1990). "Free Trade: The Need for a Definition of Small Business." *Journal of Small Business and Entrepreneurship*, 7(2) (January–March): 31–45.

——— (1992). "Ten Steps to Entrepreneurial Teaching." Second NEDI National Conference on Entrepreneurship Education.

Fontenot, Gwen (1994). "Small Business Institute, Economic Impact Study 1990–1993." Report to U.S. Small Business Administration and U.S. Congress.

Fontenot, Gwen, Michelle Haarlues, and Lynn Hoffman (1991). "The Benefits of the SBI Program: Perceptions of Former Students." *Journal of Small Business Strategy*, 9: 15–30.

Gibb, Allan (1983). "The Small Business Challenge to Management Education." *Journal of Small Business European Industrial Training*, 7: 1–41.

Jackson, W. T., G. S. Vozikis, and Emin Babakus (1992). "SBI Intervention: An Old Problem—A New Perspective." *Journal of Small Business Strategy*, 10.

Johnson, Dowey (1990). "SBIDA on the Move to Serve Small Business." SBIDA National Proceedings, Houston, TX, pp. 2–6.

Julien, Pierre-Andre, Andre Joyal, and Laurent Deshaies (1994). "SEMs and International Competition: Free Trade Agreement or Globalization?" *Journal of Small Business Management* 32(3) (July): 52–63.

Kathawala, Y., R. Judd, M. Monipamil, and M. Weirrich (1989). "Exporting Practices and Problems of Illinois Firms." *Journal of Small Business Management*, 27(1) (January): 53–59.

Kents, B. and J. Bracker (1988). "Toward a Theory of Small Firm Performances: A Conceptual Model." *American Journal of Small Business*, 12: 41–58.

Mandel, Michael J. and Aron Bernstein (1990). "Dispelling the Myths That Are Holding Us Back." *Business Week*, March 10, p. 66.

Miesenbrock, K. J. (1988). "Small Exporting: A Literature Review." *International Small Business Journal*, 6(2) (January/March): 42–61.

OECD (1991). "L'Internationalization despetites enterprises." Cartiers ILE no. 14 (January).

Oech, Roger von (1983). *A Whack on the Side of the Head*. New York: Warner Books.

Porter, Michael (1990). *The Competitive Advantage of Nations*. New York: The Free Press.

Rodríguez Costa, Sergio (1995). "Brazilian Universities: New Experiences in Training

Undergraduate Students to Become Entrepreneurs." In *Memorias. Il Mesa Redonda en la Formación y Desarrollo de Pequeñas Empresas*. IX Congreso Latinoamericano sobre Espíritu Empresarial, Mayaguez, Puerto Rico.

Romanelli, E. (1989). "Environment and Strategies of Organization Startup: Effects on Early Survival." *Administrative Science Quarterly*, 34: 1–7.

Sanfield, M. C. (1981). "Can Student Consultants Really Help a Small Business?" *Journal of Small Business Management*, 19(1): 3–9.

Shils, E. and W. Zucker (1979). "Developing a Model for Internal Corporate Entrepreneurship." *Social Sciences*, 54(4): 195–203.

Timmons, J. A. (1990). *New Venture Creation: Entrepreneurship in the 1990's*. Homewood, IL: Irwin.

U.S. Department of Commerce (1993). *Survey of Current Business* (July).

Weinstein, Art, J.A.F. Nicholls, and Bruce Seaton (1992). "An Evaluation of SBI Marketing Consulting: The Entrepreneurship Perspective." *Journal of Small Business Management*, 30(4): 62–71.

Chapter 14

International Technology Alliances: Recent Trends in the IT Sector

P. M. Rao

INTRODUCTION

The rapid growth of interfirm collaborations since the early 1980s has been the subject of a large and growing body of academic literature under the rubric of "strategic alliances." Although there is nothing new or novel about interfirm linkages per se, which are as old as the firm itself, recent trends in technology-based alliances—domestic as well as international—present something of a new phenomenon, at least in terms of their rapid growth. More important, they present an anomaly to some traditional and celebrated theories that attempt to explain vertical integration of corporate R&D activity and foreign direct investment (FDI). Prominent among them are the market failure argument and transaction cost and internalization theories grounded in the industrial organization literature (Arrow 1962; Williamson 1975; Buckley and Casson 1976; Caves 1982).

There are at least three major forces behind the rapid growth of technology-based international strategic alliances in the information technology (IT) industry. Two of these forces, which are widely noted in the literature, are brought about by the external environment. The first of these is a general shift in almost all countries toward open markets with respect to trade and FDI (Graham 1996); the second is the emergence of a vastly more competitive market structure in the global IT industry (brought about, in part, by continuing radical changes in the structure of the U.S. telecommunications industry, beginning with the 1984 breakup of the Bell system), combined with a high degree of technological rivalry that seems to characterize both the software and hardware segments of the industry (OECD 1997). The third force—brought about by the second—which is the main focus of this chapter and one that does not seem to have received much attention in the literature on strategic alliances, has to do with fundamental changes in the way in which corporate R&D activity is organized in the IT industry.

The chapter is organized into three sections. The first section provides a summary of recent empirical evidence on technology-based international strategic alliances in the IT industry. Included in this section is a brief discussion of data and definitions used in the studies reviewed. An explanation of empirical evidence in light of the vastly changed boundary of corporate R&D activity in the IT industry is provided in the second section. A summary is presented and implications of the rapid growth of technology-based alliances for future research are discussed in the third and final section.

RECENT EVIDENCE ON TECHNOLOGY ALLIANCES IN THE IT INDUSTRY

Sources, Data, and Definitions

Recent studies by Duysters (1996), Duysters and Hagedoorn (1996), Hagedoorn and Narula (1996), Hagedoorn (1993), Hagedoorn and Schakenraad (1992), and Vonortas and Safioleas (1996) provide the most extensive documentation, analysis, and hypothesis testing on technology-based international strategic alliances in the IT industry. The first four studies use a common database developed by the Maastricht Economic Research Institute on Innovation and Technology (MERIT) on Cooperative Agreements and Technology Indicators (CATI)—often referred to as the MERIT-CATI database—and focus on strategic technology partnering issues in the IT as well as other high-technology industries. The study by Vonortas and Safioleas (1996) also uses a rich database called Information Technology Strategic Alliances (ITSA), and its focus is on strategic alliances in the IT industry with developing country firms. Whereas the MERIT-CATI database was developed only from publicly announced interfirm cooperative agreements with technology content, the ITSA database was developed from all publicly announced interfirm alliances (although R&D and other alliances with technology content can be broken out) in the IT industry worldwide.

As with all databases that rely on counting and classifying information on publicly announced alliances reported in the press, MERIT-CATI and ITSA databases suffer from numerous biases. They include coverage bias (unannounced alliances are excluded), firm bias (exclusion of smaller and/or low-profile firms), and many more. More important, the two databases differ in their definitions of what constitutes a strategic alliance and what constitutes the IT industry. Briefly, in the MERIT-CATI database, only those interfirm agreements that contain some arrangements for transferring technology or joint research are included. Joint research pacts, second-sourcing, and licensing agreements are clear-cut candidates. Joint ventures in which new technology is received from at least one of the partners or joint ventures having some R&D program are also included. Production or marketing agreements are excluded, as are agreements with majority ownership. By contrast, the ITSA database contains a broader range of interfirm alliances that includes mergers and acquisitions, contractual agreements along with joint ventures, R&D agreements, and licensing and equity agreements. However, the ITS database allows categorization of alliances into three types: alliances with technological content (e.g., joint R&D agreements), alliances without R&D content (e.g., marketing and distribution), and mixed alliances. Note that neither of these definitions conforms to the one proposed by Yoshino and Rangan (1995)—who made a significant effort at clarifying the definitional issues—which excludes, among other types, all traditional contracts (e.g., licensing and cross-licensing) on the grounds that they do not call for continuous transfer of technology, products, or skills between partners. Indeed, as Vonortas and Safioleas (1996) note, the lack of a generally accepted definition of what constitutes a strategic alliance is one reason for the lack of a consistent analytical framework.

The definition of the IT industry in the MERIT-CATI database includes computers, telecommunications, and microelectronics (software and industrial automation are sometimes included). By contrast, the ITSA database covers many more industry groupings such as consumer electronics, media, and even finance, banking, and insurance, which are heavy users of IT.

Summary of Findings

Despite the difficulties for interpretation presented by the lack of consistency in the data and definitions used in the preceding studies, they nevertheless represent the most recent and most comprehensive empirical evidence available on technology-based international alliances in the IT industry. Some key findings relevant to the issues addressed in this chapter are summarized below.

Growth of Alliances. The rapid growth of both interfirm alliances and technology alliances worldwide is a phenomenon that began in the early 1980s and has been well documented (Hagedoorn and Schakenraad 1992; Duysters 1996; Vonortas and Safioleas 1996). It is important to note, however, that while total alliance records per year worldwide may run into several thousand—well over 4,000, according to Vonortas and Safioleas (1996)—technology alliances per year run to fewer than 700 and IT industry alliances are even fewer (less than 300), according to the data produced by Hagedoorn and Schakenraad (1992) and Duysters (1996) for the late 1980s and early 1990s.

Sectoral Distribution of Alliances. Firms in the IT industry dominate international technology alliance activity. Over the 1980–1993 period, they accounted for 46 percent of such alliances in the ten industrialized countries, including the U.S. and Japan (Hagedoorn and Narula 1996).

Types of Alliances. The vast majority of international technology alliances, including those in the IT industry, are of the contractual non-equity type, a departure from the traditional joint-venture equity type. Over the 1980–1993 period, depending on the particular sector, between 65 and 85 percent of international technology alliances were of this type (Duysters 1996).

Motives for Alliances. Market access/restructure followed by technological complementarity and reduction of innovation time span stand out as the most important motives for all technology alliances, including those in the IT industry in the 1980s. Market access seems to be an especially important motive for the telecommunications, computer, and microelectronics sectors, which have experienced significant restructuring (Duysters, 1996; Hagedoorn 1993).

Internationalization of R&D-Focused versus Market Alliances. There is no evidence either in the IT industry or other industries that R&D-focused alliances led to internationalization of corporate technological activities during the 1980s. Most R&D-focused international alliances in the IT industry (about 60 percent in the second half of the 1980s) are found within economic blocs (European Union, the United States, and Japan), while a majority of more market-oriented international technology alliances are found to exist between economic blocs (Duysters and Hagedoorn 1996; Duysters 1996).

Alliances with Developing Country Firms. According to heretofore unavailable data reported by Vonortas and Safioleas (1996), alliances in the IT industry involving developing country firms have grown rapidly, from fewer than 20 in 1984 to nearly 600 in 1994, and their share of total alliances during the same period nearly doubled, from 6 percent to 13 percent. Computers and telecommunications dominate the IT industry alliances involving the developing world. Moreover, the authors report a rapid rise in the cooperative R&D agreements versus licenses involving developing country firms and a dramatic increase in the share of alliances with technology content, from 54 percent in 1984 to 81 percent in 1994.

Other investigators using different methodologies and data sources—in-depth analysis of interviews with executives in 40 firms conducted by Gomes-Casseras (1996), for example—confirm the growing trend toward technology alliances in the IT industry, including the motives for such alliances, as reported earlier. As noted in the introduction, at least part of the rapid growth in the IT industry alliances, including those with the developing country firms, since the early 1980s is due to a worldwide shift, during the same period, toward open markets in the terms of trade and FDI flows combined with radical changes in the structure of the world's telecommunications and computer industries (Graham 1996; OECD 1997). Other general explanations for the rapid growth of alliances include the dispersion of technology and the high fixed costs of R&D (Ohmae (1989), deepening of industry convergence, positioning strategies of individual firms (Gomes-Casseras 1996), and entrepreneurial globalization (Yoshino and Rangan 1995). The finding that R&D-focused alliances are not the vehicle for internationalization of corporate technological activity is consistent with what we know about the location of corporate R&D activity among the industrialized countries. It is overwhelmingly confined to national borders (Graham 1996). Similarly, the finding of a trend toward non-equity agreements provides support for Ohmae's (1989) view that they offer great flexibility from the standpoint of corporate governance.

A DIFFERENT VIEW OF TECHNOLOGY ALLIANCES

A different view of technology alliances—one that is closer to Adam Smith's enduring insight, the idea of the division of labor—is that perhaps they portend the beginnings of vertical disintegration of important segments of the IT industry's R&D activity. The argument runs as follows: In the heydays of AT&T and IBM, when vertical integration was the sole model of the telecommunications industry and the dominant model of the computer industry, corporate R&D activity was totally integrated into manufacturing and was conducted in-house, all under "one roof." This is clearly not the model of corporate R&D activity in the IT industry today. Major changes in the industry structure and technology (e.g., recent voluntary divestiture of manufacturing and research at AT&T), each affecting the other, have resulted in R&D activity that is less integrated, less centralized, more specialized, and more out-sourced. The preeminent role of software in the IT industry's R&D activity, combined with the emergence of the competitive stand-alone software industry, contributed greatly to undermining the in-house R&D activity of large vertically integrated firms. According to the OECD (1997) data, in 1995 more money was spent on software and services ($275 billion or 52 percent of worldwide IT spending) than on hardware. In 1997, the top ten independent software vendors (ISVs) alone spent more on R&D ($4.2 billion or 18 percent of sales), than the combined spending by AT&T and Lucent ($3.9 billion or 5 percent of sales), whose sales are well over three times as large (Disclosure 1998). Another indicator of the dominance of software firms in terms of R&D is a comparison of the ranking of top information and communications technology (ICT) firms by R&D intensity with those ranked by the amount spent on R&D. Software firms such as Abode Systems, Cray Research, and Novell dominate the top fifteen firms ranked by R&D intensity, whereas manufacturing firms such as Lucent, Siemens, and Hitachi dominate the top fifteen firms ranked by the amount spent on R&D. Partly in response to the challenge from the competitive stand-alone software industry, significant portions of R&D activity in the large vertically integrated firms like IBM— software and computer chip development, for example—are likely to continue to come under increasing pressure to organize and run on a profit center model. Under such a model, the focus of R&D activity would shift from being an input to the production of products and services to one that produces and markets its own "final" products in the form of technologies, and marketing would become an integral part of R&D activity. More important, the shifting boundary of a firm's R&D activities (i.e., from the vertical integration model to the profit center model) is one of the major driving forces behind technology-based strategic alliances, both domestic and international (Rao 1996). Put differently, the emergence of technology-based strategic alliances may be viewed as the natural outcome of a general shift in the IT industry away from the vertical integration model of R&D activity toward market transactions. One need only consider the fact that over the 1984–1994 period, AT&T and IBM, the two "dominant" firms in their respective sectors, were also ranked as the top two in the IT industry among all the companies from OECD countries with ten or more alliances with developing country firms (Vonortas and Safioleas 1996; see Figure 14.1). The two companies combined share of alliances was a staggering 22 percent of the total. Prior to the period when the vertical integration model of R&D was unchallenged, neither company had any significant record of alliances, much less alliances with developing country firms. As Gomes-Casseras (1996) notes, a dominant firm will use an alliance only when it must.

SUMMARY AND IMPLICATIONS FOR FUTURE RESEARCH

Summary

Recent comprehensive evidence on international technology alliances in the IT industry based on MERIT-CATI and ITSA data suggests that they have grown rapidly; that the dominant motives for alliances are market access, technological complementarity, and reduction of innovation time span; that they are increasingly of the non-equity type; and that there has been a new trend, namely, the rapid growth of alliances with developing country firms. The literature on alliances provides numerous explanations for what has come to be known as the alliance revolution. They include the worldwide shift toward open markets, combined with radical changes in the structure of the world's telecommunications and computer industries, dispersion of technology, positioning strategies of individual firms, and entrepreneurial globalization. This chapter suggests a different view—one that is closer to Adam Smith's insight about the division of labor—that technology alliances portend the beginnings of a larger trend, namely, vertical disintegration of important segments of the IT industry's R&D activity as exemplified by the emergence of a competitive stand-alone software industry.

Implications for Future Research

The reality of technology-based alliances presents something of an anomaly in some celebrated theories that attempt to explain why much of corporate R&D activity is vertically integrated and why and under what circumstances multinational firms leveraging on proprietary technology engage in FDI versus other forms of foreign involvement. They include the market failure argument of Arrow (1962), internalization theory (Caves 1982, Buckley and Casson 1976), and transaction cost analysis (Williamson 1975). Although such theories still provide a useful framework for analyzing the larger issues of vertical integration and FDI, they need to be reexamined in light of the rapid growth of technology-

Figure 14.1
Companies from OECD Countries with Ten or More Strategic Alliances in Information Technology with Developing Country Firms, 1984–1994

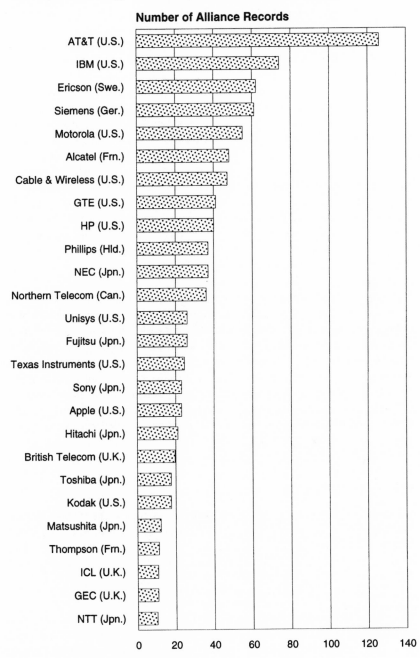

Source: Vonortas and Safioleas (1996).

based international alliances and similar other vehicles—bearing in mind that they constitute but a small fraction of worldwide corporate R&D activity— which represent externalization of corporate technology. Such reexamination could begin by asking, for example, how and in what respect the capabilities of the market have gotten ahead of the firm's capabilities, say, with respect to software development. How did the market mechanism overcome the appropriability problem associated with the production and marketing of software and turn a potential "market failure" case into a market success case? What role did marketing strategies play in the development of a competitive software industry? If technological complementary is a strong motive for alliances, as the evidence indicates, what are the characteristics of the complementary assets sought through alliances? For example, a decline in "asset specificity" (i.e., assets specific to the firm) would, in the transaction cost framework, be consistent with the growth of technology-based alliances. Similarly, if reducing innovation time span is an important motive for alliances, inter-partner learning literature may have more to offer than transaction cost analysis. As Hamel (1991) suggests, alliances may be viewed not as an alternative to market-based transactions or hierarchy but as an alternative to other modes of skill acquisition. Thus, they may be viewed as a way of short-circuiting the process of skill acquisition.

Another branch of literature that provides rich insight into the growth of technology alliances, and one that needs to be integrated more into marketing strategy literature, is the options approach suggested by Dixit and Pindyck (1995), among others. In this framework, given their irreversibility and uncertainty associated with most R&D investments, technology alliances would be viewed as value-creating options. That is, alliances give a company the option but not the obligation to make additional investments in the future. Further research along the lines suggested here could help improve our understanding of technology-based alliances and their implications for global marketing strategy.

ACKNOWLEDGMENT

This chapter is a revised version of a paper presented at the Eighth Biennial World Marketing Congress in June 1997 at Kuala Lumpur, Malaysia. The author gratefully acknowledges the partial support provided by the College of Management and the C. W. Post Research Committee.

REFERENCES

Arrow, Kenneth J. (1962). "Economic Welfare and Allocation of Resources for Invention." In R. Nelson (ed.), *The Rate and Direction of Incentive Activity*. Princeton, NJ: Princeton University Press, pp. 609–624.

Buckley, Peter and Mark Casson (1976). *The Future of Multinational Enterprise*. London: Macmillan.

Caves, Richard (1982). *Multinational Enterprise and Economic Analysis*. Cambridge: Cambridge University Press.

Coombs, Rod, Albert Richards, Pier Paolo Saviotti, and Vivien Walsh (eds.) (1996). *Technological Collaboration*. Brookfield, VT: Edward Elgar.

Day, George S. (1995). "Advantageous Alliances." *Journal of the Academy of Marketing Science*, 23(4): 297–300.

Disclosure Incorporated (1998). Annual Report Data on Diskette. Bethesda, MD.

Dixit, Avinash K. and Robert S. Pindyck (1995). "The Options Approach to Capital Investment." *Harvard Business Review* (May–June): 105–115.

Duysters, Geert (1996). *The Dynamics of Technological Innovation*. Brookfield, VT: Edward Elgar.

Duysters, Geert and John Hagedoorn (1996). "Internationalization of Corporate Technology Through Strategic Partnering: An Empirical Investigation." *Research Policy*, 25(1): 1–12.

Gomes-Casseres, Benjamin (1996). *The Alliance Revolution*. Cambridge, MA: Harvard University Press.

Graham, Edward (1996). *Global Corporations and National Governments*. Washington, DC: Institute for International Economics.

Hagedoorn, John (1993). "Understanding the Rationale of Strategic Technology Partnering: Interorganizational Modes of Cooperation and Sectoral Differences." *Strategic Management Journal*, 14: 371–385.

Hagedoorn, John and Rajneesh Narula (1996). "Choosing Organizational Modes of Strategic Technology Partnering: International and Sectoral Differences." *Journal of International Business Studies*, 27(1): 265–284.

Hagedoorn, John and Jos Schakenraad (1992). "Leading Companies and Networks of Strategic alliances in Information Technologies."*Research Policy*, 21(2): 163–190.

――― (1994). "The Effect of Strategic Technology Alliances on Company Performance." *Strategic Management Journal*, 15: 291–309.

Hamel, Gary (1991). "Competence and Inter-Partner Learning Within International Strategic Alliances." *Strategic Management Journal*, 12: 83–103.

Ohmae, K. (1989). "The Global Logic of Strategic Alliances." *Harvard Business Review* (March–April): 143–154.

Organization for Economic Cooperation and Development (OECD) (1997). *Communications Outlook 1997*. Paris: OECD.

――― (1997). *Information Technology Outlook 1997*. Paris: OECD.

Rao, P. M. (1996). "R&D and Innovation in U.S. Telecommunications: Recent Structural Changes and Their Implications." Paper presented at the International Telecommunications Society, Eleventh Biennial Conference, June 16–19, Seville, Spain.

Varadarajan, P. Rajan and Margaret H. Cunningham (1995). "Strategic Alliances: A Synthesis of Conceptual Foundations." *Journal of the Academy of Marketing Science*, 23(4): 282–296.

Vonortas, Nicholas S. and Stratos P. Safioleas (1996). Strategic Alliances in Information Technology and Developing Country Firms II: Recent Evidence. Unpublished paper. Washington, DC: The World Bank, pp. 1–27.

Williamson, Oliver E. (1975). *Markets and Hierarchies: Analysis and Antitrust Implications*. New York: Free Press.

Yoshino, Michael Y. and U. Srinivasa Rangan (1995). *Strategic Alliances*. Boston: Harvard Business School Press.

Chapter 15

Developing a Normative Framework of International Marketing for the General Insurance Industry

D. A. Yorke and Runar P. Andresen

INTRODUCTION

The continuous fast growth of services in the world economy is well supported in the literature (Edvardsson et al. 1993: Benton and Bowles 1992; Dahringer 1991), although it is suggested that, while worldwide services trade is growing faster (in real terms) than product trade, services trade accounts for a much lower proportion of total trade than the more dominating proportion of services in the gross national product of developed economies (Benton and Bowles 1992; Normann 1984; Nicolaud 1989). Such studies suggest that services represent 25–30 percent of world trade but account for 60 percent or more of GNP in developed countries. It may be hypothesized, thus, that "the internationalization of services is a different thing altogether from internationalization in the product manufacturing industries."

One problem is the lack of comparable data sources, arising from the fact that there is not the same level of activity at the frontier as in trade in manufactured goods; thus, occurrence of a service activity may not be measured. The interested reader should refer to Riddle (1986) for a summary of the problems in measuring trade in services.

THE INTERNATIONALIZATION OF SERVICES

Following the argument that the world is one marketplace, the issue of standardization versus localization of the services offering has become a field of discussion for academics and practitioners. Standardization is seen as offering benefits of lower costs and higher margins, while localization offers customized services so that differences are recognized rather than ignored. However, these opposing views should not necessarily be treated as a dichotomy, since there will be a continuum of approaches. Indeed, Edvardsson and associates (1993) argue, "it is the interplay between these two major strategic orientations that determines the outcome of the internationalisation process and companies need to learn how to balance the two successfully."

Several attempts have been made to develop conceptual models of services globalization although Cowell (1983) argues that "the principles of marketing services internationally are the same as those which apply to domestic markets." One approach has been to focus on the unique characteristics of services, namely intangibility, inseparability, heterogeneity, and perishability (Carman and Langeard 1980; Nicolaud 1989; Dahringer 1991). Thus, for example, heterogeneity makes standardization more difficult, but not impossible, for services—with Nicolaud (1989) arguing that "many service companies have turned to franchising to enable them to penetrate foreign markets with a standardized package." The core of a firm's offering may be standardized, while concessions to local factors are made using other aspects of the bundle. However, while such characteristics are important, they may not deserve to be the foundation of a theory of International Services Marketing (ISM).

Other issues to be considered are the risks involved in the international marketing of services, barriers to and motives for internationalizing, market and entry mode choice, and the role of culture. Clearly, all are interrelated; in addition, given the variety and range of services, there will necessarily be different areas of focus within each service (Vandermerwe and Chadwick 1989), and it is not possible to state general principles of ISM that apply in all specific cases.

The objective of this chapter, therefore, is to attempt to develop a normative framework for internationalization in one particular service industry, namely, the general insurance industry.

CHARACTERISTICS OF THE GENERAL INSURANCE INDUSTRY

Standardized or Customized Strategies

The issue of whether general insurance companies, as opposed to life insurance companies, have the opportunity to pursue standardized global marketing strategies or customization strategies in each geographical market of operation needs to be viewed from three perspectives, namely, industrial, customer, and regulatory.

The industrial perspective focuses on the supply side of international operations. Levitt (1983) argues that insurance is one of many industries that sell "standardised products in the same way everywhere," a commodity where price is the main differentiating factor. There is considerable scope for global strategies in general insurance, particularly with respect to the latter point. Morgan (1992) argues that "home-based advantages in the production and design of particular services can provide the initial basis for the penetration of overseas markets, that is, for globalisation." In addition, a globally integrated communications network enables coordination of worldwide operations from one national base.

However, Porter (1990) argues that the particular nature of financial services, especially the importance of trust in the supply companies, delays the process of globalization. Such a view corresponds to the need for more localized "front-office" activities, where customer contact is made and a sale initiated.

The strength of the supply argument can be witnessed by the way that certain large insurers (e.g., Allianz from Germany, Generali from Italy, UAP from France, and Prudential from the United Kingdom) have organized their international operations in order to supply the most competitive packages in terms of cost.

The speed and intensity of such developments may, however, depend upon developments in the regulatory framework governing companies' activities. Deregulation within the European Union (EU) appears to be emerging, and recent progress is now establishing the basis for genuine cross-border trading in general insurance. The "second directive" in 1988 opened up a liberalized market for commercial risks insurance whereby "above medium size" client companies were able to buy their insurance policies from insurers established in any member state. The "third directive" in 1991 liberalized domestic markets, thus enabling householders and motorists to purchase from companies licensed by any one member state.

Motives for Internationalization

Schroath (1987) states that, prior to World War II, insurers entered international markets in order to "follow the flag," that is, companies followed their governments in the process of colonization. The war, however, revealed the need for geographical diversification in order to spread risks, although more recently, as a consequence of the trend toward increasing competition, results now tend to be bad or good everywhere at the same time.

Bickelhaupt and Bar-Niv (1983) identify seven objectives for internationalization in insurance, namely:

1. Following domestic business clients
2. Seeking high profit potential in expanding economies
3. Competitive benefits (market leadership)
4. Spreading risks
5. The challenge and intrigue of foreign operations
6. Improved communication and information
7. Enhancing prestige and public relations

The first two motives are endorsed by Schroath.

Stagnation in the home market may be a strong incentive for expansion, according to Eppink and Rhijn (1989) in a study into Dutch insurance companies' international strategies. They also highlight the importance of spreading risk, economies of scale, and the existence of overcapacity.

The importance of following domestic (corporate) clients appears to be a strong motivation with most writers, although this implies a reactive approach. A superior alternative may be to develop strategies that aim to be proactive in developing a relationship with existing clients, thus pointing the way to growing mutual trust and profitability.

Barriers to Internationalization

Dahringer (1991) argues that international commerce in insurance is subject to a stronger degree and more forms of impediment than most other service industries. This observation may be related to the general concern of governments that they will lose control over their capital markets if foreign financial institutions are allowed free, unregulated entry. However, a distinction may be made between entry and operating barriers. With respect to entry, governments such as those in Thailand, Indonesia, and Paraguay, according to Detwiler (1983), simply deny access outright to foreign insurance companies. More subtle moves may be to deny entrants the appropriate license, to limit foreign presence to representative offices (with no underwriting powers), and to limit foreign equity holdings in local companies. All of these measures may be general or selective. Local operating controls may also prevent competition on equal terms. Walter (1988) identifies four such restrictions, namely:

1. Market delineation—identifying groups of clients who may or may not be served
2. Asset growth limits—gearing ratios, reserve requirements, and capitalization limits may be set at different levels for domestic and foreign companies
3. Funding limits—increasing the cost of debt and acquiring equity capital
4. Nuisance measures—limiting access to the local infrastructure (communications, building permits) and to staff, and discrimination with respect to tax.

Entry Mode

A study by Schroath (1987) is currently the only empirical study that has examined the relationship between successful entry techniques and various company and market characteristics in international general insurance. Having recognized the nine entry modes outlined by Bickelhaupt and Bar-Niv (1983), Schroath identifies the five most commonly used entry modes in international insurance as the focus for his analysis. These are:

1. Establishing a new branch office
2. Contracting with a managing general agency
3. Establishing a new (greenfield) subsidiary
4. Purchasing a local national insurer
5. Forming a joint venture

In most countries these entry techniques all require capital commitment on the part of the insurer in the form of a minimum capital deposit with the respective insurance regulatory authority and can thus be viewed as different forms of foreign direct investment in the local market. The choice of entry mode from these alternatives was found to be dependent on the ability of a company to manage a certain mode (company characteristics) and the appropriateness of the chosen mode in a given market (market characteristics).

Although Schroath found that these five entry techniques were the most commonly used in international insurance, he also points out that "restrictive regulations in the host country, business conditions in the host country, unrealistic amounts of capitalization or the need for speedy market entry would occasionally dictate that the company use other means." Thus, in order to overcome regulatory barriers in a market, insurers can enter by establishing a reinsurance company, by purchasing a minority interest in a local insurer, or by cooperative agreements.

Culture

Despite a lack of academic research into how culture will influence the provision of services internationally, it may be an important barrier in the internationalization process of the general insurance industry. Culture, as defined by Shames and Glover (1989), is "a set of life ways and orientations (including customs, beliefs, attitudes and out-of-awareness values and assumptions) that are learned and reinforced through group affiliation." Since general insurance is very much a people-based industry, where competitive advantage may be related to employees' specialist skills and know-how, it is important to recognize the need to harness a strong and flexible internal corporate culture during the internationalization process. Thus insurers should choose different entry strategies depending on the degree of flexibility required consistent with a high level of control over operations. Indeed, cooperative modes of entry may not be viable in certain markets since the corporate cultures of the partners may be too different for such a relationship to succeed. For the client, too, there will be differences in culture. Riddle's (1986) conceptual model for adapting all services to culturally defined needs in different markets should be applicable to international general insurance, whereby the explicit components of the package (availability, environment, style, and range) will be delivered and consumed through a filter of culturally defined lifestyles and orientations only if adaptations are made by both parties.

THE DEVELOPMENT OF A NORMATIVE FRAMEWORK

Objective

Given the above, research was undertaken in an attempt to develop a conceptual approach to analyze relevant issues that need to be included in a theoretical framework for internationalization in the general insurance industry.

Methodology

A qualitative exploratory approach was undertaken, as the research "is centrally concerned with understanding things rather than with measuring them" (Gordon and Langmaid 1988).

The sample of six companies was chosen from a population of international general insurers based in the United Kingdom and Scandinavia numbering eight and three, respectively. Two bases were chosen to attempt to give a representation of companies both by size and historical international activities. The UK suppliers were characterized as being the most international in Europe, drawing 44 percent of their general insurance income from abroad. With 20 percent of EU premiums, they are second only to Germany. Since the UK market has a low level of regulation by EU standards, it is vulnerable to entry by foreign suppliers. Both Sweden and Norway are mature markets, but international ambitions of supplier firms have been relatively limited (probably as a result of a lack of capital), with less than 5 percent of total premiums coming from foreign subsidiaries or branches. Again, future competition in their domestic markets is likely to be experienced from foreign suppliers. Thus, although suppliers in both areas are facing increasing competition, the Scandinavian insurers do not have the same international experience or capital base to support expansive internationalization strategies.

Moreover, as the EU becomes a single market, companies pursuing a limited international strategy within it may be able to use this experience to trigger larger-scale globalization at a later stage. The Scandinavian suppliers are not yet members of the EU and may need to adopt a different view if they are to internationalize.

Semistructured in-depth interviews lasting 75 minutes or more were held with senior personnel from four UK-based and two Scandinavian-based general insurers. Two companies suggested the presence of more than one representative during the interview, arguing that this would reduce the potential for personal bias in the responses given and also indicating high commitment to the research project.

Figure 15.1
Major Decisions in International Marketing

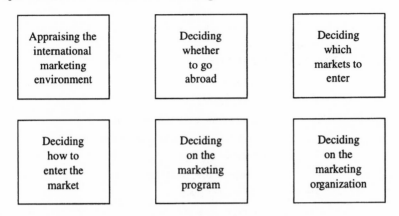

Results

1. In developing a normative framework for ISM, certain major decisions must be integrated. At the simplest level, six such decisions have been proposed by Kotler (1988) (see Figure 15.1). This framework has limited explanatory power and also assumes a company to be in the initial stages of internationalizing. Current theory in international marketing, however, reflects a need to "take into consideration the stage of a company's internationalization and also the role of entry decisions in the design of global competitive strategy" (Douglas and Craig 1992).

2. *Market Analysis and Marketing Information Systems.* Macro analysis focuses on collecting information regarding the general business environment in a particular country or region. Thus, all suppliers seem particularly preoccupied with the implications arising from the emergence of a single European general insurance market. Furthermore, a similar liberalization of trade is arguably taking place in what are termed "the triad markets" (Europe, North America, and Asia). Macro factors in total suggest that general insurers will face increasing competition irrespective of whether they expand internationally or not. In addition, industry-specific barriers to trade, such as restrictions on capital and local ownership, will force a company to be flexible in its organization structure. Demand patterns and local purchasing behavior are important issues when analyzing markets in the micro context. A distinction needs to be drawn between corporate and personal customers, with the latter requiring a relatively higher degree of local product and marketing adaptation. In addition, local customer attitudes and perceptions of suppliers (both domestic and foreign) tend to vary between countries.

All the companies pointed to quantitative factors, namely, a market's current and future profitability ratings, its economic size, and its growth potential, as

Table 15.1
Aggregate Weighted Ranking of Motives for Internationalization in General
Insurance

Ranking	Weighted Ranking	The Motives
1	26.3	Seek high profit potentials in expanding economies
2	24.2	Spread risks
3	13.2	Exploit a competitive advantage
4	11.2	Follow domestic clients to other countries
5	7.9	Economies of scope
6	4.9	Develop client relationships
7	3.8	Economies of scale
8	2.9	Communication and statistical information improvement
9	2.4	Prestige and public relations
10	2.3	Challenge and intrigue of foreign operations
11	0.8	Comparative benefits (leading firms and sizable premiums)

Note: The weighted ranking was derived by dividing the aggregate score for each factor by 6 (the
number of respondents). It is recognized that some detail is thus lost, but differences between
supplier country respondents are discussed later.

the three most important factors in assessing attractiveness. Cultural differences,
however, also play a major role. UK-based companies, with their existing international spread of operations, are likely to perceive culturally and geographically distant markets with less skepticism than their Scandinavian counterparts.
A potential substitute for experience is to use reinsurance capabilities as a spear-
head operation into distant markets.

The collected information should enable a general insurer to identify profitable
opportunities in the international arena.

3. *Motives for Internationalization.* A list of eleven motives identified from
the literature was proposed by the researcher. They were ranked and weighted
by the respondents, the weights being derived from an allocation of 100 points
(see Table 15.1).

The motive perceived as most important relates to economic and demographic
prospects capable of yielding high growth rates. A recent survey ("Insurance
Sector" 1993) points to some markets in Europe and Asia that have seen annual
growth rates of up to 25 percent. The second most important motive is internally
generated, in that it reflects the companies aim to achieve individual business
objectives by diversifying sources of income. Two benefits are related, namely,
that both economic and underwriting risks are diversified, the former offering
independent prospects irrespective of the state of each economy and the latter

notwithstanding catastrophes and related claims that may adversely affect one market.

Superior management skills, technology, underwriting and rating systems, human resources, and the insurance products themselves are some of the potential sources to exploit a competitive advantage in international general insurance. However, competitiveness will not, of itself, initiate a motivation to internationalize, but will rather act as a facilitator in situations where the more important motives make international expansion an attractive strategy.

The fourth ranked motive—following domestic clients—is closely linked with that of "developing client relationships," the more proactive approach. Respondents largely confirmed the view that following domestic clients is a strong historical motive for internationalization, but there appears to be a change in emphasis toward a more proactive approach toward their clients as they become more experienced.

Other motives were relatively unimportant, perhaps surprisingly so. Respondents seem to perceive low potential for economies of scale and only moderate potential for economies of scope. A more balanced approach may be applicable, with a positive decision *not* to dominate being used.

Although both the United Kingdom and Scandinavian markets are relatively mature in terms of premium growth and are also culturally similar, the motives for international expansion differ between respective general insurance suppliers. The underlying rationale for these differences is linked to the business environment. Thus, a lack of international experience and investment capital contributes to the Scandinavian companies' relative lack of support regarding the attractiveness of seeking high profit potential in expanding economies. They are more dependent on enjoying a more currently developed competitive advantage, particularly in culturally similar markets. The lack of international experience may also be related to the fact that Scandinavian insurers have a limited number of international commercial clients, which is reflected in the low ranking awarded to the motive of developing international client relationships. Finally, Scandinavian insurers are vulnerable targets for takeover in the European arena, which means that they look to economies of scale and scope as means of generating market power relatively more so than their UK competitors.

Thus, a company's perceptions regarding motives for internationalization are seemingly interrelated with its actual experience in international general insurance. A distinction may, therefore, be made between an *initial* decision to internationalize and continuing expansion from an existing base. Thus, a first-time entrant into a foreign market should focus its attention on areas where it is capable of understanding the local business environment and pursue a learning process before venturing into more risky areas.

4. *Barriers to Internationalization.* Market entry barriers were perceived as less important than operating barriers by all the respondents. When references were made to denial of access to markets, it was indicated that large, experienced insurers have an advantage in that they can use existing subsidiaries to gain

Table 15.2
Foreign Market Entry Modes in International Insurance

Foreign Market Entry Mode	Aggregate Weighted Ranking	Ranking Only
Establishing a new branch office	9.25	3
Wholly owned subsidiary, greenfield site	7.25	4
Wholly owned acquired subsidiary	53.00	1
Majority joint venture	24.00	2
50/50 joint venture	4.00	5
Minority joint venture	1.50	6
Contracting with a managing general agency	1.00	7

access to markets that are open only to selected foreign nationalities. In addition, large companies may have sufficient financial strength to negotiate directly with authorities to influence legislation in a favored direction.

All the restrictions discussed earlier concerning operations were referred to in varying degrees by respondents. Those relating to capital requirements and/ or local ownership were the most frequently cited, with the UK respondents arguing that organizational flexibility is essential in order to minimize the effect of such impediments. One UK respondent also argued for superior marketing skills in targeting particular segments not under tariff regulation in finding a route around pricing restrictions in U.S. motor insurance.

5. *Entry Mode.* Respondents were asked to rank and weight the seven most common entry modes (adapted from Schroath 1987), listed according to the degree of management control each offers, by allocating a total of 100 points among them (see Table 15.2).

The respondents suggest that management control is the main overriding consideration, closely followed by the speed of entry associated with the alternatives of acquisition and joint ventures. The combination of speed and control is arguably maximized when acquiring an established insurer in a foreign market, and this appears as the top-ranked option. However, recent server losses, leading to an increased focus on costs, have persuaded companies to look to majority joint ventures as an alternative that offers high control and high speed of entry, but relatively low capital outlays.

UK insurers are more experienced in using a greater variety of entry modes with a higher weighted ranking being given to the full control modes of establishing a branch office and a greenfield subsidiary. Nevertheless, both Scandinavian and UK insurers appear to indicate an equally strong preference for control, despite the difference in terms of international experience.

The entry modes suggested by general insurers can also be related to the generic model for all services suggested by Vandermerwe and Chadwick (1989). The value of their model is that it introduces the dynamic element of information technology, which makes it possible to operate in several modes simultaneously. Thus, "an insurance company can offer instant insurance from self-dispensing machines, highly differentiated services from wholly owned subsidiaries and routine insurance from a central location through a foreign telecommunications network."

6. *Culture.* All respondents stressed the importance of having a high sense of cultural awareness in international general insurance, particularly the requirement for social interaction between insurer and insured. Several respondents also highlighted the "relationship with others" dimension (Kluckholn and Strodtbeck 1961), which suggests that the acceptance of foreign firms viewed as strangers in the market will vary between cultures and will necessitate adaptation of strategies by outsiders.

Customers' expectations are also likely to vary between cultural segments, thus arguing for local marketing decisions requiring culturally attuned managers and staff in each market. The challenge of a multicultural work force was recognized by all respondents, not only in respect of different local managers but also in the coordination between such local demands and the strategic objectives and control mechanisms emanating from the head office. Qualified local managers were seen to be displacing expatriates and were equally capable of achieving "the right balance." Human resource development strategies aimed at creating culturally aware managers were viewed as beneficial in terms of facilitating communication between the head office and the various international operations.

Corporate culture is thus seen as a highly relevant management challenge for general insurers, with two issues emerging as particularly important. First, it appears that the respondents favor a balanced approach to defining the corporate culture of local operations. Thus, keeping certain core elements of the group's corporate identity intact worldwide, while allowing for local cultural conditions to be reflected in each specific market, was argued to be the most viable approach. Furthermore, the task of guiding the evolution of these separate corporate cultures was perceived to be a process that is controllable by centrally placed senior managers. The companies' defined strategic objectives and the introduced methodology for making decisions were seen as elements that reinforce a common corporate identity internationally. The respondents' concern for establishing a coherent corporate culture throughout international operations arguably reflects close commercial relationships with multinational clients, while the need for cultural affinity may reflect the interactive nature of a services experience in international general insurance. Consequently, the need to balance an international corporate identity with local responsiveness seems to be a reflection of the specific demands that exist in the international general insurance industry.

Second, all the respondents argued that joint ventures (JVs) and acquisitions offer specific management challenges for international general insurers. In the light of the fact that these were the most preferred market entry modes by the participating companies, it is not surprising that the respondents highlighted the task of managing the process of merging two distinct corporate cultures as particularly complex. The fact that the Scandinavian companies indicated that this challenge has not yet received its deserved attention does not undermine the respondents' expressed concern for the subject. The respondents' views seem to focus on the importance of selecting capable top local managers, who are capable of managing the venture according to the specified aims of the respective companies. As such, a local operation is likely to develop its own corporate identity, and a managerial capability to direct this process was argued to be the result of a learning process from similar cooperative ventures in international general insurance. Consequently, it appears that there are important issues related to a general insurer's corporate culture when expanding internationally.

The Model

The normative model proposed (Figure 15.2) recognizes a need to examine the internationalization of general insurance services within the context of existing operations. Thus, an important distinction is made between internationally experienced and inexperienced insurers. In addition, there is a need for planning to be a dynamic learning process that aims to understand and adapt to the dynamics of the marketplace and all issues are thus interconnected.

The Importance of Marketing Information

Macro-context analysis focuses on scanning countries and regions and understanding changing trade patterns and the emergence of new markets, such as the continually emerging European single market. However, such information needs to be combined with micro context insights into local demand patterns and purchasing processes.

Motives for Internationalization and Strategy Evaluation

The importance of dedicating top management resources to the challenge of evaluating motives is reflected in the model at this stage, which arguably affects the remainder of the strategic planning process. The distinction between inexperienced and experienced companies is introduced at this stage.

Inexperienced Companies

Market Selection. A company that considers a first-time entry into a foreign market should focus its attention on areas where it is capable of understanding the local business environment. Although attractive business opportunities in culturally distant markets must be forgone initially, an inexperienced insurer needs to realize the value of going through a gradual learning process in international general insurance before eventually venturing into more risky business alternatives.

Entry Mode Choice. There is a likely emphasis on acquiring an existing local company during initial international expansion, but it is crucial that firms realize that the concept of maintaining overall corporate culture offers unique challenges for them when acquiring a new corporate body.

Marketing Plans and Investments. Assuming that culturally close markets are selected for international expansion, inexperienced insurers may be able to achieve competitive advantage by pursuing operations similar to those in the domestic market. Support facilities, especially in terms of management information systems, can be utilized with a standardized approach, reducing the complexity of transferring information between the different management groups. In addition, insurers with a limited number of foreign operations are in a position where service quality programs can be coordinated from the strategic center.

Experienced Companies

Strategy at the Business Unit Level. Since a holding company structure dominates the industry, there are three methods of exercising control over an internationally expanding number of business units. First, the head office may define overall objectives but allow subsidiaries autonomy in modifying them. Second, the head office may define objectives but allow little or no autonomy. Third, and most favored, is the balance of central and local management, with financial targets being established at the center and marketing strategies at the local level.

The generic strategy may be one of cost leadership, differentiation, or focus (Porter 1980), but experiments with each may be conducted in different markets to identify ways of improving overall group profitability. Thus, decisions have to be made on both qualitative and quantitative objectives as well as the allocation of resources to various operations.

Market Entry and Consolidation Strategies. Experienced insurers are less inhibited by the difficulties involved in marketing to culturally and geographically distant markets. In addition, large companies have an advantage over smaller competitors with respect to overcoming market entry barriers, since access may be granted via a related subsidiary or by direct negotiation with local authorities.

High control and speed of entry, at low cost, are the most valued considerations favoring the acquisition of an existing company, but a variety of modes may be employed in order to circumvent operational impediments. The challenge of managing a corporate culture becomes increasingly complex, with specific demands for local responsiveness needing to be balanced with the retention of a global corporate identity.

Marketing Plans and Investments. The challenge of managing a variety of culturally differing markets necessitates delegation of responsibility to local management. Thus, an international staffing structure will require culturally aware managers to facilitate communication between the head office and subsidiary

Figure 15.2
Strategic Planning in International General Insurance

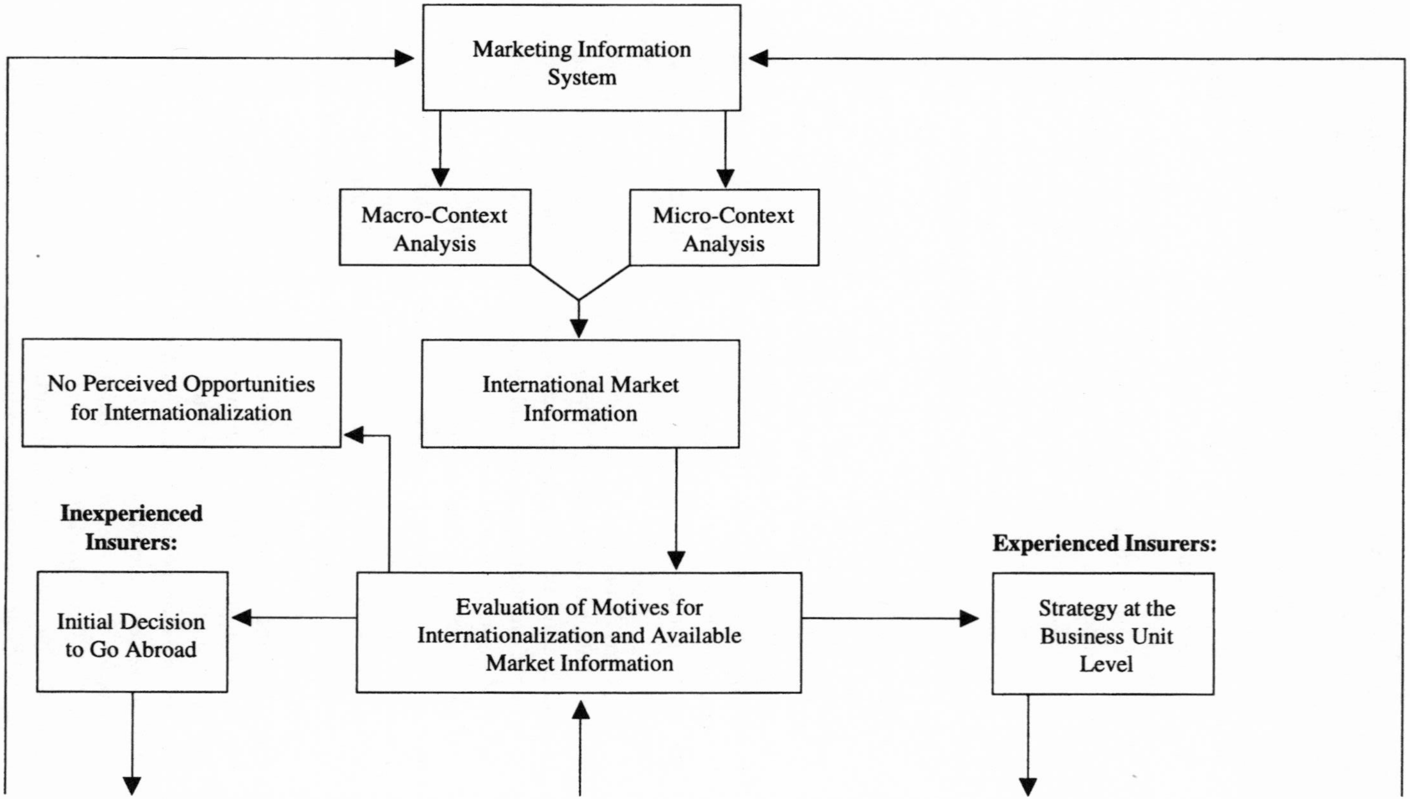

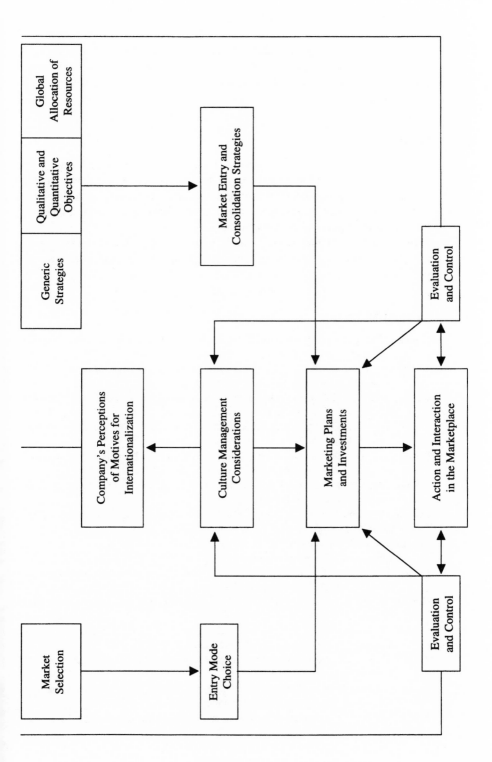

unit operations, as well as within the subsidiaries. Furthermore, the feedback links between marketing plans and action in the marketplace imply that culture management skill is a dynamic learning process in the development of long-term strategy.

SUMMARY

A model for international marketing in the general insurance industry has been proposed. The model is based on an integration of previously defined theoretical concepts on internationalization of services and the practical findings from empirical research among six major general insurance companies, both in the United Kingdom and in Scandinavia.

International marketing planning in the industry is argued to require a systems perspective, reflecting both the multifunctional and interdependent processes involved.

REFERENCES

Benton, D'Arcy M. and Bowles (1992). *Marketing: Communicating with the Customer.* New York: Mercury Books.

Bickelhaupt, D. L. and R. Bar-Niv (1983). *International Insurance: Managing Risk in the World.* New York: Insurance Information Institute.

Carman, J. M. and E. Langeard (1980). "Growth Strategies of Service Firms." *Strategic Management Journal* (January–March): 7–22.

Cowell, D. W. (1983). "International Marketing of Services." *The Services Industries Journal,* 3(3): 308–328.

Dahringer, L. D. (1991). "Marketing Services Internationally: Barriers and Management Strategies." *Journal of Services Marketing,* 5(3): 5–17.

Detwiler, J. (1983). "Foreign Trade Barriers: Hazard of International Insurance." *The Journal of Insurance* (May–June).

Douglas, S. P. and C. S. Craig (1992). "Advances in International Marketing." *International Journal of Research in Marketing,* 9(4): 291–323.

Edvardsson, B., L. Edvinsson, and H. Nystrom (1993). "Internationalisation in Service Companies." *The Services Industries Journal,* 13(1): 80–97.

Eppink, D. J. and B. M. Rhijn (1989). "International Strategies of Dutch Insurance Companies." *Long Range Planning,* 22(1).

Gordon, W. and R. Langmaid (1988). *Qualitative Market Research: A Practitioner's and Buyer's Guide.* Aldershot, UK: Gower.

"Insurance Sector: Annual Review, 1992: The Year of the CTAS; 1993: The Year of Recovery" (1993). *Hoare Govett* (February).

Kluckhohn, F. and F. Strodtbeck (1961). *Variations in Value Orientations.* Evanston, IL: Row, Peterson & Co.

Kotler, P. (1988). *Marketing Management: Analysis, Planning, Implementation, and Control,* 6th ed. Englewood Cliffs, NJ: Prentice-Hall.

Levitt, T. (1983). "The Globalization of Markets." *Harvard Business Review* (May–June).

Morgan, G. (1992). "The Globalization of Personal Financial Services: The European Community after 1992." *The Services Industries Journal*, 12(2): 193–209.

Nicolaud, B. (1989). "Problems and Strategies in the International Marketing of Services." *European Journal of Marketing*, 23(6): 55–66.

Normann, R. (1984). *Service Management: Strategy and Leadership in Service Businesses*. Chichester, UK: Wiley.

Porter, M. E. (1990). *The Competitive Advantage of Nations*. New York: Macmillan.

Riddle, D. I. (1986). *Service-Led Growth: The Role of the Service Sector in World Development*. New York: Praeger.

Schroath, F. W. (1987). "Analysis of Foreign Market Entry Techniques for Multinational Insurers." Ph.D dissertation, University of South Carolina.

Shames, G. W. and W. G. Glover (1989). *World Class Service*. Yarmouth, ME: Intercultural Press.

Vandermerwe, S. and M. Chadwick (1989). "The Internationalisation of Services." *The Services Industries Journal*, 9(1).

Walter, I. (1988). *Global Competition in Financial Services: Market Structure, Protection, and Trade Liberalization*. Cambridge, MA: Ballinger.

Part VI

Managerial Issues in Regional Markets

Chapter 16

Perceived Attribute Importance in China: An Empirical Investigation of Consumption-Oriented Personal Values

Zhengyuan Wang, C. P. Rao, and Douglas Vorhies

INTRODUCTION

In recent years, one of the most dynamic areas of research in social science disciplines, including consumer behavior, has been the measurement and functions of personal values (Kamakura and Mazzon 1991; Pitts and Woodside 1984). The pervasive role of values in all aspects of human life (Rokeach and Ball-Rokeach 1973) has motivated myriads of empirical investigations of personal values in the disciplines of psychology, sociology, cultural anthropology, and consumer behavior.

Past research has shown that personal values could be both a powerful explanation of and influence on a variety of individual and collective behaviors, including consumer consumption behavior (Henry 1976; Pitts and Woodside 1983; Schopphoven 1991; Vinson and Munson 1976), political attitude and behavior (Baum 1968; Levine 1960; Tetlock 1986), gift-giving behavior (Beatty et al. 1991), and cross-cultural differences (Munson and McIntyre 1978, 1979; Schwartz and Bilsky 1987; Grunert and Scherhorn 1990).

Several ways are currently available to measure personal values. Among the most frequently used instruments for measuring values are the Rokeach Value Survey (RVS) (Rokeach and Ball-Rokeach 1973), the Values and Lifestyles (VALS) methodology developed at SRI International (Mitchell 1983), and the List of Values (LOV) developed at the University of Michigan Survey Research Center (Kahle 1983; Veroff et al. 1981).

There has been an ongoing debate over the predictive utility associated with each of the value instruments (Beatty et al. 1985; Kahle et al. 1986; Munson and McIntyre 1988; Novak and MacEvoy 1990). So far, no conclusive empirical evidence has yet been reached.

Values provide clues about how a society operates because values are an individual's representation of a society's goals (Beatty et al. 1988). Values should thus be a central topic for cross-cultural research (Berrien 1966; Zavaloni 1980). Unfortunately, most previous attempts to develop cross-cultural value measures relevant to consumption have not been particularly productive due to conceptual differences between personal values and consumer consumption behavior (Munson 1984).

In order to fill this void, a Perceived Attribute Importance (PAI) measure has been developed and is the focus of this chapter. This new tool attempts to measure consumer consumption behavior in a personal values context. Chinese consumers are investigated in this study and used as a baseline for testing the validity of the PAI instrument.

BACKGROUND

Rokeach and Ball-Rokeach (1973, p. 5) defined a personal value as an enduring belief that a specific mode of conduct or end-state of existence is personally or socially preferable to its opposite. A value system is an enduring organization of beliefs concerning preferred modes of conduct or end-states along an importance continuum. Two kinds of values—instrumental and terminal—were defined as a person's beliefs concerning desirable modes of conduct and desirable end-states of existence, respectively (Rokeach and Ball-Rokeach 1973, p. 7).

The conceptualization of personal values in terms of social adaptation theory (Kahle et al. 1980; Kahle 1983, 1984; Kahle and Timmer 1983; Piner and Kahle 1984) posed that personal values are the most abstract type of social cognitions that function to facilitate adaptation to one's environment. The concept of regarding personal values as mediators in the social adaptation process implies that value differences between cultures can be traced back to different ethnic backgrounds and the social, economic, political, and technological environments.

A considerable amount of consumer value literature deals with the "means-end chain," linking values with behavior (Vinson and Munson 1977; Gutman 1982, 1990, 1991; Reynolds and Gutman 1984, 1988; Prakash and Munson 1985; Homer and Kahle 1988). Values are regarded as desired ends of consumption, and products and/or product attributes are perceived to be the means to realizing those values.

When discussing the relationship between values and attitudes, Rokeach and Ball-Rokeach (1973, p. 18) stated that "whereas a value is a single belief, an attitude refers to an organization of several beliefs that are all focused on a given object or situation . . . values occupy a more central position than attitudes within one's personality makeup and cognitive system, and they are therefore determinants of attitudes as well as of behavior." Their view of greater centrality of values has also been echoed by other researchers: "attitudes themselves depend on pre-existing social values" (Allport 1961, pp. 802–803); "attitudes express values" (Watson 1966, p. 215); and "attitudes are functions of values" (Woodruff 1942, p. 33).

Carman (1977) developed a model proposing a causal relationship between terminal and instrumental values and consumption behaviors. He states that values influence behaviors, such as shopping and media exposure patterns, both directly and indirectly through intervening attitudinal variables.

Due in part to the growing importance of the emerging global economy, cross-cultural value research has received greater attention during the last decade. International research on values can provide needed cross-cultural understanding of consumers. However, since values are culturally derived and determined, value instruments such as the RVS have not been consistent measures cross-culturally and tend to exhibit heterogeneity across different cultures and sub-cultures (Munson and McQuarrie 1988).

In order for values to accurately predict consumer shopping and consumption behavior, it is obviously necessary for values to be linked to product attributes. Such values should not necessarily be global human values such as those identified by Rokeach (1973), but can be less general, less abstract, and more consumption oriented. In this study, we label the special portion of the human values and value system that is relevant to and reflected by consumers' consumption behavior as consumption values.

As a matter of fact, researchers have already noted that many of the individual value items in the existing measures of personal values, including the RVS and VALS, appeared to be largely irrelevant to consumer consumption behavior (Beatty et al. 1985, 1988; McQuarrie and Langmeyer 1985; Munson and McQuarrie 1988; Prakash and Munson 1985; Vinson and Munson 1976; Vinson et al. 1977). As a consequence, values perceived to be unrelated to consumption may increase the likelihood of respondent fatigue and error and thus obscure those true relationships that are present between values and consumption (Beatty et al. 1985; Munson and McQuarrie 1988).

Moreover, most value items of existing instruments of values are viewed positively by most people, thus leading to positive bias. As Beatty and associates (1988) pointed out, "irrelevant needs, salience, superordination, impression management, social change, excessive abstractness, and ambiguity of meaning may all distort self-reports of values."

Finally, the problem of value measurement is further complicated by cultural differences when one attempts to conduct international value research.

THE CONCEPT OF PERCEIVED ATTRIBUTE IMPORTANCE

Because of the myriad of potential problems associated with the existing value instruments, we propose that consumers' Perceived Attribute Importance (PAI) be an alternative measure of cross-cultural consumption values.

There are a number of reasons for this proposition. First, PAI is an important component of a number of multi-attribute attitude models (see Lutz and Bettman

1977 for a review). In the value-attitude-behavior hierarchy, PAI reflects a lower level of abstraction than global human values such as those identified by Rokeach (1973). It is thus more likely to have higher predictive power to behavior. Its role in attitudinal models (Rosenberg 1956; Fishbein and Ajzen 1975), involvement models (Ostrom and Brock 1968), and ideal-point models of consumer preference (Lehmann 1971; Ginter 1974) reflects its importance. Second, a consumer's PAI measures his or her motivation behind the product choice and hence may reflect the cultural value he or she subscribes to. Third, most systematic models of consumer behavior (Engel et al. 1968; Howard and Sheth 1969) suggest that a consumer's attitude, in which PAI is a component, is affected by his or her social and cultural environments. This suggests that the construct of PAI may reflect the societal norms to which a consumer subscribes. Finally, the construct of PAI is conceptually simpler and more concrete than traditional measures of values. It may thus be less prone to individual interpretation, which can be a considerable problem in cross-cultural research.

Thus, the major objective of this study was to demonstrate the use of the PAI as a measure of consumption values and assess its power to predict consumer shopping and consumption behavior.

HYPOTHESES

To guide the research design and data analyses of the present study, the following research hypotheses were derived from the preceding theoretical discussions and empirical findings.

Sheth and associates (1991a, 1991b) proposed a theory of consumption values in which five values were identified. They include (1) functional, (2) social, (3) emotional, (4) epistemic, and (5) conditional values. One of the central propositions of the theory is that different consumption values make differential contributions in any given choice situation.

In the current study, consumers' consumption values along four product categories: (1) clothing, (2) household appliances, (3) household supplies, and (4) food were surveyed in China. Thus, our first hypothesis was formulated as follows:

> H1. Consumption values measured by the PAI differ across the four product categories.

As was stated previously, personal values have a causal effect upon subsequent behavior in the value-attitude-behavior hierarchy (Carman 1977; Homer and Kahle 1988). A basic problem with measures of global, transcendental Rokeach-type values has been their lack of correspondence with consumer consumption behaviors (Munson and McQuarrie 1988). Since the PAI strives to measure the less global and more consumption-relevant values, it was hypothesized that the PAI has a higher degree of predictive power than the earlier instruments utilized.

Consumer level of involvement—the degree of perceived relevance and personal importance accompanying the product and brand choice within a specific situation—has long been recognized as a crucial determinant of the type of decision process a consumer will undertake (Antil 1984; Krugman 1965; Ostrom and Brock 1968). High involvement suggests that the order of consumer decision making will follow the hierarchy of effects model—values and beliefs will be formed, attitudes will develop, and purchase and consumption behaviors will follow. With low involvement, on the other hand, consumers may behave impulsively without a priori formation of values, beliefs, and attitudes.

For highly involving choices, such as automobiles, household appliances, or expensive clothing, the role of values may be more obvious. But for less involving consumer purchases, such as household supplies and food, the predictive power of values as measured by the PAI may be less apparent. Hence, our second hypothesis states:

> H2. The power of the PAI will vary across the four product categories. The PAIs associated with household appliances and clothing will have greater predictive power than those with household supplies and food.

METHODOLOGY

The Research Instrument and Fielding Activities

The data used to test the research hypotheses resulted from personal interviews with predesigned questionnaires. Data collection was undertaken concurrently in two major Chinese cities: Beijing and Shanghai. Because of the difficulties in executing a random sampling methodology in China, a judgment sampling technique was used. Although not a probability type of sample, care was exercised in collecting a representative cross-section of the wide spectrum of the target population.

The questionnaire had three sections. The first section contained 23 Likert scales, measuring respondents' agreement to different dimensions of the respondents' shopping and consumption behavior. The second section contained perceived attribute importance (ranging from 23 to 30 attributes) in four product categories. These product categories included clothing, household appliances, household supplies, and food (fresh and unprepared). Respondents were asked to indicate on a 7-point rating scale the importance they attached to each of the product attributes, with 7 being most important and 1 being least important. The last section contained questions on respondents' gender, age, education level, and occupation.

The product attributes measured were obtained from focus group discussions by housewives of different nationalities (including Chinese) who had lived in the United States less than one year. These product attributes were then modified by professional marketing researchers in designing the descriptive study instrument.

The questionnaire was translated into Chinese by a doctoral student from China who was studying business administration at a Western university. The translated questionnaire was then reviewed by a panel consisting of another Chinese doctoral student and one of the authors whose mother tongue is Chinese. Both the English and Chinese versions of the questionnaire were pretested on convenience samples.

A total of 196 usable questionnaires were obtained: 101 originated from Beijing and 95 were obtained from Shanghai. Since interviews were generally conducted during tea breaks or leisure time, respondents had sufficient time to thoughtfully complete the survey. As a result, the response rate was quite high, approximately 85 percent.

Analysis Procedures

To test the first hypothesis, which states that consumption values measured by the PAI differ across the four product categories, separate principal components factor analysis with varimax rotation using Kaiser's criterion was run for each product category. The resulting factor structures were then compared and contrasted.

As a first step to test the second hypothesis, hierarchical cluster analysis using minimum variance or Ward's clustering method with squared Euclidean distance (Johnson 1967; Punj and Stewart 1983) was conducted to group the 196 Chinese consumers based on the raw scores of the 23 Likert scales measuring consumers' shopping and consumption behavior. Unstandardized data (the unadjusted, mean responses to each of the 23 scale items) were used, consistent with the recommendations of Funkhouser (1983) and Haley (1985), rather than factor scores or normalizing the data, which has been reported to have few effects on cluster results (Punj and Stewart 1983).

Four separate MANOVA tests based on the factor scores of the PAI for each product category were employed to assess their predictive power. Additionally, chi-square analysis was performed to see whether distinct consumer shopping and consumption groups produced by cluster analysis were dependent upon demographic variables.

RESULTS AND DISCUSSION

Comparison of Factor Analysis Results of the PAI

To test the first hypothesis that consumption values measured by the PAI differ across the four product categories, separate principal components factor analysis with varimax rotation using Kaiser's criterion was run for each product category.

Tables 16.1 through 16.4 display the factor analysis results of the PAI, respectively, for clothing, household appliances, household supplies, and food.

A comparison of these results seems to confirm our first hypothesis that consumption values as measured by the PAI are not the same across the four product

Table 16.1
Factor Analysis Results for the PAI of Clothing

Underlying Factor	Factor Loading	Percent of Variance Explained	Cronbach Alpha
Factor 1: Emotional		0.191	0.81
Luxury	0.73027		
Reflects status	0.69507		
Unique	0.65536		
Romantic	0.62987		
Self-pride	0.59810		
Glamorous	0.57925		
Having face	0.46611		
Modern	0.43476		
Factor 2: Functional/Social		0.349	0.75
Popular	0.66826		
Durable	0.66293		
Modest	0.65091		
Practical	0.63352		
Traditional	0.58669		
Mature	0.52790		
Factor 3: Emotional		0.410	0.72
Respectful	0.63465		
Fun/enjoyment	0.61150		
Neat/tidy	0.55717		
Youthful	0.55553		
Tasteful/elegant	0.50766		
Pretty	0.47387		
Factor 4: Social		0.460	0.59
Simple	0.67709		
Good value	0.65109		
Socially accepted	0.51324		
Factor 5: Functional		0.505	0.55
Convenient	0.71816		
Comfortable	0.63270		
Passionate/love	0.45252		
Factor 6: Functional		0.544	0.49
Inexpensive	0.71111		
Quality	0.63854		
Factor 7: Social		0.579	−0.41
Sexy	0.72584		
Moral	−0.39292		

Table 16.2
Factor Analysis Results for the PAI of Appliances

Underlying Factor	Factor Loading	Percent of Variance Explained	Cronbach Alpha
Factor 1: Social		0.209	0.78
Popular	0.75346		
Modest	0.72795		
Simple	0.68484		
Socially accepted	0.67663		
Traditional	0.61740		
Having face	0.51351		
Factor 2: Emotional		0.354	0.79
Luxurious	0.80358		
Unique	0.77985		
Reflects status	0.64480		
Decorative	0.60110		
Elegant	0.58658		
Self-pride	0.54613		
Factor 3: Functional		0.452	0.65
Inexpensive	0.78940		
Convenient	0.60460		
Quality	0.60053		
Good value	0.56101		
Factor 4: Functional		0.506	0.68
Practical	0.78735		
Durable	0.78246		
Safe	0.54183		
Factor 5: Functional/Emotional		0.553	0.67
High-tech	0.69591		
Modern	0.69313		
Factor 6: Functional		0.598	0.37
Family-oriented	0.70291		
Neat/tidy	0.48173		

Table 16.3
Factor Analysis Results for the PAI of Supplies

Underlying Factor	Factor Loading	Percent of Variance Explained	Cronbach Alpha
Factor 1: Emotional		0.226	0.84
Luxurious	0.81776		
Unique	0.80438		
Self-pride	0.73285		
Youthful	0.72987		
Tasteful	0.65569		
Glamorous	0.59971		
Modern	0.48953		
Factor 2: Emotional		0.374	0.74
Safe	0.73425		
Healthy	0.73402		
Family-oriented	0.66533		
Neat/tidy	0.60708		
Ornamental/pretty	0.42619		
Factor 3: Functional		0.467	0.74
Practical	0.82506		
Durable	0.73091		
Convenient	0.72217		
Quality	0.54439		
Factor 4: Functional		0.531	0.65
Good value	0.78228		
Simple	0.74991		
Having fun	0.53665		
Inexpensive	0.45808		
Factor 5: Social		0.581	0.70
Socially accepted	0.72860		
Popular	0.71053		
Factor 6: Natural		0.629	n.a.*
Natural/purity	0.69332		

*For single-item scales, Cronbach alpha cannot be calculated.

Table 16.4
Factor Analysis Results for the PAI of Food

Underlying Factor	Factor Loading	Percent of Variance Explained	Cronbach Alpha
Factor 1: Emotional		0.253	0.86
Luxurious	0.85144		
Unique	0.79535		
Self-pride	0.74790		
Glamorous	0.71346		
Elegant	0.70148		
Ornamental	0.58138		
Factor 2: Social		0.363	0.75
Socially accepted	0.71404		
Popular	0.69740		
Modest	0.66271		
Simple	0.56696		
Natural/purity	0.48263		
Neat	0.46287		
Enjoyment/fun	−0.49355		
Factor 3: Functional		0.445	0.61
Nutritious	0.73887		
Quality	0.69628		
Healthy	0.60833		
Safe	0.56037		
Factor 4: Functional		0.506	0.67
Inexpensive	0.81730		
Good value	0.79366		
Factor 5: Functional		0.557	0.38
Convenient	0.76985		
Family-oriented	0.54337		
Factor 6: Functional		0.603	0.37
Fresh	0.72979		
Appetizing	0.65518		

categories. Due to its highly visible nature, clothing was associated with more social values than the other categories. Both home appliances and clothing tend to be regarded as status symbols in China. Their importance was reflected by the more sophisticated emotional values to which the respondents attached. Food and supplies, on the other hand, appeared to be associated mostly with functional values.

Cluster Analysis Results of Shopping and Consumption Behavior

As a first step to test our second hypothesis, we conducted a hierarchical cluster analysis using Ward's clustering method with squared Euclidean distance to group the 196 Chinese consumers based on the raw scores of the 23 Likert scales measuring consumers' shopping and consumption behavior. The Cronbach coefficient alpha estimate of reliability for the 23 shopping and consumption behavior scale items was 0.70.

An examination of the dendrogram produced by the hierarchical clustering method suggests that three distinct clusters should be extracted. Cluster 1 contained 107 respondents (55%). Cluster 2 included 59 respondents (30%), while cluster 3 consisted of 30 respondents, accounting for 15 percent of the sample.

MANOVA was used to assess the adequacy of the clustering results. Table 16.5 presents both the MANOVA and univariate ANOVA test results with respect to the three clusters.

MANOVA results shown in Table 16.5 indicate that an overall group difference over the entire set of 23 shopping and consumption behavior items was present ($p < 0.01$). Among the 23 univariate ANOVA tests, 19 were statistically significant at 0.05 level. These results suggest that distinct clusters had been found.

Tables 16.6 and 16.7 show, respectively, the cluster means and multiple pairwise comparison results using Bonferroni tests. Respondents in cluster 1 can be labeled "average shoppers" since they not only represent the largest segment of the sample (55%), but also seem to take a "middle ground" position between clusters 2 and 3 in terms of their shopping and consumption behavior.

Respondents in cluster 2 represented 30 percent of the sample. They might be characterized as "enthusiastic shoppers." They enjoy shopping and like to bargain for most of the things they buy. These respondents are meticulous shoppers and always consult with friends and/or experts before making a major purchase. They check the price on an item and prepare a complete shopping list before going shopping. The "enthusiastic shoppers" tend to be innovators and/ or early adopters (Rogers 1983) in terms of their consumption behavior. They are among the first batch of consumers to try new products. Additionally, they have a good knowledge of products and/or brands and often serve as opinion leaders for their friends and neighbors.

Respondents in cluster 3, on the other hand, represent the opposite type of

Table 16.5
MANOVA Results for Three Clusters

Shopping and Consumption Behavior	F-Ratio	P-Value
Overall MANOVA Test		
Wilks' Lambda = 0.1886	9.6840	0.0001
Univariate ANOVA Tests		
I enjoy shopping in my leisure time	30.57	0.0001
I like to bargain for most of what I buy	11.00	0.0001
I always buy my favorite brand	9.41	0.0001
I prepare a complete list before shopping	10.32	0.0001
I try to stick to well-known brand names	15.06	0.0001
I always check the price on an item	25.98	0.0001
I consider myself a materialistic person	5.19	0.0064
I consult with friends/experts for major buy	3.52	0.0316
I usually buy the product of a free sample	2.48	0.0865
Advertising does help me in shopping	1.46	0.2357
A popularly advertised brand is a better buy	9.64	0.0001
My friends and neighbors seek me for advice	12.99	0.0001
Information from ads helps me make better decisions	13.53	0.0001
I like to buy new and different things	16.61	0.0001
I am an impulse buyer	20.06	0.0001
I shop a lot for specials	8.81	0.0002
A store's own brand is usually a better buy	1.61	0.2019
Shopping is fun	44.04	0.0001
Quality is far more important than price	1.08	0.3412
I am usually among the first to try new products	9.65	0.0001
I have good knowledge of famous brands	22.35	0.0001
A foreign brand is better than the local brand	12.15	0.0001
I am a meticulous shopper	36.92	0.0001

Table 16.6
Means for Each of the Three Clusters

Shopping and Consumption Behavior	Mean for Each Cluster		
	1 (107)	2 (59)	3 (30)
I enjoy shopping in my leisure time	3.74	4.80	1.87
I like to bargain for most of what I buy	3.50	3.63	1.93
I always buy my favorite brand	5.00	6.02	6.27
I prepare a complete list before shopping	4.53	5.34	3.27
I try to stick to well-known brand names	4.76	6.05	4.33
I always check the price on an item	4.98	5.47	2.73
I consider myself a materialistic person	4.28	4.90	3.60
I consult with friends/experts for major buy	5.55	6.03	4.97
I usually buy the product of a free sample	3.74	4.08	3.30
Advertising does help me in shopping	3.36	3.81	3.30
A popularly advertised brand is a better buy	2.66	3.83	3.00
My friends and neighbors seek me for advice	3.88	5.03	3.40
Information from ads helps me make better decisions	4.60	5.42	3.60
I like to buy new and different things	3.93	5.32	4.23
I am an impulse buyer	2.18	3.73	4.03
I shop a lot for specials	3.85	3.59	2.37
A store's own brand is usually a better buy	4.22	4.51	3.83
Shopping is fun	3.30	5.08	1.53
Quality is far more important than price	6.48	6.71	6.67
I am usually among the first to try new products	2.67	3.69	2.57
I have good knowledge of famous brands	4.29	5.51	3.27
A foreign brand is better than the local brand	4.24	5.64	4.73
I am a meticulous shopper	4.36	5.12	2.33

Table 16.7
Bonferroni t Tests for the Three Clusters

Shopping and Consumption Behavior	Bonferroni t Tests*
I enjoy shopping in my leisure time	2 > 1 > 3
I like to bargain for most of what I buy	2, 1 > 3
I always buy my favorite brand	2, 3 > 1
I prepare a complete list before shopping	2 > 1 > 3
I try to stick to well-known brand names	2 > 1, 3
I always check the price on an item	2, 1 > 3
I consider myself a materialistic person	2 > 3
I consult with friends/experts for major buy	2 > 3
I usually buy the product of a free sample	not significant
Advertising does help me in shopping	not significant
A popularly advertised brand is a better buy	2 > 1
My friends and neighbors seek me for advice	2 > 1, 3
Information from ads helps me make better decisions	2 > 1 > 3
I like to buy new and different things	2 > 1, 3
I am an impulse buyer	2, 3 > 1
I shop a lot for specials	2, 1 > 3
A store's own brand is usually a better buy	not significant
Shopping is fun	2 > 1 > 3
Quality is far more important than price	not significant
I am usually among the first to try new products	2 > 1, 3
I have good knowledge of famous brands	2 > 1 > 3
A foreign brand is better than the local brand	2 > 1
I am a meticulous shopper	2 > 1 > 3

*Groups are significantly different (p < 0.05) for Bonferroni t tests in multiple comparisons of means.

Table 16.8
MANOVA Results: PAI for Clothing

Product Attribute	F-Ratio	P-Value	Means for Each Cluster		
			1	2	3
Overall MANOVA Test					
Wilks' Lambda = 0.8146	2.8845	0.0004			
Univariate ANOVA Tests					
CF1	8.59	0.00	–0.19	0.43	–0.16
CF2	2.93	0.06	0.12	–0.04	–0.37
CF3	0.86	0.42	–0.08	0.12	0.07
CF4	0.07	0.93	0.02	0.00	–0.06
CF5	0.19	0.83	–0.04	0.04	0.07
CF6	6.16	0.00	0.10	0.10	–0.57
CF7	1.19	0.31	0.01	0.10	–0.24

Note: CF1 = Factor 1: Emotional; CF2 = Factor 2: Functional/Social; CF3 = Factor 3: Emotional; CF4 = Factor 4: Social; CF5 = Factor 5: Functional; CF6 = Factor 6: Functional; CF7 = Factor 7: Social.

consumers. They account for 15 percent of the sample and can be called "passive shoppers." They consider shopping to be a necessary burden; it is a chore they do not enjoy. They are casual shoppers in that they do not spend time preparing the shopping list and bargaining over price. From a diffusion-of-innovation perspective (Rogers 1983), this group tends to fall into the categories of late majority and laggards, tending to be conservative in their orientation toward and adaptation of new products. Because of their genuine disinterest in shopping, they tend to be ignorant of brand names and thus not in a position to offer advice to others regarding purchase decisions.

Assessing the Predictive Power of the Four PAIs

To test the second hypothesis, four separate MANOVA analyses based on the factor scores of the PAI for each product category were conducted to assess the predictive power associated with each of the PAIs.

Tables 16.8–16.11 summarize, respectively, the results of the MANOVA tests. An examination of the overall MANOVA test results (namely, the p-values associated with respective Wilks' lambda) shows that all the PAIs except that for food were able to discriminate among the three clusters at the 0.05 level.

Consistent with the second hypothesis, the predictive power of the PAI did

Table 16.9
MANOVA Results: PAI for Household Appliances

Product Attribute	F-Ratio	P-Value	Means for Each Cluster		
			1	2	3
Overall MANOVA Test					
Wilks' Lambda = 0.8796	2.0760	0.0177			
Univariate ANOVA Tests					
DF1	1.84	0.16	0.02	0.12	−0.30
DF2	5.17	0.01	−0.19	0.32	0.03
DF3	0.70	0.50	0.06	−0.03	−0.17
DF4	0.45	0.64	0.05	−0.01	−0.15
DF5	3.18	0.04	0.02	0.16	−0.39
DF6	1.06	0.35	−0.05	−0.04	0.24

Note: DF1 = Factor 1: Social; DF2 = Factor 2: Emotional; DF3 = Factor 3: Functional; DF4 = Factor 4: Functional; DF5 = Factor 5: Functional/Emotional; DF6 = Factor 6: Functional.

Table 16.10
MANOVA Results: PAI for Household Supplies

Product Attribute	F-Ratio	P-Value	Means for Each Cluster		
			1	2	3
Overall MANOVA Test					
Wilks' Lambda = 0.8523	2.6058	0.0024			
Univariate ANOVA Tests					
EF1	4.10	0.02	−0.13	0.31	−0.15
EF2	0.21	0.81	−0.03	0.00	0.11
EF3	1.64	0.20	0.12	−0.13	−0.17
EF4	5.71	0.00	0.01	0.24	−0.50
EF5	0.08	0.92	0.00	0.03	−0.06
EF6	3.72	0.03	−0.16	0.12	0.35

Note: EF1 = Factor 1: Emotional; EF2 = Factor 2: Functional; EF3 = Factor 3: Functional; EF4 = Factor 4: Functional; EF5 = Factor 5: Social; EF6 = Factor 6: Natural.

Table 16.11
MANOVA Results: PAI for Food

Product Attribute	F-Ratio	P-Value	Means for Each Cluster		
			1	2	3
Overall MANOVA Test					
Wilks' Lambda = 0.9110	1.4940	0.1237			
Univariate ANOVA Tests					
FF1	3.14	0.05	–0.06	0.25	–0.26
FF2	0.29	0.75	0.04	0.00	–0.12
FF3	0.70	0.50	0.00	0.10	–0.17
FF4	3.38	0.04	0.03	0.16	–0.41
FF5	0.64	0.53	–0.06	0.03	0.17
FF6	0.79	0.46	–0.07	0.04	0.18

Note: FF1 = Factor 1: Emotional; FF2 = Factor 2: Social; FF3 = Factor 3: Functional; FF4 = Factor 4: Functional; FF5 = Factor 5: Functional; FF6 = Factor 6: Functional.

seem to vary across the four product categories. The PAIs associated with cloth-ing and household appliances appeared to have greater predictive power than that with food.

An unexpected finding, however, was the significant results with household supplies. The unanticipated predictive power associated with household supplies is an interesting phenomenon that warrants further research. One possible ex-planation may have something to do with the fact that China today is still a developing economic entity. Chinese consumers may still regard purchase of household supplies such as detergent and shampoo as having high personal importance or relevance. Consequently, the high level of involvement that Chi-nese consumers associate with household supplies may have caused their PAI to have an unexpectedly high predictive power.

In order to see whether demographic variables have any relationship with the three clusters of consumers with different shopping and consumption behavior, chi-square analysis was performed for each of the demographic variables. The chi-square values for gender, age, education, occupation, and area were 0.096 (p = 0.95), 7.136 (p = 0.308), 4.838 (p = 0.57), 6.126 (p = 0.41), and 5.748 (p = 0.06), respectively. None of the demographic variables was statistically significantly related to shopping behavior cluster membership.

In order to further assess the predictive power of the four PAIs, a nonpara-metric procedure, Classification and Regression Tree (CART), was utilized. As shown in Figure 16.1. CART used 2 variables, DF2 (factor two: emotional value for appliances) and DF6 (factor six: functional value for appliances), to classify

Figure 16.1
CART Classification Tree Diagram

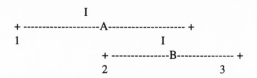

Legend: 1 = Cluster 1; 2 = Cluster 2; 3 = Cluster 3.

NODE INFORMATION

Node A was split on variable DF2: emotional for appliances.
A case went left if variable DF2 was less than or equal to 0.0305.

Node B was split on variable DF6: functional for appliances.
A case went left if variable DF6 was less than or equal to 0.034.

the respondents into the three clusters of average shoppers, enthusiastic shoppers, and passive shoppers.

Table 16.12 lists the variable importance index for the predictor variables. It is very useful in finding important variables that remain hidden when one simply examines the classification tree diagram.

It can be seen from Table 16.12 that most of the important predictor variables were those associated with household appliances and clothing. For example, if one selected 70 as a cut-point, no demographic variables would be considered important. Among the fourteen PAI values considered important, five belong to appliances, four to clothing, three to suppliers, and two to food. These findings tend to further support our final hypothesis. It appears that the PAI does have predictive power but that this predictive power varies according to the type of products examined.

Limitation of the Study

Several limitations that could be explored in future studies are worth noting. First, the present study's results are based on a relatively small and by no means representative sample of the general population in China. Hence, caution must be exercised in generalizing the findings of this study beyond the sample used, which was drawn from people living in two large Chinese cities, Beijing and Shanghai.

Second, the current study relies on general consumer perception data to define consumer shopping and consumption behavior. Future studies using more specific and objective data based on consumers' actual shopping and consumption behavior are certainly more desirable to assess the predictive utility of personal value measures.

Table 16.12
Variable Importance Index Provided by the CART Program

Variable Name	Relative Importance Index
DF5: emotional value for appliances	100
EF4: functional value for supplies	82
DF1: social value for appliances	79
CF6: functional value for clothing	78
DF6: functional value for appliances	76
CF7: social value for clothing	74
DF2: emotional value for appliances	74
FF1: emotional value for food	73
FF4: functional value for food	73
EF5: social value for supplies	73
EF6: natural value for supplies	72
CF1: emotional value for clothing	72
DF3: functional value for appliances	70
CF2: functional/social value for clothing	70
CF3: emotional value for clothing	65
CF4: social value for clothing	60
FF2: social value for food	60
EF1: emotional value for supplies	58
FF5: functional value for food	58
B17: responsible	55
DF4: functional value for appliances	54
FF3: functional value for food	50
EF3: functional value for supplies	50
CF5: functional value for clothing	50
EF2: functional value for supplies	44
Age: age of the respondent	33
B11: independent	31
FF6: functional value of food	29
EDU: education level of the respondent	27
Job: occupation of the respondent	22
Area: area in which the respondent lived	3
Sex: gender of the respondent	0

Finally, the PAIs were tested in only one country, China. The cross-cultural aspect of this instrument is still untested. In order to make the Perceived Attribute Importance a cross-cultural measure, the measurement needs to be administered in other cultures and subsequently calibrated for cross-cultural equivalence.

CONCLUSIONS

Past research has shown that personal values could be a powerful explanation of a variety of individual and collective behaviors. Yet most previous attempts to relate the global construct of personal values, as measured by existing value measures such as the RVS, to consumer choice behavior have produced less than satisfactory results.

This chapter proposes another perspective. We hypothesized and used consumers' Perceived Attribute Importance (PAI) as an alternative measure of consumption values. Consumers' consumption values along four product categories—clothing, household appliances, household supplies, and food—were surveyed in China. The results in this study seem to suggest that the PAI is an appropriate consumption value measure.

Factor analysis results showed that the PAI was able to capture the differences of the underlying consumption values along the four product categories. CART results also suggested that the PAI in general had predictive utility in assessing consumer shopping and consumption behavior. The predictive power of the PAI does, however, seem to vary across the four product categories. Consumption values measured by the PAI for household appliances, clothing, and supplies appeared to have greater predictive power than those for food. The high level of involvement that Chinese consumers are likely to attach to the purchase of appliances, clothing, and supplies may be one reason for such findings. Future research is needed to further explicate the relationships involved.

REFERENCES

Allport, G. W. (1961). *Pattern and Growth in Personality*. New York: Holt, Rinehart and Winston.

Antil, John (1984). "Conceptualization and Operationalization of Involvement." *Advances in Consumer Research*, 11: 204.

Baum, R. C. (1968). "Values and Democracy in Empirical Germany." *Sociological Inquiry*, 38: 176–196.

Beatty, Sharon E., Pamela M. Homer, and Lynn R. Kahle (1988). "Problems with VALS in International Marketing Research: An Example from an Application of the Empirical Mirror Technique." *Advances in Consumer Research*, 15: 375–380.

Beatty, Sharon E., Lynn R. Kahle, and Pamela Homer (1991). "Personal Values and Gift-Giving Behaviors: A Study Across Cultures." *Journal of Business Research*, 22: 149–157.

Beatty, Sharon E., Lynn R. Kahle, Pamela Homer, and Shekhar Misra (1985). "Alternative Measurement Approaches to Consumer Values: The List of Values and the Rokeach Value Survey." *Psychology and Marketing*, 2(3): 181–200.

Berrien, F. K. (1966). "Japanese and American Values." *International Journal of Psychology*, 71: 129–142.

Carman, J. M. (1977). "Values and Consumption Patterns: A Closed Loop." In H. K. Hunt (ed.), *Advances in Consumer Research, Vol. 5: Association for Consumer Research Annual Conference Proceedings*. College Park: University of Maryland, pp. 403–407.

Engel, James F., David T. Kollat, and Roger D. Blackwell (1968). *Consumer Behavior*. New York: Holt, Rinehart and Winston.

Fishbein, Martin and Icek Ajzen (1975). *Belief, Attitude, Intention, and Behavior: An Introduction to Theory and Research*. Boston: Addison-Wesley.

Funkhouser, G. R. (1983). "A Note on the Reliability of Certain Clustering Algorithms." *Journal of Marketing Research*, 20 (February): 99–102.

Ginter, James L. (1974). "An Experimental Investigation of Attitude Change and Choice of a New Brand." *Journal of Marketing Research*, 11 (February): 30–40.

Grunert, Susanne C. and Gerhard Scherhorn (1990). "Consumer Values in West Germany: Underlying Dimensions and Cross-Cultural Comparison with North America." *Journal of Business Research*, 20: 97–107.

Gutman, Jonathan (1982). "A Means-End Model Based on Consumer Categorization Processes." *Journal of Marketing*, 46 (Spring): 60–72.

——— (1990). "Adding Meaning to Values by Directly Assessing Value-Benefit Relationships." *Journal of Business Research*, 20: 153–160.

——— (1991). "Exploring the Nature of Linkages Between Consequences and Values." *Journal of Business Research*, 22: 143–148.

Haley, Russell I. (1985). *Developing Effective Communications Strategy: A Benefit Segmentation Approach*. New York: John Wiley and Sons.

Henry, Walter A. (1976). "Cultural Values Do Correlate with Consumer Behavior." *Journal of Marketing Research*, 13 (May): 121–127.

Homer, Pamela M. and Lynn R. Kahle (1988). "A Structural Equation Test of the Value-Attitude-Behavior Hierarchy." *Journal of Personality and Social Psychology*, 54(4): 638–646.

Howard, John A. and Jagdish N. Sheth (1969). *The Theory of Buyer Behavior*. New York: John Wiley and Sons.

Johnson, S. C. (1967). "Hierarchical Clustering Schemes." *Psychometrika*, 32: 241–254.

Kahle, L. R. (ed.) (1983). *Social Values and Social Change: Adaptation to Life in America*. New York: Praeger.

Kahle, L. R. (1984). *Attitudes and Social Adaptation: A Person-Situation Interaction Approach*, Oxford: Pergamon.

Kahle, L. R., Sharon E. Beatty, and Pamela Homer (1986). "Alternative Measurement Approaches to Consumer Values: The List of Values (LOV) and Values and Life Style (VALS)." *Journal of Consumer Research*, 13 (December): 405–409.

Kahle, L. R., R. A. Kulka, and D. M. Klingel (1980). "Low Adolescent Self-Esteem Leads to Multiple Interpersonal Problems: A Test of Social Adaptation Theory." *Journal of Personality and Social Psychology*, 39: 496–502.

Kahle, L. R. and Goff Timmer (1983). "A Theory and a Method for Studying Values." In L. R. Kahle (ed.), *Social Values and Social Change: Adaptation to Life in America*. New York: Praeger, pp. 43–69.

Kamakura, Wagner A. and Jose A. Mazzon (1991). "Value Segmentation: A Model for the Measurement of Values and Value Systems." *Journal of Consumer Research*, 18 (September): 208–218.

Krugman, Herbert (1965). "The Impact of Television Advertising: Learning Without Involvement." *Public Opinion Quarterly*, 29 (Fall): 349–356.

Lehmann, Donald R. (1971). "Television Show Preference: Application of a Choice Model." *Journal of Marketing Research*, 8 (February): 331–334.

Levine, R. A. (1960). "The Internalization of Political Values in Stateless Societies." *Human Organization*, 19: 51–58.

Lutz, Richard J. and James R. Bettman (1977). "Multi-Attribute Models in Marketing: A Bicentennial Review." In Arch G. Woodside, Jagdish N. Sheth, and Peter D. Bennett (eds.), *Consumer and Industrial Buying Behavior*. New York: North-Holland, pp. 137–149.

McQuarrie, Edward F. and Daniel Langmeyer (1985). "Using Values to Measure Attitudes Toward Discontinuous Innovations." *Psychology and Marketing*, 2 (Winter): 239–252.

Mitchell, Arnold (1983). *The Nine American Life Styles: Who We Are and Where We Are Going*. New York: Macmillan.

Munson, J. Michael (1984). "Personal Values: Considerations on Their Measurement and Application to Five Areas of Research Inquiry." In Robert E. Pitts, Jr., and Arch G. Woodside (eds.), *Personal Values and Consumer Psychology*. Lexington, MA: Lexington Books.

Munson, J. Michael and Edward F. McQuarrie (1988). "Shortening the Rokeach Value Survey for Use in Consumer Research." *Advances in Consumer Research*, 15: 381–386.

Munson, J. Michael and Shelby H. McIntyre (1978). "Personal Values: A Cross-Cultural Assessment of Self Values Attributed to a Distant Cultural Stereotype." In H. Keith Hunt (ed.), *Contributions to Consumer Research*. Chicago: Association for Consumer Research (Proceedings), pp. 160–166.

——— (1979). "Developing Practical Procedures for the Measurement of Personal Values in Cross-Cultural Marketing." *Journal of Marketing Research*, 16 (February): 55–60.

Novak, Thomas P. and Bruce MacEvoy (1990). "On Comparing Alternative Segmentation Schemes: The List of Values (LOV) and Values and Life Styles (VALS)." *Journal of Consumer Research*, 17 (June): 105–109.

Ostrom, Thomas M. and Timothy C. Brock (1968). "A Cognitive Model of Attitudinal Involvement." In R. Abelson et al. (eds.), *Theories of Cognitive Consistency*. New York: Rand McNally.

Piner, K. E. and L. R. Kahle (1984). "Adapting to the Stigmatizing Label of Mental Illness: Forgone But Not Forgotten." *Journal of Personality and Social Psychology*, 47: 805–811.

Pitts, Robert E., Jr., and Arch G. Woodside (1983). "Personal Value Influences on Consumer Product Class and Brand Preferences." *Journal of Social Psychology*, 119 (February): 37–53.

——— (eds.) (1984). *Personal Values and Consumer Psychology*. Lexington, MA: Lexington Books.

Prakash, Ved and J. Michael Munson (1985). "Values, Expectations from the Marketing

System and Product Expectations." *Psychology and Marketing*, 2 (Winter): 279–296.

Punj, Garish and David W. Stewart (1983). "Cluster Analysis in Marketing Research: Review and Suggestions for Application." *Journal of Marketing Research*, 20 (May): 134.

Reynolds, Thomas J. and Johnathan Gutman (1984). "Laddering: Extending the Repertory Grid Methodology to Construct Attribute-Consequence-Value Hierarchies." In R. E. Pitts and A. G. Woodside (eds.), *Personal Values and Consumer Psychology*. Lexington, MA: Lexington Books, pp. 155–167.

———— (1988). "Laddering Theory, Method, Analysis and Interpretation." *Journal of Advertising Research*, 28 (1): 11–34.

Rogers, Everett M. (1983). *Diffusion of Innovations*, 3rd ed. New York: Free Press.

Rokeach, Milton and Sandra J. Ball-Rokeach (1973). *The Nature of Human Values*. New York: Free Press.

Rosenberg, Milton J. (1956). "Cognitive Structure and Attitudinal Affect." *Journal of Abnormal and Social Psychology*, 53: 367–372.

Schopphoven, Iris (1991). "Values and Consumption Patterns: A Comparison Between Rural and Urban Consumers in Western Germany." *European Journal of Marketing*, 25(12): 20–35.

Schwartz, Shalom H. and Wolfgang Bilsky (1987). "Toward a Universal Psychological Structure of Human Values." *Journal of Personality and Social Psychology*, 53 (3): 550–562.

Sheth, Jagdish N., Bruce I. Newman, and Barbara L. Gross (1991a). "Why We Buy What We Buy: A Theory of Consumption Values." *Journal of Business Research*, 22: 159–170.

———— (1991b). *Consumption Values and Market Choices*. Cincinnati, OH: South-Western Publishing Company.

Tetlock, Philip E. (1986). "A Value Pluralism Model of Ideological Reasoning." *Journal of Personality and Social Psychology*, 50 (April): 819–827.

Veroff, Joseph, Elizabeth Douvan, and Richard A. Kulka (1981). *The Inner American*. New York: Basic Books.

Vinson, Donald E. and J. Michael Munson (1976). "Personal Values: An Approach to Market Segmentation." In Kenneth L. Bernhardt (ed.), *Marketing: 1877–1976 and Beyond*. Chicago: American Marketing Association, pp. 313–317.

Vinson, Donald E., J. Michael Munson, and Masao Nakanishi (1977). "An Investigation of the Rokeach Value Survey for Consumer Research Applications." *Advances in Consumer Research*, 4: 247–252.

Vinson, Donald E., J. D. Scott, and L. M. Lamont (1977). "The Role of Personal Values in Marketing and Consumer Behavior." *Journal of Marketing*, 41: 44–50.

Watson, G. (1966). *Social Psychology: Issues and Insights*. Philadelphia: Lippincott.

Woodruff, A. D. (1942). "Personal Values and the Direction of Behavior." *School Review*, 50: 32–42.

Zavaloni, M. (1980). "Values." In Harry C. Triandis and Richard W. Brislin (eds.), *Handbook of Cross-Cultural Psychology, Vol. 5: Social Psychology*. Boston: Allyn and Bacon.

Chapter 17

The European Union:
The Case of an Evolving Market

A. Ben Oumlil and Larbi Oumlil

The European Union (EU) arose from post–World War II efforts to rebuild the war-torn European economy. In 1951, six nations, consisting of West Germany, Italy, France, Belgium, Netherlands, and Luxembourg, signed the Treaty of Paris. The treaty nations pledged to work together to eliminate barriers restricting movement of goods between their countries. They pledged to harmonize the economic goals of the six nations to strengthen the economies of each (Toyne and Walters 1989). These six nations also created the European Coal and Steel Community.

The European Coal and Steel Community was an independent administrative body designed to provide the six nations with equal access to the coal and steel resources of all member nations. The Community provided the six nations with experience in working with each country's export and import laws and provided each government with experience in delegating authority to an independent European entity (Whitehead 1988).

The original Union's success resulted in the expansion of its involvement in other market areas, such as agriculture, and eventually led to the establishment of the EU. The EU currently consists of the original six countries: the United Kingdom, Ireland, and Denmark (which joined in 1973), Greece (which became a member in 1981), and Spain and Portugal (which joined the community in 1986) (Solov 1989).

The present EU has as its goals the unification of the internal economic markets of the member countries and the elimination of barriers to the crossing of borders by people or goods between member countries. The Union operates under a parliament form of government based in Brussels. The goals of free trade among member nations are reducing distribution costs and increasing the competitive edge of member nation goods. These goals require the removal of all trade barriers in the member nations with respect to other member nations' goods (Solov 1989).

Previous attempts to unify the economic markets of the member nations have been unsuccessful due to the intricate nature of each country's export and import laws. Initially, the Union attempted to draft broad regulations to be adopted by each member nation to unify the import and export laws of all members (Gut 1988). This task proved to be impossible. The Union found that trade barriers consisted not only of tariffs and other excise taxes, but also government subsidies, price supports, and public sector procurement policies (Whitehead 1988).

The English Parliament passed the Single European Act in 1985. In this act, the EU abandoned its attempts to unify all trade regulations of its member nations. Instead, the EU adopted the policy of "mutual recognition" (Sullivan 1988). This policy established that companies or goods operating or produced according to the laws of one member nation would be deemed to be operating and produced according to the laws of *any* member country. This policy transferred the responsibility for harmonizing trade regulations to the member nations themselves. Therefore, if an industry in a member country has a competitive advantage over other members' industries because of price supports or subsidies, the other members of the EU may either adopt similar price support and subsidy policies or concede the advantage (Whitehead 1988).

Despite the policy of "mutual recognition," several areas of members' trade laws and regulations must be modified to achieve the goals of a unified European market. The EU has adopted many proposals and regulations designed to identify trade barriers that must be eliminated by each member country and hopes to achieve the elimination of these barriers by the time of a fully integrated European Market. The EU has identified the following basic areas that must be coordinated. They are as follows (Price Waterhouse 1987/1988, p. 1):

1. Frontier controls and rules and procedures for the cross-border shipment of goods;
2. Freedom of movement and right of people to settle in member countries;
3. Technical and standards harmonization;
4. Opening up of governmental procurement markets;
5. Liberalization of financial services;
6. Gradual opening up of the information-services market;
7. Liberalization of transportation services;
8. Creation of suitable conditions for industrial cooperation without fear of antitrust violation in the fields of company law and intellectual and industrial property; and
9. Removal of fiscal barriers.

The concept of "mutual recognition" poses some threats to member nations since the regulatory authority of each member government is reduced to that of the lowest member country. Prior to the economic unification of the EU, goods produced in one member country and exported to another member country had to conform to the receiving country's product safety and environmental laws before entry. These laws were quite diverse among the EU members.

After full integration of the market, a member country can avoid, to some extent, the product safety and environmental laws of member countries by producing goods in other member countries where such regulations may not be as restrictive. Goods produced in Spain that satisfy the product safety and environmental laws of Spain need not conform exactly to such laws and regulations of the United Kingdom in order to be exported to the United Kingdom. Traditionally, sovereign governments would exclude goods of other countries that did not satisfy the laws of the receiving country. The idea of "mutual recognition" eliminates the sovereign governments' traditional authority to enforce domestic laws.

The concept of "mutual recognition" applies only to member countries. Therefore, goods coming directly from non-member countries will still have to comply with the myriad of laws and regulations of an EU country to gain admittance to that country (Whitehead 1988).

In addition to the government-controlled trade barriers just detailed, the EU identified fluctuations in the value of member country currencies as barriers to the free flow of goods (Solov 1989).

The dollar will remain a major global currency, with little probability of gold returning to its former status in the near future. However, international transactions in both trade and finance are increasingly likely to be denominated in nondollar terms, including regional currencies such as the European Currency Unit (ECU). (Czinkota and Ronkainen 1996)

The EU has attempted to establish a European currency as a standard for valuing trade between member countries. The currency is called the European Currency Unit (ECU) (Whitehead 1988). The ECU is not an existing issued currency, but a standard against which each member country's currency is valued. The value of each member's currency is established in a range relating to one (1) ECU (Whitehead 1988). Business located in a member country can transact business in their domestic country's currency based on the ECU. This eliminates the need for constant monitoring of the monetary markets by business entities and provides consistency regarding EU member transactions. Non-member countries, such as the United States, may trade with member countries based on ECUs if payments is to be received in the currency of a member country. Otherwise, the ECU provides no benefit to non-member countries since the ECU is expressed only in terms of value in relation to member countries' currency.

Since January of 1999, thirteen European countries have adopted the use of a common currency, called the euro. The surge of the euro as a common EU currency has led to the surge of U.S. investors' interests in targeting the euro equity markets (*Financial News*, January 3, 2000). In addition, factors such as recent strong EU countries' exports and buoyant domestic demands by EU consumers should contribute to euro strength (Major 2000). Now, many European equities are traded in euros, not local currencies. This makes it much easier for investors to compare stock vis-à-vis their peers (*Business Week*, November 8, 1999). "My capital is now diversified, and I've got institutional shareholders in places like the U.S. and Britain as well as France," says Thierry Demarest, CEO of French oil giant TotalFina (Rossant 1999, p. 60).

The European Union has resulted in a much more vibrant and pluralistic continent. The driving forces are technology and business, rather than ideology and geopolitics. The free flow of capital across EU countries' borders makes it easier to finance huge business ventures. Once sacrosanct, industries such as telecommunications are now open to competitors for investment. The adoption of the euro made the union a reality. Moreover, a wave of business mergers, partnerships, and alliances is remaking the EU corporate landscape and allowing global reach for these firms. These alliances are portrayed in mergers between firms from EU countries and between EU firms and their counterpart U.S. firms, such as the merger resulting in DaimlerChrysler (Rossant 1999).

The EU governments are striving to adjust economic regulations to a new transactional medium (i.e., e-commerce) across the Union. The rapid advance of e-commerce (i.e., Internet trade) highlights some of the challenges now facing European legislators. It would be inaccurate, however, "to imply that there is no hope for a coordinated European e-commerce regime . . . the existing structure of Europe's single market ought to provide an ideal framework for borderless e-commerce" (Vander Weyer 2000, pp. 64, 72).

Today's political realities may oblige the European Union to enlarge its membership. The next decade's greatest challenge is truly integrating the former East Bloc nations into the European fold. Bringing in nations such as Poland, Hungary, and the Czech Republic is a political pressure that faces Europe (Rossant 1999). In 1997, the Union divided the waiting list into a leading batch (including the Czech Republic, Cypriote, Estonia, Hungary, Poland, and Slovenia) and a group of laggards (including Turkey, Slovakia, Bulgaria, and Romania) (*The Economist*, October 2, 1999).

Further proof for Europe that free trade can pay big dividends is the new Mexico–EU deal. This deal will make it easier for European manufacturers to set up business operations in Mexico. As long as European products include specific amounts of Mexican labor and parts, European manufacturers will be able to export to the United States, Canada, and back to Europe. In addition, European companies will be able to export to Latin American nations with which Mexico has free trade agreements, such as Chile and Colombia (Smith and Malkin 2000).

Obviously, the EU cannot address non–government-controlled trade barriers, such as cultural and language differences, between member countries. Businesses located within EU countries will still have to modify their products and services to accommodate specific local languages, cultures, and traditions (Whitehead 1988). However, the EU's efforts to establish one European common market will greatly reduce the extent to which EU businesses must conform their products or services for sale in other EU markets.

The benefit to businesses located within the EU will be a competitive edge over other foreign firms seeking entry of their products into EU markets. Identical goods imported to Britain from the United States and Spain will not be subject to the same taxes, standards, or regulations. This difference may be sufficient to render some U.S. products unable to effectively compete in the EU market.

Besides the transfer of goods and people between EU countries, EU policies have been designed to promote the exchange of information, especially research and development, between EU-based businesses. Traditionally, antitrust laws have impeded the exchange of information between foreign and domestic-based businesses. European business have generally been subject to antitrust laws that are considerably less restrictive than those of the United States. However, the fragmentation of the European market has stunted the formation of R&D-sharing agreements between European businesses. The formation of new alliances between EU-based companies will greatly enhance such businesses' ability to compete in global markets outside the EU (Rossant 1999). In addition, the EU views opportunities in research and development in the areas of telecommunications, transportation, and energy to be among the most attractive areas of the single market to outside investors, such as U.S. businesses. For example, state-run telecommunications monopolies recognize the need to be competitive and will need American technology to update their systems for this purpose. In 1992, U.S. companies made eight deals resulting in acquisitions in Europe, including AT&T's agreement to acquire the remaining 49 percent stake in AT&T Networks Systems Espana from its Spanish partner Amper (Dykes 1993).

European firms are swiftly knitting together a real continental economy. Acquisitions and merger business deals are remaking the European corporate landscape. In 1999, the monetary value of these business deals approached $1.3 trillion. That was up fivefold from 1994 (Rossant 1999).

The resources available to EU-based businesses should not be underestimated. The once-considered small markets of Britain, France, and Italy, when combined, constitute a large integrated market. In fact, the EU market represents a market that equals and sometimes exceeds that of the United States (Solov 1989). Based on 1991 figures, Table 17.1 illustrates that the EU has a combined population of 13.9 million less than and a gross domestic product (GDP) of $119 million more than that of the NAFTA countries combined (Euromonitor 1997).

The expansion of the European domestic market to a size equivalent to that of the United States may also be detrimental to EU-based companies. Small businesses operating within an EU country will suddenly be exposed to unreg-

Table 17.1
A Comparison of the European Union (formerly the European Community) and
NAFTA

Association	Population (millions)	GNP ($millions)	Imports[1] ($millions)	Exports[1] ($millions)
European Union*	373.5	8,180	1,899,466	1,927,914
NAFTA[2]	387.4	8,061	1,014,211	852,536

*Includes fifteen countries.
[1]Includes intramember trade.
[2]Canada, Mexico, and the United States.
Sources: Crossbank Monitor (1997); Euromonitor (1997).

ulated competition from businesses based in other EU countries. These small businesses may find themselves unable to compete in their own domestic market against businesses based in EU countries with more advantageous environments (Sullivan 1988). For example, labor costs and labor regulations may be lower or less restrictive in some EU countries. Also, businesses will be subject to differing income taxes depending on their location in the EU. Businesses that do not plan effectively for adjusting to an enlarged competitive market may find themselves losing domestic market share and jeopardizing future operations.

The differences in manufacturing costs and regulations among the EU members may result in the migration of investments from highly regulated member countries to less restrictive member countries. The possibility of this migration has brought hope of expansion to the less developed economies of the EU. For instance, Portugal hopes to attract foreign investors seeking access to the EU market. Portugal, which has a relatively small market dimension and relatively unattractive consumer markets, may be transformed into a very attractive location for manufacturing or simply for distribution of goods and services into other EU countries because of its low labor costs and relatively minimal regulations. To aid in attracting foreign investment, Portugal has begun taking steps to strengthen its capital markets and provide local financing for foreign investment (Templeman 1987).

For the United States, its businesses, and its industries, the EU presents either numerous opportunities or ominous consequences. The unification of the European economy may result in both stronger and more capable competitors as well as in the loss of a market upon which U.S. firms may be dependent. The unification of the European economy may provide well-managed U.S. companies greater financial returns than previously expected from the fragmented European market.

Business strategies for reacting to the expected total integration of the European market are based upon speculation concerning the success that the EU will have in unifying, as well as the likely results from such unification. European and U.S. companies with facilities in Europe may be on equal footing in reacting to the changes brought about by unification. European companies do not have any more accurate or detailed information available to them concerning the future of the European market than do the American companies currently operating within Europe (Pottinger 1988).

To some extent, American multinational companies with operations throughout Europe may be more prepared than their European counterparts for a totally unified Europe. They already have had experience in the organization of manufacturing and distribution facilities over the large geographical market of the United States. Also, some American companies entering the European market originally designed broad strategies for entering the European market and then tailored these strategies to the local environments of individual European countries (*The Economist*, September 3, 1988). The unification of the European market may allow these companies to eliminate some of the customization of their market strategies previously required to operate within a fragmented market structure. Conversely, European companies will now find themselves having to design broad European market strategies, in some cases with little managerial experience in this area.

One such U.S. company that may be uniquely prepared for this is IBM (Gut 1988). Europe represents IBM's biggest market next to that of the United States. IBM's sales in Europe in 1987 amounted to $19.3 billion. IBM's European operations are administered out of the IBM World Trade Europe/Middle East/Africa Corp. IBM produces in Europe more than 90 percent of what it sells there. IBM's centralized operations allow it to pursue a broad European market strategy. With the elimination of trade barriers between EU countries, IBM has a greater opportunity to standardize its European market strategies. In recognition of the cultural and sociological differences that will be maintained by the EU countries, however, IBM is delegating greater decision-making ability to its local sales managers so that they may respond more quickly to changes in the individual markets (Peterson 1988).

Recently, IBM has formed numerous strategic alliances concerning its overseas affairs. A business alliance between IBM and Ford Motor Company was established to list all used Ford vehicles on the World Wide Web in Germany. This permits consumers in Germany to locate used Ford vehicles anywhere in Germany. The same system will be replicated in other European countries (Wernle 1999). In addition, IBM is teaming up with Deutsche Telekom AG, a German telecommunications services firm, to establish the world's largest data warehouse system. This system will be used for customer-relationship management applications (Whiting 1999). An example of the increasing trend between U.S. firms and companies in the EU countries for information technology outsourcing is a deal between IBM and CGU, the United Kingdom's largest composite insurer (*Financial News*, November 26, 1999). Further, IBM intends to open e-business centers in several EU nations, including Germany, the United Kingdom, France, and Italy (*Electronic Buyers News*, November 29, 1999).

U.S. companies with multinational operations in Europe which are not as well prepared as IBM should now take steps now to respond to the unification of Europe's market. Such steps should include the coordination of the companies' manufacturing, marketing, logistics, and capital allocations. Expansion or migration into more desirable manufacturing or operating environments should also be considered. Expansion can be achieved by acquiring other companies currently operating in EU member markets or by establishing new operations based in those markets (Peterson 1988).

U.S. companies with operations based in Europe must also broaden their market analysis of their competitors. U.S. companies operating in relatively protected European markets will soon be exposed to new competitors from other EU countries. Small European companies with greater access to the European market may expand and become formidable competitors for European market share (Friberg 1989).

American companies with global operations may also be faced with greater global competition from European-based companies. The currently segmented European market does not provide European-based countries with sufficient markets and capital influx to support the large research and development facilities necessary to compete on the global level. As more European-based companies financially benefit from the newly created EU market, their capabilities to establish global market share will be increased (Gelb 1989; Rossant 1999).

This global expansion of European-based companies may eventually pose a threat to U.S. companies operating exclusively within the United States (Graham 1988). U.S. companies may find their domestic market strategies, designed for competing with Japan, to be myopic. The European presence in the U.S. domestic market may be a greater threat in the twenty-first century than that of Japan, since the European companies will have a much larger domestic market from which to launch their global ventures. The large European firms are not the only ones enjoying newfound freedom. Smaller firms, mainly in high technology, are starting to multiply. Today, "the heroes are entrepreneurs going to Silicon Valley and making it big," says Dominique Moisi, a French political scientist (Rossant 1999, p. 61).

Liberalized antitrust laws in the EU have provided a greater ability for EU-based companies to contractually share in the costs and benefits of research and development ventures (Templeman 1987). As EU-based companies move quickly to form research and development alliances, U.S. companies must evaluate such opportunities so that they are not frozen out of technological advances. U.S. companies considering joining with European companies for research and development should be cognizant of the differences between U.S. and EU laws pertaining to such agreements. U.S. companies with subsidiaries based in the EU may be better positioned to take advantage of the opportunities posed by such alliances (Zwart 1987).

U.S. companies with relatively small EU-based operations are faced with a greater threat from the changes that occurred in 1992 than companies owned jointly by U.S. and European firms. These companies may currently be operating with strategies more designed toward the small fragmented market within which they operate (Zwart 1987). These strategies may be insufficient to sustain a share of that market once the access to that market expands. The companies that redesign their strategies, compensating for increased competition and expansion of the market to which the company has access, may experience growth. To take advantage of the expanded market, companies with limited operations may consider expansion before the market is fully integrated. For example, Texas Instruments, Inc. (TI), has commenced construction of a microcomputer chip manufacturing plant in Italy at a cost of $250 million. From TI's expanded Italian operations, TI may launch an expanded assault on the EU market (Gut 1988).

To protect small EU-based operations, U.S. companies with insufficient financial resources to fortify such operations in response to the total unification of Europe may consider entering into joint ventures or cooperation agreements with other companies (Peterson 1989). John F. Magee (1989), former chairman of the board of directors of Arthur D. Little, Inc., suggested that U.S. companies with relatively small EU-based operations should consider divesting themselves of such operations. Expansion requires financial commitments beyond the resources of U.S. companies. Magee wrote: "Divestiture is a difficult decision for many companies to make, but it is preferable to the slow death that can result from failing to commit the resources needed to transform a local position to a European scale."

Divestiture prior to failure will also result in a financial return more representative of the investment. Purchasers of limited operations within the EU may view such operations as a door or window to the complete EU market.

The changes that occurred in 1992 pose the greatest threat to those American companies that do not have operations based in Europe but are dependent upon exporting into EU countries. EU countries faced with a greater influx of foreign, but European, goods may react to protect their domestic companies and industries by installing greater barriers to non-EU goods. Companies exporting goods directly from the United States to EU-based purchasers must comply with the laws and regulations of each individual EU country into which they export. Such products will be subject to the differing import tariffs, duties, and excise taxes enacted by the receiving country. These goods will be competing directly against all other EU-based companies (including non-European EU-based operations), which will not be subject to such regulations and taxes (Magee 1989). These differences may result in increased price competition between American and EU-based goods.

Due to cultural and historical alliances, the United States has enjoyed an advantage in exporting goods to Europe (Sullivan 1988). The events of 1992 may have jeopardized this existing alliance with the advent of greater Euro-competition. However, publishing companies in the United Kingdom currently view the occurrences of a unified Europe as a greater threat than their U.S. counterparts. W. Gordon Graham (1988) stated, "the British *have* to respond; the Americans can *choose* to respond." Graham recognized that the UK market provides additional revenue to the U.S. industry, whereas in the UK market the publishing industry is its lifeblood.

U.S. companies that do not have operations based in any EU member countries but desire to either maintain or cultivate sales in the EU market may wish to consider establishing an EU base (Graham 1988). A U.S. manufacturer exporting goods to the EU may wish to choose an EU country, such as Spain or Portugal, with relatively few restrictive laws and regulations and a less expensive labor pool to establish an EU distribution post. Once the U.S.-manufactured goods gain access to an EU country, they may then be distributed as any other EU good.

Assistance may be available for companies considering expanding or entering EU markets. New firms are appearing throughout Europe to provide consulting services to companies ill equipped to design strategies for entering or maintaining a European presence (Gut 1988). Consulting firms providing European unification informational services are believed to number approximately 200 in Brussels alone. Interestingly enough, in the late 1980s, U.S. firms with experience in European markets were estimated to comprise between one-third and one-half of the consulting firms offering such services (*The Economist*, September 3, 1988).

In analyzing future market opportunities and threats posed by the EU and the events of 1992, U.S. companies must not ignore the effect of the European Free Trade Association (EFTA). The EFTA consists of six non–EU-member countries that maintain a free trade agreement with the EU (*The Economist*, September 3, 1988). The EFTA member countries are Iceland, Finland, Norway, Sweden, Austria, and Switzerland. EFTA members enjoy duty-free access to EU markets and provide reciprocal access to EFTA markets for EU goods and services. EFTA provides nonaligned countries with the ability to conduct unrestricted trade with EU countries without compromising their neutrality (*The Economist*, January 23, 1988). The relationship between the EU and EFTA may not remain stable, however. EFTA is viewed by some to be a freeloader, since EFTA members enjoy the benefits available to EU members without the corresponding expenditures (Gut 1988).

EFTA membership may provide significant benefits to member countries in industries such as financial services. As the financial markets of the EU become more unified, the climate for EU banks to do business throughout the EU market will become more amenable (*The Economist*, January 23, 1988). The non-EU bank's home country must enter into a reciprocal agreement with the EU, opening the home market to EU banking institutions in order for non-EU banks to expand their business activities from one EU member country to another (Whitehead 1988). EFTA countries have already established the required reciprocal agreements necessary to expand throughout the EU (Gut 1988). The highly regulated U.S. financial services market may be unable to deliver the necessary reciprocal agreements and may be foreclosed from operating throughout the unified EU market. However, non-EU banks may still expand throughout the EEC market by separately complying with each country's individual laws and regulations (Gut 1988).

Japanese companies also have much at stake as the EU unifies. The EU has already adopted stringent automobile and microcomputer chip import quotas that will have a direct impact upon Japan's ability to compete in these markets (Whitehead 1988). As EU administrative operations become more centralized, the EU's ability to respond punitively to the dumping of low-cost foreign goods increases; the risks to Japan in conducting "dumping" competitive strategies correspondingly increase (Keller 1988).

The U.S. government must also consider options available for assisting U.S. businesses in adapting to the changing environment in Europe. If EU member countries erect additional access barriers to their domestic markets for non-EU member goods and services, the United States should retaliate against such protectionist actions (*The Economist*, July 25, 1987). Also the United States should consider pursuing free trade agreements with the EU similar to those existing between the EU and EFTA (Vernon 1989). Free trade agreements could also be pursued with non-EU countries.

One example of a free trade agreements that have been pursued by the United States is the United States–Israel Free Trade Agreement (Gut 1988). The United States–Israel Free Trade Agreement provided for the staged reduction of tariffs by January 1, 1995, on all goods exchanged between the two countries (Jensen 1985). Exchanged goods will essentially have a duty-free status. Another example of free trade agreements that has been pursued by the United States is NAFTA. This trade agreement is between the United States, Canada, and Mexico. By pursuing a number of these agreements, the U.S. government can assure competitive access to valuable markets for U.S. goods and services.

The development of a single European market has been called "the business opportunity of the century" (Stitt 1991; Rossant 1999), and companies, both large and small, are positioning to gain competitive advantage in that market (Forman 1991; KPMG Peat Marwick 1990; Magee 1989; Quelch et al. 1990; Rossant 1999). It has been suggested that "U.S. firms will have greater opportunities to enter or expand in the EU market through mergers, acquisitions and joint ventures" (Rossant 1999). Although some firms decided not to compete in the European Union, they are being forced to rethink their strategy as European companies, strengthened by new efficiencies and economies of scale, enter new non-European markets (Magee 1989; Stitt 1991). Wisse Dekker, chairman of N. V. Philips, has stated "there are no second chances for companies that fail to win a share of the world market quickly" (Stone 1989).

As it was stated, the state of the EU represents significant opportunities and threats for American businesses. They must act now to establish themselves firmly in the new European marketplace or leave the field to their European and Japanese counterparts. If the latter scenario should occur, U.S. firms will not only face more intense competition in the global marketplace but also within the United States when strengthened pan-European competitors target opportunities in the American market. The continuous implementation of the directives guiding the integration process and the changing political and economic environment of Europe require constant updating and review to ensure that the original premises and assumptions are still valid. The nature of the European marketplace has been changed significantly by the unification of European nations into the EU (Cateora and Graham 1999). Further, the effect of the Berlin Wall's collapse on European attitudes has been so tremendous that, for the first time, there is hope for even more radical change. The outcomes of 1989 are still being felt throughout Europe. Europe cannot afford to stay still. More cross-frontier business mergers, more market opening moves by European governments, and more opportunities for restless entrepreneurs are all part of today's Europe (Rossant 1999).

In summary, every U.S. company has been forced to face the new marketing realities brought on by the unification of the European Union. Although the full consequences of European unification cannot be known, companies can take steps now to prepare to operate within the newly structured EU market. Not only will effective marketing strategies be needed; there will also be a need for contingency planning. Additionally, companies should be poised to react to major changes in the marketing environment as the EU market evolves. Such flexible marketing strategies will be necessary in the global, European, and domestic markets to prevent them from being "trampled underfoot" by the rising EU economic giant. Marco Tronchetti Provera, chief executive of tire maker Pirelli, states that, "after the Wall, the single European market became a possible reality. And in the last 24 months, it has become reality" (Rossant 1999). To U.S. international business organizations, the EU single market means business opportunity through access to a greatly enlarged market with reduced or abolished country-by-country tariff barriers and restrictions. Production, financing, labor, and marketing decisions are shaped by the transformation of Europe into a European Union (Cateora and Graham 1999).

According to Cateora and Graham (1999), business competition will become more intense in the EU as European businesses become stronger and more experienced in dealing with a large market group (i.e., the EU). Further, European and non-European multinational firms are preparing to deal with the changes in competition in a fully integrated Europe. It is not wrong to imply that, in an integrated Europe, U.S. multinationals may have an initial advantage over expanded European firms; U.S. firms have more experience in operating in a large, diverse market (i.e., the U.S. market) and are accustomed to looking at Europe as one market. The advantage, however, is only temporary as mergers, acquisitions, and joint ventures consolidate operations of European business firms in anticipation of the benefits of a single EU market. Also, it is accurate to imply that individual national markets will still confront international managers with the same problems of language, customs, and instability, even though they are packaged under the umbrella of a common market (Cateora and Graham 1999). For example, new automobile prices may vary by more than 40 percent between Great Britain and the rest of the EU countries. Other examples include France's refusal to import British beef, lack of a common language, different legal systems and cultures, and consumer attitudes toward the issue of privacy and e-commerce (Vander Weyer 2000).

As stated previously, however, there have been many advances made toward the unification of Europe. The most important one has been the launch of the euro in January 1999. Other points of progress include growth in the areas of cross-border mergers and, at the most practical level, the well-developed, competitively priced distribution services developed by Europe (Vander Weyer 2000). So, as barriers come down and multicountry markets are treated as one common market, a fully integrated European Union (i.e., economic and political unions) will be one step closer to reality. Further, despite the problems and complexities of dealing with the new markets (e.g., the EU), astute global marketers can still reap the benefits of business opportunities and greater profit potential.

REFERENCES

Business Week (1999). "Europe: Ten Years Later." November 8, pp. 56–88.

Cateora, Philip R. and John L. Graham (1999). *International Marketing*, 10th ed. Boston: Irwin/McGraw-Hill.

Crossborder Monitor (1997). "Indicators of Market Size for 115 Countries" (August).

Czinkota, Michael R. and Ilkka A. Ronkainen (1996). *Global Marketing*. Fort Worth, TX: The Dryden Press.

Darling, John R. and Danny R. Arnold (1988). "Foreign Consumers' Perspective of the Products and Marketing Practices of the United States versus Selected European Countries." *Journal of Business Research*, 17: 237–248.

Dykes, Hugh (1993). "Watch on the EC: Investment Opportunities." *Journal of Business Strategy*, 14(2) (March/April): 22–25.

Economist, The (1999). "Enlarging the European Union: A New Pace?" October 2, pp. 54–55.

——— (1988). "The EEC's Internal Market, Ask Us Another." September 3, pp. 50–51.

——— (1988). "European Trade, Twelve and Six Make What?" January 23, pp. 42–43.

——— (1987). "Japan-Bashing Catches On." July 25, p. 54.

Electronic Buyers News (1999). "IBM Opens E-business Centers." November 29, p. 68.

Euromonitor (1997). *International Marketing Data and Statistics*. London: Euromonitor.

Financial News (2000). "US Investors Target European Equities." January 3.

——— (1999). "CGU Signs Outsource Deal with IBM." November 26, p. 26.

Forman, Craig (1991). "EC Leaders Move toward Unity on Currency but Discord Remains." *Wall Street Journal*, December 10, p. A10.

Friberg, Eric G. (1989). "1992: Moves Europeans Are Making." *Harvard Business Review*, 67 (May/June): 85–89.

Gelb, Norman (1989). "The Practical Problems, Europe without Frontiers." *The New Leader*, January 9, pp. 7–8.

Graham, W. Gordon (1988). "The Shadow of 1992." *Publishers Weekly*, December 23, pp. 24–26.

Gut, Rainer E. (1988). "The Impact of the European Communities 1992 Project." *Vital Speeches of the Day*, November 1, pp. 34–37.

Holstein, William J., Maria Mallory, and Resau King (1988). "Should Small U.S. Exporters Take the Big Plunge?" *Business Week*, December 12, p. 64.

Jensen, Gordon W. V. (1985). "The United States–Israel Free Trade Agreement: A Model for Canada?" *The Canadian Business Review* (Autumn): 24–27.

Keller, Maryann N. (1988). "Car Wars in 1992." *Across the Board* (December): 6–7.

KPMG Peat Marwick (1990). "U.S. Gains in Foreign Acquisitions." *Accounting Today*, February 19, p. 14.

Magee, John F. (1989). "1992: Moves America Must Make." *Harvard Business Review*, 67 (May/June): 78–84.

Major, Tony (2000). "Underestimated Euro Looks to Higher Ground ECB Watch." *Financial Times*, January 4, p. 20.

Peterson, Thane (1988). "Mike Armstrong Is Improving IBM's Game in Europe." *Business Week*, June 20, pp. 96–101.

——— (1989). "The EC Just Says No to Japan's Cheap Chips." *Business Week*, January 30, pp. 46–47.

Pottinger, Kenneth (1988). "Shallow Roots." *The Banker* (December): 21–22.

Price Waterhouse (1987/1988). *EC Bulletin* (December/January): 1.

Quelch, John A., Robert D. Buzzell, and Eric R. Salama (1990). *The Marketing Challenge of 1992*. New York: Addison-Wesley.

Rossant, John (1999). "Europe: Ten Years Later. . . ." *Business Week*, November 8, pp. 57–61.

Smith, Geri and Elizabeth Malkin (2000). "Mexico Pulls Off Another Trade Coup." *Business Week*, February 7, p. 56.

Solov, Diane (1989). "1992 Stars: Will Dayton Companies Shine When Europe Becomes One?" *Dayton Daily News*, May 22, pp. 10–11.

Stitt, Iain (ed.) (1991). *Arthur Andersen European Community Sourcebook*. Chicago: Triumph Books.

Stone, Nan (1989). "The Globalization of Europe: An Interview with Wisse Dekker." *Harvard Business Review*, 67 (May/June): 90–95.

Sullivan, Scott (1988). "Who's Afraid of 1992?" *Newsweek*, October 31, pp. 32–34.

Templeman, John (1987). "Hands across Europe: Deals That Could Redraw the Map." *Business Week*, May 18, pp. 17–19.

Toyne, Brian and Peter G. P. Walters (1989). "The International Environment: Major Dimensions and Institutions." In *Global Marketing Management: A Strategic Perspective*. Boston: Allyn and Bacon, p. 97.

Vander Weyer, Martin (2000). "Europe: Despite Unification, Local Laws Might Take the 'E' out of 'EU.' " *Strategy & Business*, 18 (January–April): 63–64, 69–72.

Vernon, Raymond (1989). "Can the U.S. Negotiate for Trade Equality?" *Harvard Business Review*, 67 (May/June): 96.

Wernle, Bradford (1999). "Ford, IBM Launch Web Project." *Automotive News Europe*, 4(26) (December 20): 1.

Whitehead, David D. (1988). "Moving toward 1992: A Common Financial Market for Europe?" *Economic Review* (November/December): 42–49.

Whiting, Rick (1999). "IBM to Bring Deutsche Telekom Data Warehouse to 100 Terabytes." *Information Week*, December 20, p. 40.

Zwart, Sara G. (1987). "The New Antitrust: An Aerial View of Joint Ventures and Mergers." *Journal of Business Strategy*, 7 (Spring): 68–76.

Index

Achievement motive, 157

Acquisitions, 237, 243–44, 280, 283, 284

Adelman, M., 161

Administrative routine, 78, 81, 85, 87, 90–91

Adobe Systems, 227

Advantage, 166

Adverse selection, 124

Advertisement testing: effectiveness measurement, 166–68; exposure effect, 174, 177; liking the ad, 170–72; model-based, 173–82; mood and emotion, 177–78, 179; quantitative, 168–69, 172; recall, 170, 177–78, 178–79; recognition, 169–70, 174–77; sales results, 172

Advertising: in Denmark, 196–97, 198; in Greece, 196, 198; in India, 196, 198; in New Zealand, 196, 198; perceptions of, 186; pros and cons, 186; in Singapore, 187–88, 197, 198; standardization, 198–99

Advertising Research Foundation, 166–67

Affiliation motive, 157

Africa. See Kenya

After-sales service, 81, 139

Agency theory, 122, 123

Agents: contracts, 122–24; cultural factors, 124–35; monitoring, 123–24; negotiating with, 124, 131; post-negotiation relationship, 133–35; problems, 124

Al-Khalifa, Ali, 139

Alliances, 31–35, 40–41

Allianz, 235

Alston, Jon P., 129

Ambiguity, 125. See also Uncertainty

Andrews, Craig, 185–86, 199

Apple Computer, 40

Arabs, 159, 160, 161. See also Saudi Arabia

Armenia, 61–62, 65, 68

Arnold, Ulli, 101–2

Article of commerce test, 50–51, 56

Asia: communication style, 161; crisis, 36–38; cultural factors, 129; former Soviet republics in, 64–65; insurance, 240; Muslim countries, 66; newly industrializing countries, 29–30. See also specific countries

Asset specificity, 230

Astra, 40

AT&T, 228

Attitudes, 254–55

Autonomy, 34, 90

Azerbaijan, 62, 65, 68

About the Contributors

RUNAR P. ANDRESEN joined marketing research consultancy as a research executive in Norway, working particularly in the field of brand building. He worked at the Coca-Cola Company as manager of the Strategic Marketing Research and Trends Department. More recently he assumed the role of Nordic Trends Manager throughout Scandinavia.

R. K. ASUNDI is Professor at the College of Business Administration, University of Puerto Rico, Mayaguez. His research and publication interests include management of small and medium-sized enterprises and strategic management.

ERIN A. C. BRELAND was a graduate student at the Fisher Graduate School of International Management, Monterey Institute of International Studies, Monterey, California.

IRVINE CLARKE III is on the faculty of Marketing and International Business at the Meinders School of Business, Oklahoma City University. His research interests are in international marketing. He also has extensive industry experience in marketing.

VICTOR V. CORDELL is Professor of International Business at the Fisher Graduate School of International Management, Monterey Institute of International Studies, Monterey, California. His research and publication interests include international marketing, globalization issues, and country-of-origin studies.

SRINIVAS DURVASULA is an Associate Professor in Marketing at Marquette University and a Senior Fellow at the National University of Singapore. He was a visiting professor at Vrije University and also at Tinbergen Institute in the Netherlands. His research interests include measurement theory, model development, cross-national consumer behavior, advertising perceptions, and industrial marketing. He has published in the *Journal of Consumer Research*, the *Journal of Marketing Research*, the *Journal of Retailing*, and the *Journal of Advertising*.

PERVEZ N. GHAURI is Professor and Head of Marketing at the University of Groningen, the Netherlands. He has published extensively in the areas of international joint ventures, international strategic alliances, international marketing, and international business negotiations. He is the Editor-in-Chief of the *International Business Review*. He has extensive experience in conducting executive development programs in many overseas countries.

FLEMMING HANSEN is Professor, Department of Marketing, Faculty of Economics and Business Administration, Copenhagen Business School, Denmark. He has published widely in the areas of consumer behavior, marketing communications, and cross-cultural communications research.

LESTER W. JOHNSON is Professor of Marketing at the Monash Mt. Eliza Business School, Australia. He teaches in the postgraduate programs and supervises graduate research students. His research and publication interests are consumer choice modeling, service marketing, and international marketing channels.

JACOB JOU is Professor of Marketing, Department of Business Administration, National Sun-Yat-Sen University, Taiwan, Republic of China. His research and publication interests include importer-exporter interaction studies, cross-cultural consumer behavior, and international marketing.

AMAL KARUNARATNA is a member of the Faculty of Management and Economics, University of Adelaide, Australia. His research interests are in the areas of importer-exporter interaction process, cross-cultural issues, and international marketing.

STEVEN LYSONSKI is an Associate Professor at Marquette University. Earlier he was on the faculty at the University of Rhode Island, Copenhagen School of Business and Economics, and University of Canterbury, New Zealand. He has published in the *Journal of Marketing*, the *Journal of Consumer Research*, the *Journal of Advertising*, the *Journal of Consumer Affairs*, and the *International Journal of Research in Marketing*. His research interests are in the areas of cross-cultural marketing, product management, consumer behavior, and content analysis.

A. BEN OUMLIL is Associate Professor of Marketing at the University of Dayton, Ohio. He has published widely in the areas of international marketing and inflation-related consumer behavior. He has published a book on inflation-induced shopping behavior, and he has also taught in overseas countries.

LARBI OUMLIL (deceased) was an international business consultant in Cincinnati, Ohio.

MARGARET OWENS is a member of the Oklahoma Bar Association and in private practice with a law firm in Oklahoma. She is a past member of the American Bar Association, the Oklahoma Trial Lawyers Association, and the Oklahoma Country Bar Association.

KUMAR C. RALLAPALLI is Senior Analyst, Promotion Resource Strategies at Glaxo Wellcome Inc. Prior to joining Glaxo Wellcome he was on the faculty of the School of Business at Troy State University. He is an active researcher and has presented marketing research papers at national and international conferences. He has published in the *Journal of the Academy of Marketing Science*, the *Journal of Business Research*, the *Journal of Business Ethics*, *International Marketing Review*, and the *Journal of Pharmaceutical Marketing and Management*.

C. P. RAO is Professor of Marketing and Director of the Case Research & Teaching Unit, College of Administrative Sciences, Kuwait University. He was Eminent Scholar and William B. Spong Chair, Old Dominion University, Wal-Mart Lecturer in Strategic Marketing, and University Professor, University of Arkansas at Fayetteville. He has published extensively in the areas of marketing and international business.

P. M. RAO is on the faculty of the College of Management, Long Island University/C. W. Post campus. Prior to working in academia he worked in the telecommunications industry. His research writings have been in the area of intellectual property protection.

PER SERVAIS' is an Associate Professor in the Department of Marketing, Odense University, Denmark. His research and publication interests are in the areas of purchasing management, international marketing, and industrial marketing.

D. DEO SHARMA is Professor of Marketing at the Copenhagen Business School, Denmark. His research interests have focused on strategic alliances, government-TNC relationships, and internationalization processes. His research has been published in the *Journal of International Business Studies*, *International Marketing Review*, the *Journal of Global Marketing*, *International Business Review*, and *Advances in International Marketing*.

ANGELA D'AURIA STANTON is on the faculty of the Department of Marketing, James Madison University. She is also the President of the Strategy Group, a full-service marketing research and consulting firm. Her research interests are in the areas of international marketing, cross-cultural consumer behavior, and measurement issues.

DOUGLAS VORHIES is a faculty member in the Department of Marketing at the Illinois State University. He also worked as Marketing faculty member at the University of Wisconsin–Oshkosh. His research and publication interests are in the areas of strategic marketing management and strategy implementation issues.

ZHENGYUAN WANG is a faculty member in the Department of Marketing at the Sydney Technologocial University, Sydney, Australia. His research and publication interests are in the areas of health care marketing, cross-cultural consumer behavior, and international marketing.

JEROME WITT is a faculty member in the Department of Marketing, School of Business, Philadelphia Institute of Textile Technology. His research and publication interests include international marketing, East European studies, and country-of-origin studies.

DAVID A. YORKE is Senior Lecturer in Marketing, UMIST, Manchester, England. His principal interests and publications include services marketing strategy and internationalization of services. For a number of years he was a member of the IMP group of researchers, which developed the interaction approach to business-to-business marketing and which he adapted to services marketing.